T0212924

Lecture Notes in Computer Science   8848

Commenced Publication in 1973
Founding and Former Series Editors:
Gerhard Goos, Juris Hartmanis, and Jan van Leeuwen

More information about this series at http://www.springer.com/series/7412

Bjoern Menze · Georg Langs
Albert Montillo · Michael Kelm
Henning Müller · Shaoting Zhang
Weidong (Tom) Cai · Dimitris Metaxas (Eds.)

Medical Computer Vision: Algorithms for Big Data

International Workshop, MCV 2014
Held in Conjunction with MICCAI 2014
Cambridge, MA, USA, September 18, 2014
Revised Selected Papers

 Springer

Editors

Bjoern Menze
Technische Universität München
Munich
Germany

Georg Langs
Medical University of Vienna
Vienna
Austria

Albert Montillo
GE Global Research
Niskayuna, NY
USA

Michael Kelm
Siemens AG
Erlangen
Germany

Henning Müller
University of Applied Sciences
Sierre
Switzerland

Shaoting Zhang
University of North Carolina
Charlotte
USA

Weidong (Tom) Cai
School of Information Technologies
Biomedical and Multimedia Information
    Technology (BMIT) Research Group,
    University of Sydney
Sydney, NSW
Australia

Dimitris Metaxas
Rutgers University
Piscataway, NJ
USA

ISSN 0302-9743   ISSN 1611-3349 (electronic)
Lecture Notes in Computer Science
ISBN 978-3-319-13971-5   ISBN 978-3-319-13972-2 (eBook)
DOI 10.1007/978-3-319-13972-2

Library of Congress Control Number: 2014958150

Springer Cham Heidelberg New York Dordrecht London

Printed on acid-free paper

Springer International Publishing AG Switzerland is part of Springer Science+Business Media
(www.springer.com)

Preface

The MICCAI 2014 Workshop on Medical Computer Vision: Algorithms for Big Data (MICCAI-bigMCV 2014) was held in conjunction with the 17th International Conference on Medical Image Computing and Computer Assisted Intervention (MICCAI 2014) on September 18, 2014 in Boston, USA. It succeeds the Workshops on Medical Computer Vision that were held in September 2010 in conjunction with MICCAI 2010 in Beijing, in June 2012 in conjunction with CVPR 2012 in Providence, in October 2012 in conjunction with MICCAI 2012 in Nice, and in September 2013 in conjunction with MICCAI 2013 in Nagoya.

With the ever-increasing amount of annotated multimodal medical data consisting of imaging and textual information, large-scale, data-driven methods provide the promise of bridging the semantic gap between images and diagnoses. The one-day workshop aimed at exploring the use of modern computer vision technology and "big data" algorithms in tasks such as automatic segmentation and registration, localization of anatomical features, and detection of anomalies. We emphasized questions of harvesting, organizing, and learning from large-scale medical imaging datasets and general-purpose automatic understanding of medical images. We were especially interested in modern, scalable, and efficient algorithms that generalize well to previously unseen images and can be applied to large-scale datasets that are arising, for example, from studies with significant populations, through the use of wide-field-of-view imaging sequences at high-spatial resolution, or when compiling hospital-scale databases. In addition, the bigMCV 2014 hosted a VISCERAL session for presentation and discussion of methods for anatomical structure segmentation and localization. The session highlights the results of the VISCERALanatomy2 challenge, and provided a forum to discuss the individual approaches and their comparative evaluation.

Our call for papers resulted in 29 submissions of up to 12 pages. Each paper received two to four reviews. Based on these peer reviews, we accepted 13 papers that were regular oral presentations, and 5 papers for the VISCERAL session.

October 2014

Bjoern Menze
Georg Langs
Albert Montillo
Michael Kelm
Henning Müller
Shaoting Zhang
Weidong (Tom) Cai
Dimitris Metaxas

Organization

Organization Committee

General Co-chairs

Bjoern Menze — Technische Universität München, Munich, Germany

Georg Langs — Medical University of Vienna, Vienna, Austria and MIT, Cambridge, MA, USA

Albert Montillo — GE Global Research, USA

Michael Kelm — Siemens, Erlangen, Germany

Henning Müller — University of Applied Sciences Western Switzerland (HES-SO) and University Hospitals and University of Geneva, Switzerland

Shaoting Zhang — UNC Charlotte, USA

Weidong (Tom) Cai — University of Sydney, Australia and Harvard Medical School, Boston, MA, USA

Dimitris Metaxas — Rutgers University, USA

Publication Chair

Henning Müller — Switzerland

International Program Committee

Adrien Depeursinge — Stanford University, USA

Allan Hanbury — Technical University of Vienna, Austria

Allison Noble — University of Oxford, UK

Alvina Goh — National University, Singapore

Christian Wachinger — MIT, USA

Daniel Rueckert — Imperial College London, UK

Darko Zikic — Microsoft Research Cambridge, UK

Diana Mateus — Technische Universität München, Munich, Germany

Dinggang Shen — UNC Chapel Hill, USA

Ender Konukoglu — Harvard Medical School, USA

Ertan Cetingul — Siemens Corporate Research, USA

Herve Lombaert — Inria, France

Jan Margeta — Inria, France

Jurgen Gall — University of Bonn, Germany

Kilian Pohl — Stanford University, USA

Koen Van Leemput	Technical University of Denmark, Denmark
Le Lu	National Institutes of Health, USA
Marius Erdt	Fraunhofer/NTU, Germany
Marleen de Bruijne	Erasmus MC, The Netherlands
Matthias Schneider	ETH Zurich, Switzerland
Matthew Toews	Harvard Medical School, USA
Maxime Sermesant	Inria, France
Michael Wels	Siemens Healthcare, Germany
Milan Sonka	University of Iowa, USA
Paul Suetens	KU Leuven, Belgium
Philippe Cattin	University of Basel, Switzerland
Pingkun Yan	Chinese Academy of Sciences, China
Ron Kikinis	Harvard Medical School, USA
Sebastian Ourselin	University College London, UK
Stefan Wesarg	Fraunhofer Gesellschaft, Germany
Stefan Bauer	University of Bern, Switzerland
Tammy Riklin-Raviv	Ben-Gurion University of the Negev, Israel
Tobias Gass	ETH Zurich, Switzerland
Tom Vercauteren	Mauna Kea Technologies, France
Xavier Pennec	Inria, France
Xinghua Lou	Microsoft Research, UK
Yang Song	University of Sydney, Australia
Yefeng Zheng	Siemens Corporate Research, USA

Sponsors

European Commission 7th Framework Programme, VISCERAL (318068) and Khresmoi (257528) projects.

Contents

Workshop Overview

Overview of the 2014 Workshop on Medical Computer Vision—Algorithms
for Big Data (MCV 2014) 3
   Henning Müller, Bjoern Menze, Georg Langs, Albert Montillo,
   Michael Kelm, Shaoting Zhang, Weidong (Tom) Cai, and Dimitris Metaxas

Segmentation of Big Medical Data

Joint Segmentation and Registration for Infant Brain Images 13
   Guorong Wu, Li Wang, John Gilmore, Weili Lin, and Dinggang Shen

LINKS: Learning-Based Multi-source IntegratioN FrameworK for Segmentation
of Infant Brain Images....................................... 22
   Li Wang, Yaozong Gao, Feng Shi, Gang Li, John H. Gilmore, Weili Lin,
   and Dinggang Shen

Pectoralis Muscle Segmentation on CT Images Based on Bayesian Graph Cuts
with a Subject-Tailored Atlas 34
   Rola Harmouche, James C. Ross, George R. Washko,
   and Raúl San José Estépar

Advanced Feature Extraction

Learning Features for Tissue Classification with the Classification
Restricted Boltzmann Machine 47
   Gijs van Tulder and Marleen de Bruijne

Dementia-Related Features in Longitudinal MRI: Tracking Keypoints
over Time 59
   Elisabeth Stühler and Michael R. Berthold

Object Classification in an Ultrasound Video Using LP-SIFT Features...... 71
   Mohammad Ali Maraci, Raffaele Napolitano, Aris Papageorghiou,
   and J. Allison Noble

Unsupervised Pre-training Across Image Domains Improves Lung
Tissue Classification 82
   Thomas Schlegl, Joachim Ofner, and Georg Langs

Multi-atlas and Beyond

Atlas-Guided Multi-channel Forest Learning for Human Brain Labeling 97
  Guangkai Ma, Yaozong Gao, Guorong Wu, Ligang Wu, and Dinggang Shen

Fast Multiatlas Selection Using Composition of Transformations
for Radiation Therapy Planning 105
  *David Rivest-Hénault, Soumya Ghose, Josien P.W. Pluim, Peter B. Greer,
Jurgen Fripp, and Jason A. Dowling*

Classifier-Based Multi-atlas Label Propagation with Test-Specific Atlas
Weighting for Correspondence-Free Scenarios 116
  Darko Zikic, Ben Glocker, and Antonio Criminisi

Translational Medical Computer Vision

CT Prostate Deformable Segmentation by Boundary Regression 127
  Yeqin Shao, Yaozong Gao, Xin Yang, and Dinggang Shen

Precise Lumen Segmentation in Coronary Computed
Tomography Angiography 137
  Felix Lugauer, Yefeng Zheng, Joachim Hornegger, and B. Michael Kelm

Confidence-Based Training for Clinical Data Uncertainty
in Image-Based Prediction of Cardiac Ablation Targets 148
  *Rocío Cabrera-Lozoya, Jan Margeta, Loïc Le Folgoc, Yuki Komatsu,
Benjamin Berte, Jatin Relan, Hubert Cochet, Michel Haïssaguerre,
Pierre Jaïs, Nicholas Ayache, and Maxime Sermesant*

VISCERAL Session

Rule-Based Ventral Cavity Multi-organ Automatic Segmentation
in CT Scans 163
  Assaf B. Spanier and Leo Joskowicz

Multi-atlas Segmentation and Landmark Localization in Images
with Large Field of View 171
  Tobias Gass, Gabor Szekely, and Orcun Goksel

Automatic Liver Segmentation Using Statistical Prior Models
and Free-form Deformation 181
  *Xuhui Li, Cheng Huang, Fucang Jia, Zongmin Li, Chihua Fang,
and Yingfang Fan*

Hierarchic Multi–atlas Based Segmentation for Anatomical Structures:
Evaluation in the VISCERAL Anatomy Benchmarks.................. 189
  Oscar Alfonso Jiménez del Toro and Henning Müller

Automatic 3D Multiorgan Segmentation via Clustering and Graph Cut
Using Spatial Relations and Hierarchically-Registered Atlases............ 201
  Razmig Kéchichian, Sébastien Valette, Michaël Sdika, and Michel Desvignes

Author Index 211

Workshop Overview

Overview of the 2014 Workshop on Medical Computer Vision—Algorithms for Big Data (MCV 2014)

Henning Müller[1,2]([✉]), Bjoern Menze[3,4], Georg Langs[5,6],
Albert Montillo[7], Michael Kelm[8], Shaoting Zhang[9], Weidong (Tom) Cai[10,11],
and Dimitris Metaxas[12]

[1] University of Applied Sciences Western Switzerland (HES–SO), Sierre, Switzerland
`henning.mueller@hevs.ch`
[2] University Hospitals and University of Geneva, Geneva, Switzerland
[3] Technical University of Munich, Munich, Germany
[4] INRIA, Sophia Antipolis, France
[5] Medical University of Vienna, Vienna, Austria
[6] MIT, Cambridge, MA, USA
[7] GE Global Research, Niskayuna, USA
[8] Siemens Healthcare, Erlangen, Germany
[9] UNC Charlotte, Charlotte, USA
[10] University of Sydney, Sydney, NSW, Australia
[11] Harvard Medical School, Boston, USA
[12] Rutgers University, Piscataway, USA

Abstract. The 2014 workshop on medical computer vision (MCV): algorithms for big data took place in Cambridge, MA, USA in connection with MICCAI (Medical Image Computing for Computer Assisted Intervention). It is the fourth MICCAI MCV workshop after those held in 2010, 2012 and 2013 with another edition held at CVPR 2012. This workshop aims at exploring the use of modern computer vision technology in tasks such as automatic segmentation and registration, localisation of anatomical features and extraction of meaningful visual features. It emphasises questions of harvesting, organising and learning from large-scale medical imaging data sets and general-purpose automatic understanding of medical images. The workshop is especially interested in modern, scalable and efficient algorithms which generalise well to previously unseen images.The strong participation in the workshop of over 80 persons shows the importance of and interest in Medical Computer Vision. This overview article describes the papers presented in the workshop as either oral presentations or short presentations and posters. It also describes the invited talks and the results of the VISCERAL session in the workshop on the use of big data in medical imaging.

Keywords: Medical image analysis · Medical computer vision · Segmentation · Detection

© Springer International Publishing Switzerland 2014
B. Menze et al. (Eds.): MCV 2014, LNCS 8848, pp. 3–10, 2014.
DOI: 10.1007/978-3-319-13972-2_1

1   Introduction

The Medical Computer Vision workshop (MCV) took place in conjunction with MICCAI (Medical Image Computing for Computer-Assisted Interventions) on September 18, 2014 in Cambridge, MA in the USA. This fifth workshop on medical computer vision was organised in connection with MICCAI after the workshops in 2010 [12], 2012 [10] and 2013 [11] and with CVPR in 2012. The workshop received 29 paper submissions of which five were submitted to the VISCERAL session. All papers were reviewed by at least three external reviewers of the scientific committee of the workshop. Then, all borderline papers were reviewed in addition by at least one member of the workshop organisers. The 13 best papers were presented as oral presentations and authors had the possibility to also present a poster on their techniques for discussions during the lunch break.

With the increasing importance of large datasets (and the addition of big data in the workshop title) it was also decided to again add a session on an evaluation campaign called VISCERAL[1] (VISual Concept ExtRaction challenge in RAdioLogy) in 2014. The VISCERAL project [5] is creating large amounts of manually annotated 3D medical data, and is making them available to the research community in four benchmark challenges. The first two benchmarks were focussed on the automatic detection of organs in the body and include annotations of over 20 organs and 50 landmarks in multiple modalities. The third benchmark is on lesion detection and the fourth on the retrieval of similar cases in very large data sets.

This text also gives an overview of the most important discussions that took place during the medical computer vision workshop and the challenges that were identified in the field. Participants gave very good feedback and all agreed to again organize the workshop during future MICCAI conferences.

2   Papers Presented at the Workshop

The oral presentations were separated into four topic areas, papers on segmentation, feature extraction, multi-atlas techniques and the last session on translational medical computer vision.

2.1   Segmentation of Big Medical Data

Wu et al. [21] addressed the problem of segmentation and registration of infant brains from subjects at different ages. They estimated tissue probability maps separately using only training at the respective age and used the probability maps as a good initialization to guide the level set segmentation.

Then, Wang et al. [20] presented a random forest based approach for infant brain image segmentation that fuses multi-contrast MRI and tissue probability maps. Next, Harmouche et al. [3] proposed a method to segment the pectoralis

---

[1] http://visceral.eu/.

muscle in CT. Their approach constructs a likelihood using a multivariate distribution of pairwise registered similar training subjects while the posterior tissue map probability is used to drive a graph cuts segmentation.

2.2 Advanced Feature Extraction

In the first paper in this section, van Tulder and de Bruijne [19] adapted a convolutional classification restricted Boltzmann machine to learn features well suited for discriminative feature learning and apply it for texture-based tissue classification on two lung CT problems. Then, Stühler [17] argued that for large scale longitudinal key point tracking in brain MRI of dementia studies, time-consuming non-rigid registration could be avoided by employing local invariant features that are independent of image scale and orientation. Maraci et al. [9] then showed how they combined techniques from the computer vision and medical imaging communities to increase the degree of automation in ultrasound acquisition. They introduced new symmetric SIFT features and used them to represent the acquired image for classification of fetal image anatomical structures. Next Schlegl et al. [14] addressed the need to learn from data collected across multiple hospitals with heterogeneous medical imaging equipment. Using unsupervised pre-training of convolutional neural networks they inject information from hospitals or image classes for which no annotations are available and they show how this can lead to improved classification accuracy in the classification of lung tissue.

2.3 Multi Atlas and Beyond

Ma et al. [8] kicked off our Multi-Atlas section by presenting a hybrid approach for brain anatomy segmentation that combines multi-atlas and learning based methods. Different from traditional learning-based labelling methods, their atlas-guided multi-channel forest learning method utilized information from both the target image and the aligned atlas for a voxel-wise labelling. Next the task of reducing registration cost for radiation therapy planning was addressed by Rivest-Henault et al. [13]. Their approach finds a proxy that can be used to hop from a given image A to a target image B with minimal distortion and they also defined both a clustering scheme and the transitivity error function. Last, Zikic et al. [22] adapted the Atlas Forest approach for the case when target and test brain images lack correspondences such as the case when there is a tumor in one. By training on only atlases similar to the test, they managed to overcome the inherent overtraining problem as shown in the results they presented on BraTS 2013 (Multimodal Brain Tumor Segmentation Challenge).

2.4 Translational Medical Computer Vision

The translation of concepts from computer vision to applications in the medical imaging domain was well represented in our workshop. Shao et al. [15] let off this section by describing a prostate boundary delineation method that forms an estimate of voxel boundary likelihood using votes cast by a regression forest and then form a discrete segmentation by fitting a deformable model. Next Lugauer et al. [7] proposed a model-guided segmentation approach to segment the lumen in coronary computed tomography angiography. Their method builds a Markov Random Field model with convex priors to ensure tubular solutions, which they optimize through a graph-cut based approach. Finally, a method for identifying local image characteristics capable of predicting the presence of local abnormal ventricular activities in the heart was proposed by Cabrera Lozoya et al. [1]. While determining the optimum intensity and texture-based local image features using a random forest, they developed an approach for integrating uncertainties due to errors in the training set and describe how this improves algorithm performance.

3   Invited Speakers

3.1   Xiang Sean Zhou

The first invited speaker was *Xiang Sean Zhou*, Head of Innovations at Siemens Medical Solutions in Malvern, PA, USA who presented his experiences in Medical Imaging research from a large company perspective. He described main lines of his research approach that has lead him to develop rapid and robust anatomy localization. This accomplishment has in part lead him to recently be awarded Inventor of the Year at Siemens. Emphasizing the principle of "robustness through redundancy", he argued that the three keys to achieve high robustness in medical image analysis are *"redundancy, redundancy, redundancy"*, (which reminded us of the saying that "the three key aspects in buying a house are 'location, location, location'"). The perspective on implementing or exploiting redundancy was also inspired by the space and aeronautics industries that are well known for pioneering work in fault tolerant design. Dr. Zhou described multiple ways in which he has successfully designed redundancy into his solutions. Redundancy through ensemble learning was an approach he adopted early on which increases reliability through aggregating multiple machine learning models, while redundancy through modality leverages multiple modalities when providing a clinical interpretation such as was prevalent in the Health-e-Child project. Redundancy through algorithm fusion entails using all of the best methods for image interpretation including detection, registration and segmentation. These as well as several other redundancies have formed the hallmarks of his research which lead to stimulating discussions about what academia might provide for industrial research. Dr. Zhou described how while many algorithms might achieve success on 80–90 % of the cases, to find truly robust solutions that can work on 98–99 % of the cases requires quantitative evaluation on large-scale standardized datasets, such as those represented in the large challenges now becoming popular at MICCAI or other events.

3.2 Eric G. Learned-Miller

The second invited speaker was *Eric G. Learned-Miller*, Associate Professor of Computer Science at the University of Massachusetts in Amherst, MA, USA who presented a talk entitled "Experience with Big Data: A Decade of Research in Face Recognition". In it he both presented an overview of computer vision techniques for face recognition and provided a historical perspective. A central theme in his research has been in the reduction of the face recognition problem to its salient components. Towards this aim he has created a widely used public resource for the community in the form of a curated face database, Labeled Faces in the Wild. This has over 13,000 faces collected from the web, each labeled with the name of the person pictured. Every face was identified with the Viola-Jones face detector making detection less of a concern. Additionally he provides subsets of the database in which the faces have been cropped, scaled and aligned to a standard reference frame, leaving only the core recognition task. As a nice complement to the discussion we had with Dr. Zhou, Dr. Learned-Miller described how he sees a primary benefit coming from maintaining the database online, so that researchers can at any time benchmark their approaches to the state of the art. The system maintains a ranking of all methods submitted. This has enabled Dr. Learned-Miller to uncover trends in the approaches being applied. For example he has observed that, while at first computer vision researchers submitted the best methods, the recent trend has been that researchers from the machine learning community have attained top scores. Additionally, multiple ranking strategies are employed. In one, methods are allowed to train only from data in the database, while in another training data can come from any additional source, including Facebook which several methods employed successfully. This has enabled further insights including an understanding of the relative value in training on more data versus the development of new methodological models and approaches. This provided an excellent tutorial example to complement the MICCAI debate session "Signal Processing or Machine learning: What's right for MICCAI?".

4 VISCERAL Session

The VISCERAL session started with an overview of the challenges in multi-organ detection and the data that were annotated and made available in the VISCERAL project. An overview of the results was presented without detailing the various techniques of the participants. This included a description of the cloud-based evaluation infrastructure that avoids to physically distribute the data. The session also included five presentations of participants on the techniques employed in the benchmark.

Spanier et al. [16] presented their approach for multi-organ segmentation starting with the simplest organs and then going towards harder organs in the process. The process includes identification of the region of interest for each organ, thresholding, seed point identification and then slice growing. Gass et al. [2] used a multi-atlas approach for the segmentation of multiple organs and also the identification of landmarks. The goal was a data-driven and modality-independent approach for multi-organ segmentation.

Only liver segmentation is done by Li et al. in [6]. The approach uses multiple prior knowledge models and an Adaboost classifier, reaching good results on the liver. Jimenez del Toro et al. [18] presented an approach to multi-organ segmentation that is entirely data driven and does not use any organ-specific optimizations. It uses first a global registration and then successive local registrations. For large organs with much contrast a single local registration is used and then for small organs with less contrast the registration of the larger organs is refined in a successive manner. Segmentation reached best results in several of the organs. Kechichian et al. [4] employed multiple graph cut optimization for multi-organ segmentation. Spatial relationships of organs are modelled and registration was done using SURF key points to reach good segmentation results.

5   Discussions at the Workshop

The large number of over 80 participants at the workshop also led to a large number of very interesting questions during the discussions after the talks and also the lunch and coffee breaks. Many comments after the two invited talks highlighted both the importance of data availability and systematic testing. For commercial applications it is clear that robustness is much more important than only pure performance on very specific data sets as pointed out by Sean Zhou. The case of face recognitions also highlights the importance that standardised and publicly available data sets have as well as standardized performance comparisons on the development of algorithms. This can really show advances over the years and it was highlighted that popular believe on best techniques often does not correspond to the reality of systematic evaluations of it.

The discussions also made clear that theoretical novelty is not necessarily the main point when building real applications in medical imaging as stability is important or *redundancy* as Erik Learned-Miller emphasised. Several of the approaches show that clinical impact and importance gain in importance in the field and that computer vision and machine learning approaches can now well be applied to large and heterogeneous data sets in medical imaging.Registration and segmentation remain very important underlying techniques that can help clinical applications. The session on translational medical imaging also highlights that there are many potential application areas with a potential real impact. At this point we would also like to thank the speakers and the workshop participants for the many discussions and exchange of ideas.

6   Conclusions

The fourth edition of the workshop on medical computer vision at MICCAI was a clear success. High quality papers and posters were presented and many discussions on challenges and techniques in medical imaging emerged at the workshop. The workshop gives a forum for exchange at the crossing of medical imaging, computer vision, machine learning and techniques to manage large data sets of heterogeneous nature. Based on the positive experience we foresee to again hold similar workshops at MICCAI in the coming years to follow up on developments in this quickly changing research area.

Acknowledgments. This work was supported by the EU in the FP7 through the VISCERAL (318068) and Khresmoi (257528) projects.

References

1. Cabrera Lozoya, R., et al.: Confidence-based training for clinical data uncertainty in image-based prediction of cardiac ablation targets. In: Menze, B., et al. (eds.) MCV 2014. LNCS, vol. 8848, pp. 148–159. Springer, Heidelberg (2014)
2. Gass, T., Szekely, G., Goksul, O.: Multi-atlas segmentation and landmark localization in images with large field of view. In: Menze, B., et al. (eds.) MCV 2014. LNCS, vol. 8848, pp. 171–180. Springer, Heidelberg (2014)
3. Harmouche, R., Ross, J., Washko, G., San Jose Estepar, R.: Pectoralis muscle segmentation on CT images based on bayesian graph cuts with a subject-tailored atlas. In: Menze, B., et al. (eds.) MCV 2014. LNCS, vol. 8848, pp. 34–44. Springer, Heidelberg (2014)
4. Kéchichian, R., Valette, S., Sdika, M., Desvignes, M.: Automatic 3D multiorgan segmentation via clustering and graph cut using spatial relations and hierarchically-registered atlases. In: Menze, B., et al. (eds.) MCV 2014. LNCS, vol. 8848, pp. 201–209. Springer, Heidelberg (2014)
5. Langs, G., Müller, H., Menze, B., Hanbury, A.: Visceral: towards large data in medical imaging - challenges and directions. In: Medical Content-based Retrieval for Clinical Decision Support, MCBR-CDS 2012, October 2012
6. Li, X., Huang, C., Jia, F., Li, Z., Fang, C., Fan, Y.: Automatic liver segmentation using statistical prior models and free-form deformation. In: Menze, B., et al. (eds.) MCV 2014. LNCS, vol. 8848, pp. 181–188. Springer, Heidelberg (2014)
7. Lugauer, F., Zheng, Y., Hornegger, J., Kelm, B.M.: Precise lumen segmentation in coronary computed tomography angiography. In: Menze, B., et al. (eds.) MCV 2014. LNCS, vol. 8848, pp. 137–147. Springer, Heidelberg (2014)
8. Ma, G., Gao, Y., Wu, G., Wu, L., Shen, D.: Atlas-guided multi-channel forest learning for human brain labeling. In: Menze, B., et al. (eds.) MCV 2014. LNCS, vol. 8848, pp. 97–104. Springer, Heidelberg (2014)
9. Maraci, M.A., Napolitano, R., Papageorghiou, A., Noble, J.A.: Object classification in an ultrasound video using LP-SIFT features. In: Menze, B., et al. (eds.) MCV 2014. LNCS, vol. 8848, pp. 71–81. Springer, Heidelberg (2014)
10. Menze, B., Langs, G., Lu, L., Montillo, A., Tu, Z., Criminisi, A. (eds.): MCV 2012. LNCS, vol. 7766. Springer, Heidelberg (2013)
11. Menze, B., Langs, G., Montillo, A., Kelm, M., Müller, H., Tu, Z. (eds.): MCV 2013. LNCS, vol. 8331. Springer, Heidelberg (2014)
12. Menze, B., Langs, G., Tu, Z., Criminisi, A. (eds.): MICCAI 2010 Workshop MCV. LNCS, vol. 6533. Springer, Heidelberg (2010)
13. Rivest-Hénault, D., Ghose, S., Pluim, J.P.W., Greer, P.B., Fripp, J., Dowling, J.A.: Fast multiatlas selection using composition of transformations for radiation therapy planning. In: Menze, B., et al. (eds.) MCV 2014. LNCS, vol. 8848, pp. 105–115. Springer, Heidelberg (2014)

14. Schlegl, T., Ofner, J., Langs, G.: Unsupervised pre-training across image domains improves lung tissue classification. In: Menze, B., et al. (eds.) MCV 2014. LNCS, vol. 8848, pp. 82–93. Springer, Heidelberg (2014)

15. Shao, Y., Gao, Y., Yang, X., Shen, D.: CT prostate Deformable segmentation by boundary regression. In: Menze, B., et al. (eds.) MCV 2014. LNCS, vol. 8848, pp. 127–136. Springer, Heidelberg (2014)

16. Spanier, A.B., Joskowicz, L.: Rule-based ventral cavity multi-organ automatic segmentation in CT scans. In: Menze, B., et al. (eds.) MCV 2014. LNCS, vol. 8848, pp. 163–170. Springer, Heidelberg (2014)

17. Stühler, E., Berthold, M.R.: Dementia-related features in longitudinal MRI: tracking keypoints over time. In: Menze, B., et al. (eds.) MCV 2014. LNCS, vol. 8848, pp. 59–70. Springer, Heidelberg (2014)

18. Jimenez del Toro, O.A., Müller, H.: Hierarchic multi-atlas based segmentation for anatomical structures: evaluation in the VISCERAL anatomy benchmarks. In: Menze, B., et al. (eds.) MCV 2014. LNCS, vol. 8848, pp. 189–200. Springer, Heidelberg (2014)

19. van Tulder, G., de Bruijne, M.: Learning features for tissue classification with the classification restricted boltzmann machine. In: Menze, B., et al. (eds.) MCV 2014. LNCS, vol. 8848, pp. 47–58. Springer, Heidelberg (2014)

20. Wang, L., Gao, Y., Shi, F., Li, G., Gilmore, J.H., Lin, W., Shen, D.: LINKS: learning-based multi-source integration framework for segmentation of infant brain images. In: Menze, B., et al. (eds.) MCV 2014. LNCS, vol. 8848, pp. 22–33. Springer, Heidelberg (2014)

21. Wu, G., Wang, L., Gilmore, J., Lin, W., Shen, D.: Joint segmentation and registration for infant brain images. In: Menze, B., et al. (eds.) MCV 2014. LNCS, vol. 8848, pp. 13–21. Springer, Heidelberg (2014)

22. Zikic, D., Glocker, B., Criminisi, A.: Classifier-based multi-atlas label propagation with test-specific atlas weighting for correspondence-free scenarios. In: Menze, B., et al. (eds.) MCV 2014. LNCS, vol. 8848, pp. 127–136. Springer, Heidelberg (2014)

Segmentation of Big Medical Data

Joint Segmentation and Registration
for Infant Brain Images

Guorong Wu[1], Li Wang[1], John Gilmore[2], Weili Lin[1],
and Dinggang Shen[1(✉)]

[1] Department of Radiology and BRIC, University of North Carolina,
Chapel Hill, NC 27599, USA
dgshen@med.unc.edu
[2] Department of Psychiatry, University of North Carolina,
Chapel Hill, NC 27599, USA

Abstract. The first year of life is the most dynamic and perhaps the most critical phase of postnatal brain development. The ability to accurately characterize structure changes is very critical in early brain development studies, which highly relies on the performance of image segmentation and registration techniques. However, either infant image segmentation or registration, if deployed independently, encounters much more challenges than the adult brains due to dynamic appearance change with rapid brain development. Fortunately, image segmentation and registration of infant images can assist each other to overcome the above difficulties by harnessing the growth trajectories (temporal correspondences) learned from a large set of training subjects with complete longitudinal data. To this end, we propose a joint segmentation and registration algorithm for infant brain images. Promising segmentation and registration results have been achieved for infant brain MR images aged from 2-week-old to 1-year-old, indicating the applicability of our joint segmentation and registration method in early brain development studies.

1 Introduction

Human brain undergoes rapid physical growth and functional development from birth to 1 year old. The ability to accurately measure the structural changes from MR (Magnetic Resonance) images at this period is indispensable for shedding new light on the exploration of brain development and also the early detection of neurodevelopmental disorder. For example, infants with autism were found to have 5 %–10 % abnormal enlargement in total brain volume at early development stage [1].

However, the automatic image segmentation and registration tools for processing a large amount of infant brain MR images lag behind the demands from ongoing neuroscience/clinical studies. Both image segmentation and registration are challenged by: (1) the dynamic appearance changes of brain tissues from birth to 1 year old [1], and (2) the fast and spatially-varied developments of brain anatomy and size, especially in the first year of life [1]. Consequently, either segmentation or registration, if deployed independently, is difficult to handle the above challenges.

© Springer International Publishing Switzerland 2014
B. Menze et al. (Eds.): MCV 2014, LNCS 8848, pp. 13–21, 2014.
DOI: 10.1007/978-3-319-13972-2_2

Since the imaging-based study on early brain development becomes more and more popular, a sufficient number of longitudinal infant brain images have been collected in the past years. Many subjects with complete longitudinal images have been well segmented by either human interactions or automatic methods with multi-modality information [2]. As demonstrated by many literatures, appropriate joint segmentation and registration could significantly improve both of their performances [3]. Motivated by this, we aim to develop joint segmentation and registration method to overcome the above challenges. The leverage to achieve this goal is the availability of a large number of longitudinal infant data (scanned at 2 weeks, 3 months, 6 months, 9 months, and 1 year of age) and their respective segmentation results. It is worth noting that these valuable data are often ignored when performing segmentation/registration for the new infant images by current methods.

In this paper, we present an accurate and robust approach for joint segmentation and registration of any two given infant brain images by using the knowledge learned from the training infant subjects with the complete longitudinal data and segmentation results. Specifically, we first establish accurate temporal correspondences for each training subject with complete longitudinal images, in order to learn the subject-specific growth trajectories [4]. Then, to deal with the potential large age gap between two new infant images, we first segment them separately with a sparse patch-based level set approach that allows each patch in the new infant image to look for similar patches in the respective training subjects with similar age and further combine the labels of matched patches in the training subjects to provide a good initialization for the level set segmentation. Afterwards, deformations between two new infant images can be esti-mated by deformable registration upon their segmented images, thus avoiding the challenge of directly registering two new infant images with large appearance differ-ence. The refined registration allows all matched patches of longitudinal training images (regardless of their ages) to improve the segmentation of each new infant image. By alternating these segmentation and registration steps, we can iteratively refine both segmentation and registration results of two new infant images. The advantages of our method include: (1) avoiding the direct registration between two new infant images with dynamic appearance changes, and (2) improving both segmentation and registration performances by fully using the available information from a number of training infant subjects with complete longitudinal data and their subject-specific growth models. In experiments, improved segmentation and registration results have been achieved for the infant images aged from 2-week-old to 1-year-old.

2   Methods

Our goal here is to register a moving infant brain image M_{t_2} with a fixed infant brain image F_{t_1} and also simultaneously determine tissue maps for F_{t_1} and M_{t_2}, where t_1 and t_2 are two different ages, each of which could be as young as 2-week-old or as old as 1-year-old. Assume that we have N training subjects I^s ($s = 1, \ldots, N$) with longitudinal data $I^s = \{I_t^s | t = 1, \ldots, T_s\}$. For each image sequence I^s, we can apply state-of-the-art 4D segmentation method [2] to segment 3D image at each time-point into WM (white matter), GM (gray matter), and CSF (cerebral-spinal fluid), which can be denoted as

$L^s = \{L_t^s | t = 1, \ldots, T_s\}$. With some human inspection, we can regard these segmentation results of longitudinal training images as the ground truth.

Next, we first estimate the growth trajectory (Sect. 2.1) to determine temporal correspondences for each point in the longitudinal data I_s, as designated by the purple dash curves in Fig. 1. Second, we use sparse patch-based label fusion method to calculate the tissue probability maps for F_{t_1} and M_{t_2} separately, by using only the training images at the respective time-point as the atlas images. For example, the label fusion on F_{t_1} selects only the image patches from training images $\left\{ I_{t_1}^s | s = 1, \ldots, N \right\}$ at time-point t_1 (as shown in the dash pink box of Fig. 1) to form the dictionary. The obtained tissue probability maps can be used as a good initialization for level-set approach for tissue segmentation (Sect. 2.2). In this way, we can just register the two segmented images, thus avoiding the difficulty of directly registering the original two images with different appearances (Sect. 2.3). Given the spatial correspondences between F_{t_1} and M_{t_2}, we can further improve the segmentation accuracy by augmenting the dictionary with additional image patches from training images at all other time-points, not simply the similar time-point(s) (Sect. 2.4). By alternating these segmentation and registration steps, we can iteratively refine both segmentation and registration results for F_{t_1} and M_{t_2}.

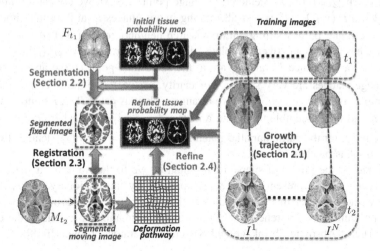

Fig. 1. The overview of joint segmentation and registration for infant brain images.

2.1 Learning Subject-Specific Growth Trajectories

For each training subject with complete longitudinal data I^s and segmentations L^s, a conventional way is to independently register all follow-up images to the baseline image (first time-point). However, such independent image registration may tear down the coherence of temporal correspondences in each longitudinal data. Hence, we go one step further to apply a 4D image registration method [5] for jointly estimating the deformation fields $\mathbf{U}^s = \{u_t^s | t = 1, \ldots, T_s\}$ that can bring the image at each time-point to the latent common space. Thus, the temporal deformations $\varphi_{t \to t'}^s$ from time-point t to time-point t' can be efficiently computed as the composition of inverse deformation $(u_t^s)^{-1}$ (from I_t^s toward common space) and the forward deformation $u_{t'}^s$ (from common space to $I_{t'}^s$): $\varphi_{t \to t'}^s = (u_t^s)^{-1} \circ u_{t'}^s$, where $\circ$ denote for the deformation composition. In this way, we can use the estimated temporal deformation fields to form the growth trajectories of each training subject I^s, as indicated by the purple dash curves in Fig. 1.

2.2 Sparse Patch-Based Level Set Segmentation

Estimation of Tissue Probability Maps: The initial tissue probability maps for each new infant image are very important to initialize the level set approach for achieving accurate tissue segmentation. Here, we use a patch-based label fusion method to estimate the tissue probability maps for each new infant image by considering the training images with same age as the atlases.

Let's take F_{t_1} as example, where we consider all training images at t_1 time-point, $\{(I_{t_1}^s, L_{t_1}^s)|s = 1, \dots, N\}$, as the atlases. We first affine register all atlases to F_{t_1} and then apply deformable registration method to deform all atlases to F_{t_1} image space. To determine the tissue type (WM, GM, or CSF) for each image point x in F_{t_1}, we extract a referent patch $Q(x, t_1) \subset F_{t_1}$ centered at image point x. Next, we collect a number of atlas patches $P_s(v, t_1) \subset I_{t_1}^s$ across all training infant images $I_{t_1}^s$ at the same time-point t_1, with the center point v sitting within a search neighborhood $n(x)$. Thus, all of these atlas patches form an over-complete dictionary $D(x, t_1) = \{P_s(v, t_1)|v \in n(x), s = 1, \dots, N\}$. Since F_{t_1} and $I_{t_1}^s$ are at the same time-point t_1, the appearances of these image patches are very similar. For clarity, we vectorize the reference patch $Q(x, t_1)$ into a column vector b. Also, we arrange each atlas patch $P_s(v, t_1)$ into a column vector a_p and then assemble them into a matrix $A = [a_p]_{p=1,\dots,\eta}$, where $p = (v, s)$ is a bivariate index for the particular atlas patch $P_s(v, t_1)$ and $\eta = N \cdot |n(x)|$ denotes the total number of atlas patches.

Inspired by the power of sparse representation, we further look for a sparse coefficient vector w to represent the reference patch b by the dictionary matrix A, i.e., $b \leftarrow Aw$, where each element in w indicates the contribution of a particular atlas patch a_p in representing the reference patch b. Thus, the estimation of w falls to the classic LASSO (Least Absolute Shrinkage and Selection Operator) problem [6–8]:

$$\widehat{w} = \min_w \|b - Aw\|^2 + \lambda \|w\|_1, s.t. w > 0, \tag{1}$$

where λ controls the sparsity of the coefficient vector w. Here, we specifically use $\widetilde{D}(x, t_1)$ to denote the set of selected image patches in $D(x, t_1)$ with the sparse coefficient $w_p > 0$. Since the tissue type for each a_p is known, we can calculate the tissue probability w.r.t. WM, GM, and CSF, respectively. After repeating this procedure for every point in the fixed image F_{t_1}, we can obtain the tissue probability maps (as shown by a pink box in Fig. 1) to initialize the level set algorithm for segmenting F_{t_1}.

Level Set Segmentation: In level set algorithm, we employ three level sets, with their zero-level surfaces, respectively, denoting for interfaces of WM/GM, GM/CSF, and

CSF/background. The tissue probability maps can be integrated as prior knowledge into the coupled level set segmentation algorithm to improve the segmentation accuracy. Similarly, we can repeat the above procedure to segment the moving image M_{t_2}, except building the patch dictionary from the training images at time-point t_2. The tentative segmentation results of F_{t_1} and M_{t_2} are shown in the blue boxes of Fig. 1.

2.3 Symmetric Feature-Based Image Registration

Given segmentations for the fixed and moving images, we can deploy the state-of-the-art registration method, i.e., HAMMER [9], to register the two segmented images. Since geometric invariant moment (GMI) features are extracted from the segmented images, image registration is free of dynamic appearance changes in the original intensity images. Here, we further improve HAMMER by using the symmetric deformation estimation strategy, where we simultaneously estimate the deformation pathways ϕ_1 (from fixed image) and ϕ_2 (from moving image). It is worth noting that the deformed fixed image w.r.t. ϕ_1 and the deformed moving image w.r.t. ϕ_2 should be similar in the end of registration.

Since ϕ_1 and ϕ_2 are iteratively refined during registration, we use k ($k = 0,.., K$) to denote the iteration. In the beginning of registration ($k = 0$), $F^{(0)} = F_{t_1}$ and $M^{(0)} = M_{t_2}$, along with the identity deformation pathways $\phi_1^{(0)}$ and $\phi_2^{(0)}$. In the following, we adopt the hierarchical deformation mechanism in HAMMER for establishing the correspondence between the deformed fixed image $F^{(k)} = F_{t_1}\left(\phi_1^{(k)}\right)$ and the deformed moving image $M^{(k)} = M_{t_2}\left(\phi_2^{(k)}\right)$, instead of always using $F^{(0)}$ and $M^{(0)}$ in HAMMER. Also, only a small number of key points with distinctive features are selected from $F^{(k)}$ and the $M^{(k)}$ to establish anatomical correspondences by matching the GMI features. The entire deformation pathways $\phi_1^{(k)}$ and $\phi_2^{(k)}$ are steered by the correspondences on these key points by requiring all other non-key points following the deformations on the nearby key points. With progress of registration, more and more key points are selected to refine the deformation pathways $\phi_1^{(k)}$ and $\phi_2^{(k)}$ regarding to $F^{(k)}$ and $M^{(k)}$, which is repeated until $F^{(k)}$ and $M^{(k)}$ become very similar in the end of registration. Finally, the deformation pathway from fixed image to moving image can be calculated by $\phi = \phi_1^K \circ (\phi_2^K)^{-1}$, where '$\circ$' denotes the composition of deformation pathway ϕ_1^K and the inverse deformation pathway $\left(\phi_2^K\right)^{-1}$.

2.4 Joint Segmentation and Registration by Using Growth Trajectories

Given the tentatively estimated deformations, we can further refine the tissue segmentation and then continue to improve the registration results with more accurate segmentation results. The key to achieve this goal is the augmented dictionary in tissue segmentation step since the refined registration will allow all matched image patches in other time-points to assist the segmentation, while these additional image patches are not included in the initial dictionary.

Taking F_{t_1} as example, the initial dictionary used to segment each image point $x \in F_{t_1}$ uses only the image patches in time-point t_1 of training subjects (the dash pink box in Fig. 1). After registration, we assume the tentative corresponding location of x in the moving image M_{t_2} is $\phi(x)$. Since we know the growth trajectory in each training image, we can construct an augmented dictionary $D^*(x, t_1)$ for image point x, by now including: (1) *image patches at time-point t_1*: the training image patches from the initial dictionary $D(x, t_1)$ (at *time-point t_1*); (2) *image patches at time-point t_2*: the selected image patches in $\widetilde{D}(\phi(x), t_2)$ that is used to represent the moving image patch $Q(\phi (x), t_2)$, and (3) *image patches at all other time points*: all temporally corresponded image patches derived from $\widetilde{D}(\phi(x), t_2)$. Thus, we also know the appearance information at all other time points for each image patch in $\widetilde{D}(\phi(x), t_2)$ by traversing the growth trajectory learned in Sect. 2.1.

As shown in Fig. 1, in our joint segmentation and registration framework, segmenting infant image at a particular time-point can now utilize the information in the entire training images (pink and red boxes in Fig. 1). Since such additional subject-specific image patches are more pertinent to the image point x than the training image patches from the entire population, the augmented dictionary can provide more useful information to guide tissue segmentation. By alternating the segmentation and registration steps, we can achieve state-of-the-art performance for both segmentation and registration for the infant brain images.

3   Experiments

In the training stage, we collect 24 infant subjects with complete longitudinal data as the training subjects, where each subject has T1- and T2-weighted images at 2 weeks, 3 months, 6 months, 9 months, and 12 months of age. All images were acquired from a Siemens head-only 3T MR scanner. T1-weighted images were acquired with 144 sagittal slices at resolution of $1 \times 1 \times 1$ mm^3. T2-weighted images with 64 axis slices were obtained at resolution of $1.25 \times 1.25 \times 1.95$ mm^3. For each subject, the T2-weighted image is aligned to the T1-weighted image at the same time-point and then further resampled to $1 \times 1 \times 1$ mm^3. Note that we use T2-weighted images for segmenting 2-week-old and 3-month-old infant images, while use T1-weighted images to segment 6-, 9-, and 12-month-old infant images, considering the strong tissue contrast in the respective time-points for the respective MR images.

Since most of early brain development studies use the infant image at 1-year-old or older age as the atlas to discover structure development, we apply our joint segmentation and registration method to align 27 images at 2-week-old and 28 images at 3-month-old as moving images onto a 1-year-old infant image that is used as the fixed image (top right of Fig. 2). In the following, we evaluate the segmentation and registration performances one by one.

3.1 Evaluation of Segmentation Results

For each testing infant image, we have the manual segmentation results of WM, GM, and CSF. Here, we use Dice ratio to quantitatively measure the overlap degree between manual segmentations (used as ground truth) and our estimated tissue segmentations. The sparse patch-based level set segmentation algorithm (without using registration to refine) is used as the baseline method for comparison. The Dice ratios on each tissue type for 2-week-old and 3-month-old infant brain images are listed in Tables 1 and 2, respectively. After joint segmentation and registration, our method achieves overall 2.38 % and 1.95 % improvement in segmenting 2-week-old and 3-month-old infant brain images, respectively. Some typical improvements on 2-week-old infant brain image (top left of Fig. 2) are displayed in Fig. 2. It is clear that the initial mis-segmentations (in the blue boxes of Fig. 2) have been successfully corrected based on more and more accurate image registration (in the red boxes of Fig. 2).

Table 1. The Dice ratios of WM, GM, and CSF on 2-week-old infant brain images

	WM	GM	CSF	Overall
Sparse-level set	82.04 ± 5.17	81.02 ± 4.10	73.02 ± 5.77	78.69 ± 3.33
Our method	84.12 ± 2.38	83.53 ± 1.97	76.48 ± 2.98	81.07 ± 1.49

Table 2. The Dice ratios of WM, GM, and CSF on 3-month-old infant brain images

	WM	GM	CSF	Overall
Sparse-level set	82.53 ± 4.61	81.25 ± 3.53	75.14 ± 3.38	79.77 ± 2.68
Our method	84.35 ± 1.76	82.44 ± 2.11	77.00 ± 2.12	81.94 ± 1.27

3.2 Evaluation on Registration Results

A typical result of registering 2-week-old image to 1-year-old image is shown in the bottom right of Fig. 2. Since we have the manually labeled hippocampus region for both fixed image (1-year-old image as shown in the top right of Fig. 2) and eight 2-week-old infant brain images, we can further quantitatively evaluate the registration accuracy on 2-week-old images, by measuring the overlap degree between manual ground-truth and our estimated hippocampus (by deforming the hippocampal region of the fixed image to the image space of each individual 2-week-old image). In order to demonstrate the power of joint segmentation and registration, we apply HAMMER [9] on the baseline segmentations, obtained by using the sparse patch-based level set only (without refinement by joint registration). The average and standard deviation of Dice ratios on hippocampus is 70.13 ± 4.69 by HAMMER (based on the baseline segmentations) and 73.48 ± 2.05 by our joint segmentation and registration method, achieving almost 4.7 % increase in Dice ratio by our proposed method.

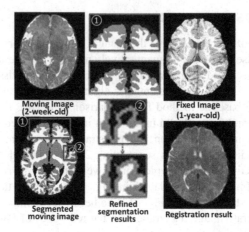

Fig. 2. Segmentation improvements on 2-week-old infant brain images, from results in blue boxes to the results in red boxes (Colour figure online).

4 Conclusion

In this paper, we propose a novel joint segmentation and registration method for infant brain images by using the growth trajectories learned from a large number of training subjects with complete longitudinal data. Specifically, image segmentation assists the registration by providing accurate tissue segmentations, which avoid the challenge of directly registering the two infant brain images with large appearance changes. In return, the refined image registration can bring more useful information to provide better tissue probability maps for guiding the level set based segmentation. Promising results for both segmentation and registration have been achieved, indicating the potential applicability of our method for early brain development study.

References

1. Knickmeyer, R., Gouttard, S., Kang, C., Evans, D., Wilber, K., Smith, J., Hamer, R., Lin, W., Gerig, G., Gilmore, J.: A structural MRI study of human brain development from birth to 2 years. J. Neurosci. **28**, 12176–12182 (2008)
2. Wang, L., Shi, F., Yap, P.-T., Gilmore, J.H., Lin, W., Shen, D.: 4D Multi-Modality Tissue Segmentation of Serial Infant Images. PLoS ONE **7**, e44596 (2012)
3. Pohl, K., Fisher, J., Grimson, W.E.L., Kikinis, R., Wells, W.M.: A bayesian model for joint segmentation and registration. Neuroimage **31**, 228–239 (2006)
4. Miller, M.I.: Computational anatomy: shape, growth, and atrophy comparison via diffeomorphisms. NeuroImage **23**, S19–S33 (2004)
5. Shen, D., Davatzikos, C.: Measuring temporal morphological changes robustly in brain MR images via 4-dimensional template warping. NeuroImage **21**, 1508–1517 (2004)
6. Tibshirani, R.: Regression shrinkage and selection via the lasso. J. R. Stat. Soc. Ser. B (Stat. Methodol.) **58**, 267–288 (1996)

7. Zhang, S., Zhan, Y., Dewan, M., Huang, J., Metaxas, D.N., Zhou, X.S.: Towards robust and effective shape modeling: Sparse shape composition. Med. Image Anal. **16**, 265–277 (2012)
8. Zhang, S., Zhan, Y., Metaxas, D.N.: Deformable segmentation via sparse representation and dictionary learning. Med. Image Anal. **16**, 1385–1396 (2012)
9. Shen, D., Davatzikos, C.: HAMMER: hierarchical attribute matching mechanism for elastic registration. IEEE Trans. Med. Imaging **21**, 1421–1439 (2002)

LINKS: Learning-Based Multi-source IntegratioN FrameworK for Segmentation of Infant Brain Images

Li Wang[1], Yaozong Gao[1,2], Feng Shi[1], Gang Li[1], John H. Gilmore[3],
Weili Lin[1], and Dinggang Shen[1(✉)]

[1] Department of Radiology and BRIC, University of North Carolina,
Chapel Hill, NC, USA
{li_wang, dinggang_shen}@med.unc.edu
[2] Department of Computer Science, University of North Carolina,
Chapel Hill, NC, USA
[3] Department of Psychiatry, University of North Carolina,
Chapel Hill, NC, USA

Abstract. Segmentation of infant brain MR images is challenging due to insufficient image quality, severe partial volume effect, and the ongoing maturation and myelination processes. In particular, the image contrast inverts around 6–8 months of age, and the white and gray matter tissues are isointense in both T1- and T2-weighted MR images and thus exhibit the extremely low tissue contrast, which poses the significant challenges for automated segmentation. Most previous studies used multi-atlas label fusion strategy, which has the limitation of equally treating the available multi-modality images and is often computationally expensive. In this paper, we propose a novel learning-based multi-source integration framework for infant brain image segmentation. Specifically, we employ the random forest technique to effectively integrate features from multi-source images together for tissue segmentation. The multi-source images include initially only the multi-modality (T1, T2 and FA) images and later also the iteratively estimated and refined tissue probability maps of gray matter, white matter, and cerebrospinal fluid. Experimental results on 119 infant subjects and MICCAI challenges show that the proposed method achieves better performance than other state-of-the-art automated segmentation methods, with significantly reduction of running time from hours to 5 minutes.

1   Introduction

The first year of life is the most dynamic phase of the postnatal human brain development, with the rapid tissue growth and development of a wide range of cognitive and motor functions. Accurate tissue segmentation of infant brain MR images into white matter (WM), gray matter (GM), and cerebrospinal fluid (CSF) in this phase is of great importance in studying the normal and abnormal early brain development [1, 2]. However, the segmentation of infant brain MRI is challenging due to the reduced tissue contrast [3], increased noise, severe partial volume effect [4], and the ongoing white matter myelination [3, 5]. In fact, there are three distinct stages in the first-year brain

B. Menze et al. (Eds.): MCV 2014, LNCS 8848, pp. 22–33, 2014.
DOI: 10.1007/978-3-319-13972-2_3

MR images, (1) infantile stage (≤5 months), (2) isointense stage (6–8 months), (3) early adult-like stage (≥9 months). Especially, in the isointense stage, the infant brain image appears isointense and exhibits the extremely low tissue contrast in both T1- and T2-weighted MRI, thus posing significant challenges for automated segmentation [6–8]. While, the other two stages show a relatively good contrast in T2-weighted MRI (the infantile stage) and T1-weighted MRI (the early adult-like stage), respectively.

Atlas-based segmentation has been one of the most popular techniques developed for brain MR image segmentation. As an extension, multi-atlas label fusion (MALF) makes use of more than one reference atlas to compensate potential biases and errors imposed by using a single atlas [9–14]. Such MALF methods have recently enjoyed the increased attention in the infant brain segmentation [15, 16]. However, one limitation of current MALF methods is that they employ a single modality image for segmentation. For example, Wang et al. [15] utilized 20 atlases from T2-weighted MRI for neonatal image segmentation, achieving promising results. However, to better address the challenge of segmenting isointense infant images, other modalities such as fractional anisotropy (FA) image from diffusion tensor imaging (DTI) could also be utilized to improve the segmentation on WM bundle as well as the subcortical region [17]. However, previous methods involved with multi-modality images usually consider each modality equally, which may not hold true since certain modalities may provide better guidance for some varying local brain regions. Another limitation of previous methods is that they are computationally expensive (e.g., taking hours), due to their requirement of multiple nonlinear registrations between atlases and the target image. Moreover, the larger number of atlases used, the longer computational time is expected. This disadvantage limits the number of atlases that could be utilized by MALF. To this end, some methods have been proposed to reduce the computational time by employing simple linear registration, which were unfortunately proved with compromised performance [18].

To address these limitations, we propose a novel Learning-based multi-source IntegratioN frameworK for Segmentation of infant brain images (LINKS). The proposed framework is able to integrate information from multi-source images together for efficient tissue segmentation. Specifically, the multi-source images used in our work initially include multi-modality (T1, T2 and FA) images, and later also the iteratively estimated and refined tissue probability maps for GM, WM and CSF. As a learning-based approach, our framework consists of two stages: training and testing stages. In the training stage, we first use the classification forest [19] to train a multi-class tissue classifier based on the training subjects with multiple modalities. The trained classifier provides the initial tissue probability maps for each training subject. Inspired by the auto-context model [20, 21], the estimated tissue probability maps are further used as additional input images to train the next classifier, which combines the high-level multi-class context features from estimated tissue probability maps with the appearance features from multi-modality images for refining the tissue classification. By iteratively training the subsequent classifiers based on the updated tissue probability maps, we can finally obtain a sequence of classifiers. Similarly, in the testing stage, given a target subject, the learned classifiers are sequentially applied to iteratively refine the estimation of tissue probability maps by combining multi-modality information with previously-estimated tissue probability maps. There are three advantages of our method, compared to previous methods:

(1) *Effective Integration of Multi-Modality Images.* Instead of either treating different modalities equally or explicitly defining different weights for them, we use random forest to learn the contribution of each modality automatically by fully exploring the power of each modality.

(2) *Spatially Consistent Labeling by using Multi-class Context Features.* The tissue probability maps of previous classifier provide rich context features (e.g., tissue types of nearby voxels), which are critical for addressing the spatial inconsistency caused by independent voxel-wise classification.

(3) *Computational Efficiency.* In contrast to the previous methods, which often require nonlinear registration between the training subjects (used as atlases) and the target subject, our method involves only the linear registration to ensure all subjects to have same orientation.

Validated on 119 infant subjects collected from 0-, 3-, 6-, 9- and 12-month old infants, the proposed method has achieved the state-of-the-art accuracy with significant reduction of runtime, compared to previous methods. Further validation has been performed on the MICCAI2012 challenge and our method has achieved the best performance among all the competing methods. In addition, our method can also be used in other important applications, such as the diencephalon labeling (MICCAI2013 challenge), in which our method has achieved the overall good performance, only slightly short of the leading accuracy. To alleviate possible anatomical errors, our method can be also combined with the anatomically-constrained multi-atlas labeling approach [17] for further improving the segmentation accuracy.

For related work, many previous methods based on the random forest have been proposed for image segmentation [22–26]. For example, Han [24] first performed the traditional multi-atlas label fusion and then employed random forests to refine structure labels at "ambiguous" voxels where labels from different atlases do not fully agree. This method has been applied to the segmentation of head and neck images with promising results. However, this method still requires nonlinear registrations as in MALF. Criminisi et al. proposed a random forest-based method for efficient detection and localization of anatomical structures within CT volumes [27]. Zikic et al. proposed a novel method based on the random forests for automatic segmentation of high-grade gliomas and their sub-regions from multi-channel MR images [26]. Similar work was also presented in [25], in which an atlas forest was introduced for efficient brain labeling. Our proposed method differs from the above mentioned methods [24–27] in two aspects: (1) our method allows integration of multi-source information, i.e., original multi-modality images and tissue probability maps, which are important for the optimal performance, and (2) an iterative classification scheme is adopted for achieving spatially consistent tissue segmentation by adaptively integrating knowledge from the previously-estimated tissue probability maps.

2 Method

2.1 Data and Image Preprocessing

This study has been approved by institute IRB and the written informed consent forms were obtained from all parents. In the training stage, for each time-point (0-, 3-, 6-, 9-, and 12-months of age), we have 10 training atlases with all T1, T2 and FA modality images. T1- and T2-weighted images were acquired on a Siemens head-only 3T scanners with a circular polarized head coil. During the scan, infants were asleep, unsedated, fitted with ear protection, and their heads were secured in a vacuum-fixation device. T1-weighted images were acquired with 144 sagittal slices using parameters: TR/TE = 1900/4.38 ms, flip angle = 7°, resolution = $1 \times 1 \times 1$ mm^3. T2-weighted images were obtained with 64 axial slices: TR/TE = 7380/119 ms, flip angle = 150° and resolution = $1.25 \times 1.25 \times 1.95$ mm^3. Diffusion weighted images consist of 60 axial slices: TR/TE = 7680/82 ms, resolution = $2 \times 2 \times 2$ mm^3, 42 non-collinear diffusion gradients, and b = 1000 s/mm^2. Seven non-diffusion-weighted reference scans were also acquired. The diffusion tensor images were reconstructed and the respective FA images were computed. Data with moderate or severe motion artifacts was discarded and a rescan was made when possible [28].

For image preprocessing, T2 images were linearly aligned to their corresponding T1 images. FA images were first linearly aligned to T2 images and then propagated to T1 images. All images were resampled into an isotropic $1 \times 1 \times 1$ mm^3 resolution. Afterwards, standard image preprocessing steps were performed before segmentation, including skull stripping [29], intensity inhomogeneity correction [30] and histogram matching, and removal of the cerebellum and brain stem by using in-house tools. To generate the manual segmentations, we first generated an initial reasonable segmentation by using a publicly available software iBEAT[1] [31]. Then, manual editing was carefully performed by an experienced rater to correct segmentation errors by using ITK-SNAP[2] [32] based on T1, T2 and FA images.

2.2   Multi-source Classification with Multi-class Auto-Context

In this paper, we formulate the tissue segmentation problem as a tissue classification problem. In particular, random forest [19] is adopted as a multi-class classifier to produce a tissue probability map for each tissue type (i.e., WM, GM, CSF) by voxel-wise classification. The final segmentation is accomplished by assigning the tissue label with the largest probability at each voxel location. As a supervised learning method, our method consists of training and testing stages. The flowchart of training stage is shown in Fig. 1. In the training stage, we will train a sequence of classification forests, each with the input of multi-source images/maps. In the first iteration, the classification forest takes only the multi-modality images as input, and learn the optimal image appearance features from different modalities for voxel-wise classification. In the later iterations, the three tissue probability maps obtained from the previous iteration will act as additional source images. Specifically, high-level multi-class context features are extracted from three tissue probability maps to assist the classification, along with multi-modality images. Since multi-class context features are informative about the nearby tissue structures for each voxel, they encode the spatial constraints into the

---

[1] http://www.nitrc.org/projects/ibeat.

[2] http://www.itksnap.org/.

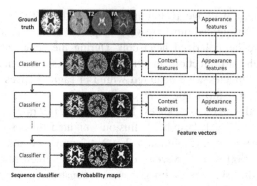

Fig. 1. Flowchart of the training procedure for our proposed method with multi-source images, including T1, T2, and FA images, along with probability maps of WM, GM and CSF.

classification, thus improving the quality of tissue probability maps estimated, as also demonstrated in Fig. 1.

In the testing stage, a target subject with multi-modality images is first linearly aligned to the atlas space. Similar to the training stage, in the first iteration, three tissue probability maps are estimated by voxel-wise classification with only the image appearance features obtained from multi-modality images. In the later iterations, the tissue probability maps estimated from previous iteration are also fed into the next classifier for refinement. Figure 2 shows an example by applying a sequence of learned classifiers on a target subject. As we can see from Fig. 2, the tissue probability maps are gradually improved with iterations and become more and more accurate.

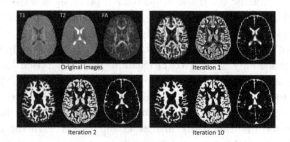

Fig. 2. The estimated tissue probability maps by applying a sequence of learned classifiers on a target subject in the isointense stage with T1, T2 and FA modalities. The probability maps become more and more accurate and sharp with iterations.

2.3 Appearance and Context Features

Our framework can utilize any kind of features from multi-modality and tissue probability maps for tissue classification. In this work, we use 3D Haar features [33] due to its efficiency. Specifically, for each voxel x, its Haar features are computed as the local mean intensity of any randomly displaced cubical region R_1 or the mean intensity difference over any two randomly displaced, asymmetric cubical regions (R_1 and R_2) within the image patch R [24]:

$$f(x, I) = \frac{1}{|R_1|}\sum_{u \in R_1} I(u) - b\frac{1}{|R_2|}\sum_{v \in R_2} I(v), R_1 \in R, R_2 \in R, \quad b \in \{0, 1\} \quad (1)$$

where R is the patch centered at voxel x, I is any kind of source image and the parameter $b \in \{0, 1\}$ indicates whether one or two cubical regions are used (as shown in Fig. 3, $b = 1$). In the image patch R, its intensities are normalized to have the unit $\ell 2$ norm [34, 35]. In theory, for each voxel we can determine an infinite number of such features. For simplicity, we employ 3D Haar features for both image appearance features and multi-class context features.

Fig. 3. Haar features, a 2D illustration. The red rectangle indicated the patch centered at x. Haar-like features are computed as the local mean of any randomly displaced cubical region R_1 or the mean difference over any two randomly displaced, asymmetric cubical regions (R_1 and R_2) within the image patch R.

Implementation. In our implementation, for each tissue type, we select 10000 training samples for each training subject. Then, for each training sample with the patch size of $7 \times 7 \times 7$, 10000 random Haar features are extracted from all source images: T1, T2, FA images, and three probability maps of WM, GM and CSF. In each iteration, we train 20 classification trees. We stop the tree growth at a certain depth (i.e., $d = 50$), with a minimum of 8 sample numbers for each leaf node ($s_{min} = 8$), according to the setting in [25].

Imposing Anatomical Constraint into the Segmentation. Based on the estimated probability maps by the classification forest, the final segmentation of the target subject could be obtained by assigning the label with the maximal probability for each voxel. However, as noticed in, due to the extremely low tissue contrast in the isointense infant image, the probability maps obtained by the classification forest might introduce artificial anatomical errors in the final segmentation results. To deal with this possible limitation, we can use sparse representation [36, 37] technique to impose the anatomical constraint into the segmentation. Specifically, by applying the trained classification forests, each training subject can obtain its corresponding *forest-based tissue probability maps*. Then, for each voxel in the *forest-based tissue probability maps* of the target subject, its patch can be sparsely represented by the neighboring patches in all aligned *forest-based tissue probability maps* of all training subjects, by minimizing a non-negative Elastic-Net problem [38]. Then, the new segmentation for the target subject can be computed by using the obtained sparse coefficients to estimate the new tissue probabilities [17], which are often more accurate as confirmed by experimental results below as well as in [39].

3 Experimental Results

Due to the dynamic changes of appearance pattern in the first year of life, it is difficult to train the random forest jointly for all time-points. Therefore, we trained the random forest for each time-point separately. The validations are performed on 119 *target* subjects consisting of 26, 22, 22, 23, and 26 subjects at 0-, 3-, 6-, 9- and 12-months of age, respectively. The manual segmentation for each subject is provided and considered as the ground truth for quantitative comparison. In the following, we will mainly focus on describing results for the 6-month images, since they are the most difficult for segmentation due to insufficient image contrast. Besides, we will also validate the proposed method on the MICCAI2012 and MICCAI2013 grand challenges.

3.1   Importance of the Multi-source Information

Figure 4 shows the Dice ratios on 22 isointense subjects by sequentially applying the learned classifiers. It can be seen that the Dice ratios are improved with the iterations and become stable after a few iterations (i.e., 5 iterations). Specially, in the second iteration, the Dice ratios are improved greatly due to the integration of the previously-estimated tissue probability maps for guiding classification. These results demonstrate the importance of using multi-class context features for segmentation.

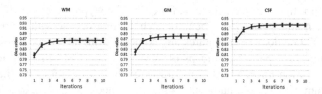

Fig. 4. Changes of Dice ratios of WM, GM and CSF on 22 isointense subjects, with the increase of iteration number.

We further evaluate the importance of the different modalities: T1, T2 and FA. Since the multi-class context feature is important for the segmentation, as shown in Fig. 4, we integrate it with different combinations of three modalities for training and testing. Figure 5 demonstrates the Dice ratios of the proposed method with different combinations of three modalities. It is can be seen from Fig. 5 that any combination of modalities generally produce more accurate results than any single modality, which proves that the multi-modality information is useful for guiding tissue segmentation [17].

3.2   Comparison with Other Methods on 119 Infant Subjects

We make comparison with (a) the majority voting (MV), (b) Coupe et al.'s patch-based method [40], (c) Zikic et al.'s atlas forests [25], and (d) Wang et al.'s multimodality

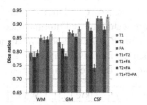

Fig. 5. Average Dice ratios of the proposed method with different combinations of 3 modalities.

sparse anatomical labeling [17]. Majority voting method assigns the most appeared label to each voxel based on the warped segmentations. Coupe et al.'s method employs the non-local mean patch-based strategy for the label fusing. Wang et al.'s method utilizes the patch-based sparse representation strategy. As demonstrated in [18], the use of nonlinear registrations to warped all the training subjects onto the target image space can produce more accurate results than the use of linear registrations. Therefore, to achieve the best performance for majority voting, Coupe et al.'s patch-based method and Wang et al.'s method, we applied a nonlinear registration method [41] to align all atlases to the target subject based on the multi-modality images. But, for our method, we still use the linear registration to ensure all the subjects have the same orientation. Zikic et al. [25] used atlas forests to train the atlas-specific classifiers. Similar with our method, their method does not require the nonlinear registration to warp the training subjects onto the target image space. However, one nonlinear registration is required to align the probabilistic atlas to the target. Due to the unavailability of their code, in our implementation, we used ANTs to warp the probabilistic-atlas to the target image space, where the probabilistic-atlas was estimated by using [42] based on our training subjects. Note that for all above comparison methods, they were performed on the multi-modality images and have been optimized the parameters via cross validation based on the training subjects. The Dice ratios of different method are shown in Table 1. It can be clearly seen that, even for the proposed method without anatomical constraint (last second column), it produces a competitive accuracy at all time-points. Especially, a significantly better (p-value < 0.05) accuracy for segmenting the 6-month infant brain images is achieved, as all other methods cannot effectively utilize the multi-source information for guiding the segmentation. Importantly, the proposed method (last second column) requires only the simple registration (linear registration) and also the least computational time (5 m) for a typical infant brain image with multi-modality images, as listed in Table 1.

3.3 Comparison with Other Methods on the MICCAI2012 Challenge

We further validate our algorithm on preterm born infants acquired at 40 weeks gestation corrected age, as provided by the MICCAI Grand Challenge on Neonatal Brain

Table 1. Segmentation accuracies (DC) of 6 different methods on 119 infant subjects, along with information of both registration technique and runtime used by each method. Proposed1 and Proposed2 denote the proposed method *without* and *with* anatomical constraint, respectively. Numbers (0, 3, 6, 9, and 12) denote months of age for the target subjects. Bold indicates statistically significantly larger than the other existing methods (p-value < 0.05).

Methods		MV	Coupe [40]	Zikic [25]	Wang [17]	Proposed1	Proposed2
Time cost		1h	1.2h	12m	2h	5m	1.8h
WM	0	81.6±0.28	89.0±0.74	88.9±0.60	89.7±0.59	**91.7±0.64**	92.1±0.62
	3	76.6±1.48	85.0±1.21	85.1±1.33	85.3±1.71	**88.8±1.09**	89.1±0.95
	6	80.1±0.83	83.6±0.80	82.1±0.91	84.2±0.78	**86.4±0.79**	87.9±0.68
	9	79.2±0.98	86.1±2.00	84.2±1.34	87.1±1.89	**89.0±0.78**	89.4±0.56
	12	82.5±1.05	88.6±1.22	87.2±1.29	90.3±1.42	90.7±0.74	91.8±0.65
GM	0	78.6±1.02	85.1±0.78	87.1±0.76	86.7±0.81	**89.6±0.66**	90.8±0.42
	3	77.3±1.42	83.4±0.78	85.5±1.12	85.3±0.51	**88.1±1.00**	88.3±0.90
	6	79.9±1.04	83.9±0.83	83.1±0.93	84.8±0.77	**88.2±0.77**	89.7±0.59
	9	83.6±0.69	88.1±0.75	87.4±0.66	87.4±0.54	**90.0±0.49**	90.3±0.54
	12	84.9±1.01	89.3±0.90	88.8±1.02	88.9±0.57	**90.3±0.74**	90.4±0.68
CSF	0	76.6±1.57	80.2±1.87	77.7±4.52	76.1±2.59	**83.9±2.20**	84.2±2.02
	3	80.6±1.55	84.1±1.88	82.4±2.17	80.1±1.10	83.7±1.52	85.4±1.49
	6	71.2±0.71	79.2±1.69	86.7±1.16	83.0±0.77	**92.7±0.63**	93.1±0.55
	9	68.7±1.27	80.6±2.40	84.1±1.57	81.0±2.27	85.8±1.53	86.7±1.09
	12	65.2±3.69	81.5±1.66	83.6±1.83	81.7±2.59	84.1±1.90	85.2±1.69

Segmentation (NeoBrainS12[3]). We segment the neonatal brain into 6 classes: unmyelinated and myelinated whiter matter (WM), cortical grey matter (CGM), basal ganglia and thalami (BGT), brainstem (BS), cerebellum (CB), ventricles and cerebrospinal fluid in the extracerebral space (CSF). The Dice ratios and modified Hausdorff distance by our method (3rd row, LINKS) and also other competing methods are shown in Table 2. It can be clearly seen that our methods achieves the superior performance and is ranked top among all the competing methods.[4]

3.4 Comparison with Other Methods on the MICCAI2013 Challenge

Besides the infant brain segmentation, our method can be also used in other applications. For example, we applied it on the MICCAI2013 SATA challenge[5] for the adult diencephalon labeling, in which the diencephalon is labeled into 14 ROIs. The accuracy measured by the mean (±standard deviation) Dice ratio by our method on this challenge data is 0.8613 (±0.0261). For reference, the accuracy by Zikic et al.'s atlas-forest method [25] is 0.8282 (±0.0495) while the leading accuracy is 0.8686 (±0.0237). It can be seen that our result is still very good, only slightly short of the leading accuracy.

---

[3] http://neobrains12.isi.uu.nl.

[4] http://neobrains12.isi.uu.nl/mainResults_Set1.php.

[5] https://masi.vuse.vanderbilt.edu/workshop2013.

Table 2. Dice ratios (DC) and modified Hausdorff distance (MHD) of different methods on NeoBrainS12 MICCAI Challenge data (**Bold** indicates the best performance).

Team Name	WM		CGM		BGT		BS		CB		CSF		Placed
	DC	MHD	DC	MHD	DC	MHD	DC	MHD	DC	MHD	DC	MHD	
LINKS	**0.92**	**0.35**	**0.86**	**0.47**	**0.92**	**0.47**	**0.83**	**0.9**	**0.92**	**0.5**	**0.79**	**1.18**	1
Imperial	0.89	0.70	0.84	0.73	0.91	0.8	0.84	1.04	0.91	0.7	0.77	1.55	2
Oxford	0.88	0.76	0.83	0.61	0.87	1.32	0.8	1.24	0.92	0.63	0.74	1.82	3
UCL	0.87	1.03	0.83	0.73	0.89	1.29	0.82	1.3	0.9	0.92	0.73	2.06	4
UPenn	0.84	1.79	0.80	1.01	0.8	4.18	0.74	1.96	0.91	0.85	0.64	2.46	5

4 Conclusion

We have presented a learning-based method to effectively integrate multi-source images and the tentatively estimated tissue probability maps for infant brain image segmentation. Specifically, we employ a random forest technique to effectively integrate features from multi-source images, including T1, T2, FA images and also the probability maps of different tissues estimated during the classification process. Experimental results on 119 infant subjects and NeoBrainS12 MICCAI grand challenge show that the proposed method achieves better performance than other state-of-the-art automated segmentation methods. We further applied our method on MICCAI2013 SATA challenge and also achieved a good performance. In this work, we extract only the Haar features, which may be not the optimal choice. In our future work, we will explore other types of features and also validate the proposed method on more subjects. The source code for our work will be publicly available.[6]

References

1. Nie, J., Li, G., Wang, L., Gilmore, J.H., Lin, W., Shen, D.: A computational growth model for measuring dynamic cortical development in the first year of life. Cereb. Cortex **22**, 2272–2284 (2012)
2. Li, G., Nie, J., Wang, L., Shi, F., Lyall, A.E., Lin, W., Gilmore, J.H., Shen, D.: Mapping longitudinal hemispheric structural asymmetries of the human cerebral cortex from birth to 2 years of age. Cereb. Cortex **24**, 1289–1300 (2013)
3. Weisenfeld, N.I., Warfield, S.K.: Automatic segmentation of newborn brain MRI. NeuroImage **47**, 564–572 (2009)
4. Xue, H., Srinivasan, L., Jiang, S., Rutherford, M., Edwards, A.D., Rueckert, D., Hajnal, J. V.: Automatic segmentation and reconstruction of the cortex from neonatal MRI. NeuroImage **38**, 461–477 (2007)
5. Gui, L., Lisowski, R., Faundez, T., Hüppi, P.S., Lazeyras, F., Kocher, M.: Morphology-driven automatic segmentation of MR images of the neonatal brain. Med. Image Anal. **16**, 1565–1579 (2012)
6. Wang, L., Shi, F., Yap, P.-T., Gilmore, J.H., Lin, W., Shen, D.: 4D multi-modality tissue segmentation of serial infant images. PLoS ONE **7**, e44596 (2012)

---

[6] http://www.unc.edu/~liwa.

7. Wang, L., Shi, F., Yap, P., Lin, W., Gilmore, J.H., Shen, D.: Longitudinally guided level sets for consistent tissue segmentation of neonates. Hum. Brain Mapp. **34**, 956–972 (2013)

8. Wang, L., Shi, F., Lin, W., Gilmore, J.H., Shen, D.: Automatic segmentation of neonatal images using convex optimization and coupled level sets. NeuroImage **58**, 805–817 (2011)

9. Wang, H., Suh, J.W., Das, S.R., Pluta, J., Craige, C., Yushkevich, P.A.: Multi-atlas segmentation with joint label fusion. IEEE Trans. PAMI **35**, 611–623 (2013)

10. Rohlfing, T., Russakoff, D.B., Maurer Jr., C.R.: Performance-based classifier combination in atlas-based image segmentation using expectation-maximization parameter estimation. IEEE Trans. Med. Imaging **23**, 983–994 (2004)

11. Aljabar, P., Heckemann, R.A., Hammers, A., Hajnal, J.V., Rueckert, D.: Multi-atlas based segmentation of brain images: Atlas selection and its effect on accuracy. NeuroImage **46**, 726–738 (2009)

12. Heckemann, R.A., Hajnal, J.V., Aljabar, P., Rueckert, D., Hammers, A.: Automatic anatomical brain MRI segmentation combining label propagation and decision fusion. NeuroImage **33**, 115–126 (2006)

13. Warfield, S.K., Zou, K.H., Wells, W.M.: Simultaneous truth and performance level estimation (STAPLE): an algorithm for the validation of image segmentation. IEEE Trans. Med. Imaging **23**, 903–921 (2004)

14. Lötjönen, J.M.P., Wolz, R., Koikkalainen, J.R., Thurfjell, L., Waldemar, G., Soininen, H., Rueckert, D.: Fast and robust multi-atlas segmentation of brain magnetic resonance images. NeuroImage **49**, 2352–2365 (2010)

15. Wang, L., Shi, F., Li, G., Gao, Y., Lin, W., Gilmore, J.H., Shen, D.: Segmentation of neonatal brain MR images using patch-driven level sets. NeuroImage **84**, 141–158 (2014)

16. Srhoj-Egekher, V., Benders, M.J.N.L., Viergever, M.A., Išgum, I.: Automatic neonatal brain tissue segmentation with MRI. Proc. SPIE **8669**, 86691K (2013)

17. Wang, L., Shi, F., Gao, Y., Li, G., Gilmore, J.H., Lin, W., Shen, D.: Integration of sparse multi-modality representation and anatomical constraint for isointense infant brain MR image segmentation. NeuroImage **89**, 152–164 (2014)

18. Rousseau, F., Habas, P.A., Studholme, C.: A supervised patch-based approach for human brain labeling. IEEE Trans. Med. Imaging **30**, 1852–1862 (2011)

19. Breiman, L.: Random forests. Mach. Learn. **45**, 5–32 (2001)

20. Tu, Z., Bai, X.: Auto-context and its application to high-level vision tasks and 3D brain image segmentation. PAMI **32**, 1744–1757 (2010)

21. Loog, M., Ginneken, B.: Segmentation of the posterior ribs in chest radiographs using iterated contextual pixel classification. IEEE Trans. Med. Imaging **25**, 602–611 (2006)

22. Shotton, J., Johnson, M., Cipolla, R.: Semantic texton forests for image categorization and segmentation. In: IEEE Conference on Computer Vision and Pattern Recognition, CVPR 2008, pp. 1–8 (2008)

23. Montillo, A., Shotton, J., Winn, J., Iglesias, J., Metaxas, D., Criminisi, A.: Entangled decision forests and their application for semantic segmentation of CT images. In: Székely, G., Hahn, H.K. (eds.) IPMI 2011. LNCS, vol. 6801, pp. 184–196. Springer, Heidelberg (2011)

24. Han, X.: learning-boosted label fusion for multi-atlas auto-segmentation. In: Wu, G., Zhang, D., Shen, D., Yan, P., Suzuki, K., Wang, F. (eds.) MLMI 2013. LNCS, vol. 8184, pp. 17–24. Springer, Heidelberg (2013)

25. Zikic, D., Glocker, B., Criminisi, A.: Atlas encoding by randomized forests for efficient label propagation. In: Mori, K., Sakuma, I., Sato, Y., Barillot, C., Navab, N. (eds.) MICCAI 2013, Part III. LNCS, vol. 8151, pp. 66–73. Springer, Heidelberg (2013)

26. Zikic, D., Glocker, B., Konukoglu, E., Criminisi, A., Demiralp, C., Shotton, J., Thomas, O.M., Das, T., Jena, R., Price, S.J.: Decision forests for tissue-specific segmentation of high-grade gliomas in Multi-channel MR. In: Ayache, N., Delingette, H., Golland, P., Mori, K. (eds.) MICCAI 2012, Part III. LNCS, vol. 7512, pp. 369–376. Springer, Heidelberg (2012)

27. Criminisi, A., Shotton, J., Bucciarelli, S.: Decision forests with long-range spatial context for organ localization in CT Volumes. In: MICCAI-PMMIA (2009)

28. Blumenthal, J.D., Zijdenbos, A., Molloy, E., Giedd, J.N.: Motion artifact in magnetic resonance imaging: implications for automated analysis. NeuroImage 16, 89–92 (2002)

29. Shi, F., Wang, L., Dai, Y., Gilmore, J.H., Lin, W., Shen, D.: Pediatric brain extraction using learning-based meta-algorithm. NeuroImage 62, 1975–1986 (2012)

30. Sled, J.G., Zijdenbos, A.P., Evans, A.C.: A nonparametric method for automatic correction of intensity nonuniformity in MRI data. IEEE Trans. Med. Imaging 17, 87–97 (1998)

31. Dai, Y., Shi, F., Wang, L., Wu, G., Shen, D.: iBEAT: a toolbox for infant brain magnetic resonance image processing. Neuroinformatics 11, 211–225 (2013)

32. Yushkevich, P.A., Piven, J., Hazlett, H.C., Smith, R.G., Ho, S., Gee, J.C., Gerig, G.: User-guided 3D active contour segmentation of anatomical structures: significantly improved efficiency and reliability. NeuroImage 31, 1116–1128 (2006)

33. Viola, P., Jones, M.: Robust real-time face detection. Int. J. Comput. Vision 57, 137–154 (2004)

34. Cheng, H., Liu, Z., Yang, L.: Sparsity induced similarity measure for label propagation. In: Proceedings of the ICCV, pp. 317–324 (2009)

35. Wright, J., Yi, M., Mairal, J., Sapiro, G., Huang, T.S., Shuicheng, Y.: Sparse representation for computer vision and pattern recognition. Proc. IEEE 98, 1031–1044 (2010)

36. Zhang, S., Zhan, Y., Dewan, M., Huang, J., Metaxas, D.N., Zhou, X.S.: Towards robust and effective shape modeling: sparse shape composition. Med. Image Anal. 16, 265–277 (2012)

37. Zhang, S., Zhan, Y., Metaxas, D.N.: Deformable segmentation via sparse representation and dictionary learning. Med. Image Anal. 16, 1385–1396 (2012)

38. Zou, H., Hastie, T.: Regularization and variable selection via the elastic net. J. Roy. Stat. Soc. B 67, 301–320 (2005)

39. Bai, W., Shi, W., O'Regan, D., Tong, T., Wang, H., Jamil-Copley, S., Peters, N., Rueckert, D.: A probabilistic patch-based label fusion model for multi-atlas segmentation with registration refinement: application to cardiac MR images. IEEE Trans. Med. Imaging 32, 1302–1315 (2013)

40. Coupé, P., Manjón, J., Fonov, V., Pruessner, J., Robles, M., Collins, D.L.: Patch-based segmentation using expert priors: application to hippocampus and ventricle segmentation. NeuroImage 54, 940–954 (2011)

41. Avants, B.B., Tustison, N.J., Song, G., Cook, P.A., Klein, A., Gee, J.C.: A reproducible evaluation of ANTs similarity metric performance in brain image registration. NeuroImage 54, 2033–2044 (2011)

42. Joshi, S., Davis, B., Jomier, M., Gerig, G.: Unbiased diffeomorphic atlas construction for computational anatomy. NeuroImage 23(Supplement 1), S151–S160 (2004)

Pectoralis Muscle Segmentation on CT Images Based on Bayesian Graph Cuts with a Subject-Tailored Atlas

Rola Harmouche$^{(\boxtimes)}$, James C. Ross,
George R. Washko, and Raúl San José Estépar

Brigham and Women's Hospital and Harvard Medical School, Boston, MA, USA
rharmo@bwh.harvard.edu

Abstract. This paper proposes a method to segment the pectoralis muscles in CT scans of patients within a Bayesian framework. First, a subject-tailored probabilistic atlas is constructed using affine registered label-maps of subjects that are highly similar to the test subject from a database of pairwise registered training subjects. The likelihood is constructed using a multivariate distribution taking intensities and distance to the atlas into account. The posterior probability is used to drive a graph cuts segmentation for classifying the CT into left major, left minor, right major, right minor pectoralis and non-pectoralis taking neighborhood information into account. The probabilistic prior is built using 400 CT scans and the method is tested on 50 independent CT scans. Results are reported on each muscle separately and show a statistically significant improvement when the subject-tailored prior is incorporated into the model. This automatic method can be used to objectively and efficiently asses clinical outcomes for patients with COPD.

Keywords: Pectoralis muscle segmentation · Graph cuts · Subject-tailored atlas

1 Introduction

Chronic obstructive pulmonary disease (COPD) affects approximately 28.9 million people in the United States. It is increasingly recognized that altered body composition is common in COPD and represents a clinically relevant process in patients suffering from this condition [1]. For example, a low body mass index (BMI) is associated with increased mortality. While measures of BMI are non-invasive and easy to perform in any clinical setting, they are limited by their insensitivity to body composition. Recently, it was demonstrated that in COPD subjects low fat free mass prevalence was higher than low BMI [2]. Furthermore, [3] observed that computed tomography (CT) measures of pectoralis muscle area (PMA) on a single axial slice are significantly associated with COPD-related traits and may be a more clinically relevant measure of COPD-related outcomes than BMI. They also note that the relationship between PMA and

© Springer International Publishing Switzerland 2014
B. Menze et al. (Eds.): MCV 2014, LNCS 8848, pp. 34–44, 2014.
DOI: 10.1007/978-3-319-13972-2_4

clinically relevant outcomes requires further investigation. Such further investigation can benefit from the consistency inherent to automated segmentation as opposed to the presently used manual segmentation. In this paper, we propose an approach to automatically segment pectoralis muscles (pecs) on axial CT images.

Segmenting the pectoralis muscle group is challenging due to their thin and variable shape, proximity between the major and minor muscles, and low contrast and overlapping intensity distributions with surrounding tissue (Fig. 1). Reference [4] reviews methods for segmenting pectoralis muscles on mamograms; these include a range of techniques that apply intensity and edge-based segmentation methods. In the presence of low contrast, it can be helpful to apply *a priori* information about structure location. This *a priori* information can have the form of a statistical atlas. However, mis-registrations between the test subject and the subjects used to construct the atlas can diminish the quality of the segmentation. More importantly, the shape of the pectoralis muscles varies significantly between subjects, and registration is not always sufficient to compensate for these variations. A few works have proposed the use of clustering based on similarity metrics in order to identify modes of the distribution of atlases and to build an atlas for each mode [5–7]. For example, [8] uses an atlas-based approach in order to segment the pectoralis muscles from MRIs. They use a data set consisting of 26 images and register the labelmap of the closest training case for the segmentation. The intensity characteristics on MRIs are better suited to distinguish soft tissues, and thus the contrast problem is not as prominent as in the case of CT data. Most multi-atlas based approaches generate the segmentation directly from atlas labels and do not take image intensity into account. We believe that intensity information is beneficial in areas of low similarity between the test case and the training data. We are not aware of any pectoralis muscle segmentation efforts on CT data.

In this paper, we propose a pectoralis segmentation method within a graph cuts framework which incorporates the intensity and shape variabilities both between patients and within a patient's pectoralis muscle. A subject-tailored *a priori* statistical atlas is built online from multiple labeled training CT data that share high similarity with the test patient from within a large training dataset. The subject-tailored atlas diminishes the segmentation errors that occur due to shape differences between the atlas and the patient. We build a likelihood model based on intensities and distances from an expected pectoralis constructed from the atlas, in order to explicitly model low density regions inside the muscles. We build on the multi-shape graph cuts idea proposed in [5] by proposing a direct scheme with the following original contributions. First, our graph-cut approach maximizes a posterior probability that takes into account both intensity and shape by means of encoding the distance to an expected pec shape based on an atlas. Second, the probabilistic atlas that we propose is built based on selecting the most similar cases from a training set by means of a fast retrieval approach based on affine registrations.

The paper is organized as follows: Sect. 2 describes the segmentation method. Section 3 compares the results obtained with our method to one with likelihood and prior probabilities generated from a random set of patients. Conclusions and future works are discussed in Sect. 4.

2 Methods

The proposed approach aims to segment each CT image into left major, left minor, right major, right minor pecs and non pec, by means of a posterior probability that takes into account intensity, shape, and prior information. This is accomplished using graph cuts by assigning a label l from the set of labels $\mathcal{L} = \{leftMajor, leftMinor, rightMajor, rightMinor, nonPec\}$ to each pixel i in the CT image given its neighbor $\mathcal{N}_i$. The optimal labeling for each of the pectoralis muscles is obtained by minimizing the overall energy

$$E_l(f) = \sum_i A_i^l + \alpha \sum_{(i,j) \in \mathcal{N}_i} B_{i,j}, \tag{1}$$

where f is the labeling of the entire set of pixels, A_i is the data term and $B_{i,j}$ is the smoothness term. We model the intensity variability by taking into account the distance $d_i | m_k$ emanating from the *expected pec* with label $m_k \in \mathcal{L}$ to pixel i. The *expected pec* from a label m_k is defined as $P_{m_k}(i) > 0.5$. The data term is given by the negative log of the posterior probabilities defined as:

$$A_i^l = -\ln \left[\frac{p(I_i, d_i | L_i) P(L_i)}{P(I_i, d_i)} \right] = -\ln \left[\frac{\sum_{k=1}^{N} p(I_i, d_i | L_i, m_k) p(m_k) P(L_i)}{P(I_i, d_i)} \right],$$

where L_i is the random variable describing the label, I_i is the CT density at pixel i, $P(L_i)$ is the *a priori* probability distribution for the label classes at pixel i, $P(I_i, d_i | L_i)$ is the likelihood of each of the labels, and $P(I_i, d_i)$ is the joint probability defined as

$$P(I_i, d_i) = \sum_{l \in \mathcal{L}} P(I_i, d_i | L_i) P(L_i). \tag{2}$$

The smoothness term incorporates first and second order neighborhood information. This is useful to segment small, low density regions within the pectoralis. Labeling of each pectoralis class is done by minimizing Eq. 1 using the alpha expansion method [9]. A final labelmap is computed by merging the labeling from the four graph cuts. Pixels with multiple labels are assigned to the label with a higher posterior probability in order to produce a proper splitting. We now describe the likelihood and prior probability computations.

2.1 Modeling the Likelihood

Based on experimental observations of the training data (Fig. 2), the joint likelihood of intensity and distance to a pectoral muscle $l_k \in \mathcal{L}$ conditioned on a

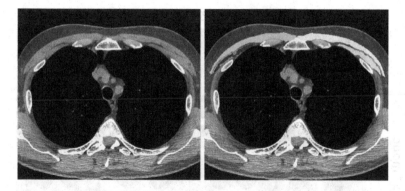

Fig. 1. Example of a CT image of the pectoralis muscles and corresponding segmentation. The major pectoralis (left and right) sits on top of the minor, the latter being closer to the chest wall.

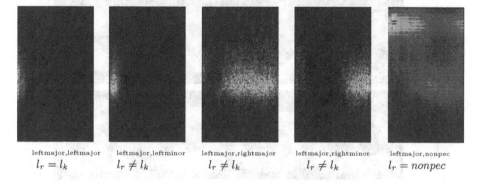

leftmajor,leftmajor	leftmajor,leftminor	leftmajor,rightmajor	leftmajor,rightminor	leftmajor,nonpec
$l_r = l_k$	$l_r \neq l_k$	$l_r \neq l_k$	$l_r \neq l_k$	$l_r = nonpec$

Fig. 2. Histograms based on intensity (vertical) and distance (horizontal) obtained from the training dataset for the three different families that are defined. These histograms are used in order to estimate the parametric likelihoods used for the classification.

given pectoral muscle $l_r \in \mathcal{L}$ belongs to three different families depending on whether $l_r = l_k$, $l_r \neq l_k$ and $l_r =$ nonpec. We chose this model since the actual intensity distributions vary based on the distance to the pecs. This is particularly true for the non-pec intensities, which are obtained from a variety of structures. Also, given that there is intensity overlap between non-pec structures and the pecs themselves, the distance can provide location-specific intensity information which is complementary to the spatial information that is encoded in the a priori atlas.

Likelihood for $l_r = l_k$. This likelihood has a fast decay with distance while the intensity at a given distance follows more or less a normal distribution. We thus model this likelihood with an exponential distribution in distance and a Gaussian distribution in intensity, where the means and variances are linearly dependent on distance.

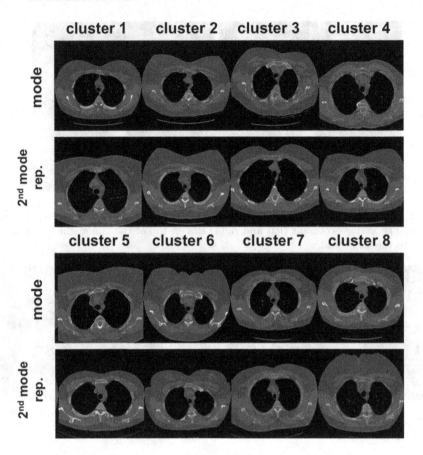

Fig. 3. Training cases selected as cluster modes to serve as reference for the initial registration to compute the probabilistic prior. Each cluster shows a different anatomical shape in the pec muscles.

$$p(I, d|l_r, l_k) = \frac{\lambda^2}{\sqrt{2\pi}(\gamma + \kappa\lambda)} e^{-\frac{(I_{l_r} - (\alpha d_{l_k} + \beta))^2}{2(\gamma d_{l_k} + \kappa)^2}} e^{-\lambda d_{l_k}}. \tag{3}$$

The parameters of this distribution $\alpha, \beta, \gamma, \kappa, \lambda$ are estimated using a maximum likelihood (ML) estimator. The ML is maximize using the limited-memory quasi-Newton algorithm with bounds constrains (L-BFGS-B). We have experimentally verified that the exponential model is a good fit to sampled distribution.

Likelihood for $l_r \neq l_k$**.** The likelihood between structure intensity and distance to a different pec structure exhibits a mode not centered at $d = 0$, and the decay with distance is smoother than in the previous case. Our model of choice for this likelihood is the same modified Gaussian as in the previous case, but with a Rice distribution modeling the variation in distance. This fits the non-symmetric distributions that we have obtained when observing the training data. In this case the likelihood is defined as:

$$p(I, d | l_r, l_k) = \frac{1}{C} e^{-\frac{(I_{l_r} - (\alpha d_{l_k} + \beta))^2}{2(\gamma d_{l_k} + \kappa)^2}} \frac{d_{l_k}}{\sigma^2} e^{-\frac{(d_{l_k}^2 + \eta^2)}{2\sigma^2}} I_0 \left(\frac{d\eta}{\sigma^2} \right) \tag{4}$$

where α, β, γ, κ are the Gaussian parameters, η and σ are the Rice parameters, and C is a normalization constant

$$C = \frac{\sqrt{\pi}}{2\sqrt{2}\sigma} \left(4\sigma(\kappa - \gamma\eta) + \sqrt{2\pi}\gamma e^{-\frac{\eta^2}{4\sigma^2}} \left(\eta^2 I_1 \left(\frac{\eta^2}{4\sigma^2} \right) + (\eta^2 + 2\sigma^2) I_0 \left(\frac{\eta^2}{4\sigma^2} \right) \right) \right) \tag{5}$$

Non-pec likelihoods. Finally, since multiple structures with different intensity distributions comprise the non-pec class, each non-pec distribution is estimated using a bivariate mixture of Gaussians in I and d. The Gaussian mixture model parameters are obtained using the expectation maximization algorithm. We emperically found three modes in the distributions and modeled the likelihoods accordingly.

2.2 Modeling the Prior Probability

The prior probability is defined using a probabilistic atlas that is built for the test subject to be segmented by selecting a most suitable subset of cases from a training dataset based on a normalized cross correlation similarity metric. This atlas tries to overcome the main problem of general atlas approaches, namely, the difficulty in modeling large variations in anatomy as is typically encountered in the pecs. We compute the similarity only in the pec muscles and surrounding fat area. This allows us to generate organ specific atlases that are not biased by the overall appearance beyond the region of interest. In this section we describe how we build the subject-specific atlas.

Let us define $\mathcal{C} = \{c_1, c_2 \cdots, c_M\}$ as a training set of M segmented pec labelmaps. The goal of our approach is to find a subset of K training cases that are the best fit to the test case. These K cases are obtained by measuring the similarity between the CTs of the training data and the test CT, CT_{test}. To this end, we first performed an offline pairwise affine registration between the labelmaps of all the training cases. Let us define T_{mn} as the affine registration from training cases c_m to c_n. We then register CT_{test} to a reference case, c_k, from the training set, CT_{c_k} to obtain T_{test}. Then, normalized cross correlation (NCC) between the test subject and the registered training CT image corresponding to the labelmap c_m is obtained in a computational efficient manner by means of transformation concatenation:

$$\mathrm{NCC}(\mathrm{CT}_{test}, \mathrm{CT}_{c_m}) = \mathrm{NCC}\left(\mathrm{CT}_{test}, \mathrm{CT}_{c_m}(T_{test}^{-1} \circ T_{mk}) \right). \tag{6}$$

The subset of K training cases, $\mathcal{C}_{test} = \{c_m\}$ that yield the K highest (NCC) scores is selected to build our atlas. The subject specific probabilistic atlas at pixel location i in the test CT image domain is then defined as

$$w_r = \frac{\mathrm{NCC}(\mathrm{CT}_{test}, \mathrm{CT}_{c_r})}{\sum_{m \in \mathcal{C}_{test}} \mathrm{NCC}(\mathrm{CT}_{test}, \mathrm{CT}_{c_m})} \qquad (7)$$

are weights based on the similarity metric that assign a higher probability to the most similar training cases. G_σ is a Gaussian kernel with standard deviation σ that is used to smooth the atlas to account for the uncertainty in the affine registration. It is worth noting that the proposed approach only requires a single registration between the test CT image, CT_{test}, and the reference CT image from the training set, CT_{c_k}.

$$P_l(i) = G_\sigma(i) * \frac{1}{K} \sum_{r \in \mathcal{C}_{test}} w_r c_r ((T_{test}^{-1} \circ T_{rk})i) \qquad (8)$$

The choice of a reference case from the training set can greatly affect the result of the similarity calculation. If the reference case and the test case are highly dissimilar, the quality of the registration between the two cases and, consequently, to the remaining training dataset is reduced. In order to reduce such errors, we compile offline a group of reference cases that are fairly representative of the training dataset. In order to obtain these reference cases, spectral clustering is performed using the pairwise normalized cross-correlation values between all the training cases. For each cluster, the mode selected is the training case which has maximum average similarity with the other cluster members. The different modes obtained in our training set and the second mode exemplar for each cluster are displayed in Fig. 3. These modes form our reference cases. For each new test case, the reference case that has the highest similarity to one of the modes is selected as the reference case.

3   Results

3.1   Experimental Setup

We validate our approach using a training set of 450 high resolution CT scans of patients with COPD spanning a range of disease stages. The method is validated using 50 CT scans. The training labels were generated using manual labeling by experts. Validation is performed by computing the Dice score between the automatic and the manual segmentations. True positive (TPR) and positive predictive rates (PPR) values are also computed. Since pectoralis segmentation on CT has not been attempted to date, we could not justify a single method for comparison. The task itself is difficult mainly due to a low contrast between the pecs and surrounding tissues on CT, rendering the comparison to methods applied to other image modalities or structures (such as edge-based approaches) less relevant. However, in order to test the effectiveness of the personalized atlas, we compare results obtained using our proposed method to the same method but with an atlas generated using a randomly selected set of cases from within the training data set. We also test the effect of varying the number of cases used in order to build our atlas.

3.2   Qualitative Results

Figures 4 and 5 show segmentations for a few cases obtained using each of the experiments. In Fig. 4, all methods fail to properly distinguish the boundary

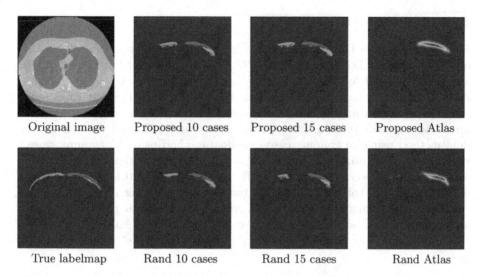

Fig. 4. Classification of the right major (orange), right minor (red), left major (cyan) and left minor (green) pectoralis muscles using atlases generated with the random and proposed method, and using 10 and 15 cases. The right major pectoralis atlases are displayed on the right (Color figure online).

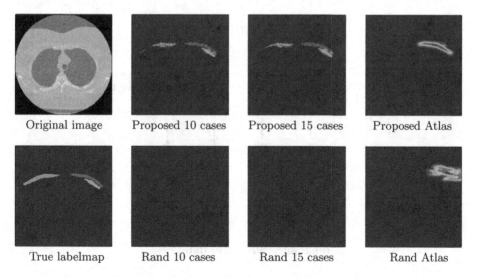

Fig. 5. Classification of the pectoralis muscles (same color scheme as Fig. 4) (Color figure online).

between the lower and upper pectoralis muscles seen on the left side of the image. However, the proposed method better captures the shape of the upper pectoralis muscle on the right side of the image, due to a better atlas in that area. In Fig. 5, the random atlas is erroneous leading to a segmentation failure.

3.3   Quantitative Results

Figure 6(a) displays Dice overlap values for the test cases using the two methods. The average Dice values are 0.672 ± 0.18, 0.669 ± 0.18, 0.738 ± 0.110 and 0.739 ± 0.109 for the random method using 10 training cases, random method using 15 training cases, proposed method using 10 closest cases, and proposed method using 15 closest cases, respectively. The average TPR values are 0.744 ± 0.0209, 0.736 ± 0.0210, 0.867 ± 0.08 and 0.873 ± 0.08 for the random method using 10 training cases, random method using 15 training cases, proposed method using 10 closest cases, and proposed method using 15 closest cases, respectively. The average PPR values are 0.629 ± 0.18, 0.737 ± 0.209, 0.652 ± 0.122 and 0.652 ± 0.123 for the random method using 10 training cases, random method using 15 training cases, proposed method using 10 closest cases, and proposed method using 15 closest cases, respectively. An ANOVA analysis shows differences between the four groups for TPR ($p < .0001$) and PPR

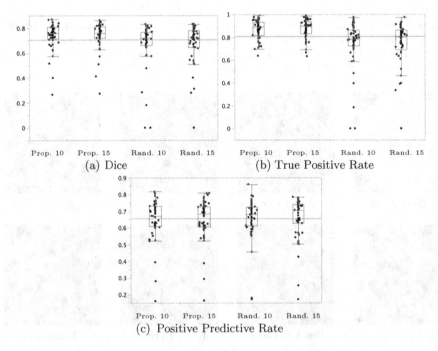

(a) Dice

(b) True Positive Rate

(c) Positive Predictive Rate

Fig. 6. Bloxplots comparing the proposed and the random methods. Dice, TPR and PPR are reported for the 50 testing cases.

($p = 0.025$) but not for Dice ($p = 0.053$). When looking at the pair-wise differences between the groups using a Tukey-Kramer HSD test, the results using the subject-tailored atlas (for both 10 and 15 training cases) were different to the random counterparts. However, there were no differences between the subject-tailored atlas using 10 or 15 training cases indicating that our method performs equally well with a prior based on 10 training cases. The subject-tailored atlas is less susceptible to failure which may occur when the training dataset is not representative of the test case. In particular, the true positive rate was particularly better when our method is used, which means that the alignment between the atlas and the structure to be segmented allowed for the structure's shape to be captured. We believe that our segmentation results are sufficient for studies with large sample sizes.

With regards to the time efficiency of the method, it requires on average 200 seconds per patient (including atlas building and segmentation) with a python implementation (OSX 10.8.3 machine, Intel Core i7 2.7 GHz processor). This is comparable to manual segmentation, but can be run in parallel on clusters thus saving man-hours in the long run. The automatic method also provides an objective segmentation, which is important when dealing with a large cohort in the context of a clinical investigation.

4   Conclusions

A method was proposed to segment pectoralis muscles from CT scans using graph cuts and subject-tailored atlases. The overall energy was minimized by taking into account the posterior probability at each voxel and neighborhood information. In addition to intensity information, the distance to an expected pectoralis based on the atlas is incorporated into the likelihood. The prior is built using a subset of a training cases that best fit the test case based on normalised cross correlation. Results were reported on 50 scans and show a statistically significant improvement when the atlas is built using our proposed method and when the distance to the pectoralis muscles is incorporated in the likelihood. The proposed method allows for the segmentation of the pectoralis and serves as an important first step in the analysis of COPD. Future work includes using a larger database which will allow us to construct an atlas with a much higher similarity to the test case and therefore improving the overall segmentation result. In addition, faster comparison methods between the test case and the database will be explored in order to reduce computational time, which will be essential when leveraging large databases.

Acknowledgements. This work has been supported by NIH NHLBI award number 1R01HL116931, 1R01HL122464-01A1 and K25-HL104085. The content is solely the responsibility of the authors and does not necessarily represent the official views of the NIH.

References

1. Schols, A.M., et al.: Body composition and mortality in chronic obstructive pulmonary disease. Am. J. Clin. Nutr. **82**(1), 53–59 (2005)
2. Kim, S., et al.: Body mass index and fat free mass index in obstructive lung disease in korea. Int. J. Tuberc. Lung Dis. **18**(1), 102–108 (2014)
3. McDonald, M.L.N., et al.: Quantitative computed tomographic measures of pectoralis muscle area and disease severity in chronic obstructive pulmonary disease: A cross-sectional study. Ann. Am. Thorac. Soc. **11**, 326–334 (2014)
4. Ganesan, K., et al.: Pectoral muscle segmentation: a review. Comput. Meth. Programs Biomed. **110**(1), 48–57 (2013)
5. Shimizu, A., Nakagomi, K., Narihira, T., Kobatake, H., Nawano, S., Shinozaki, K., Ishizu, K., Togashi, K.: Automated segmentation of 3D CT images based on statistical atlas and graph cuts. In: Menze, B., Langs, G., Tu, Z., Criminisi, A. (eds.) MICCAI 2010. LNCS, vol. 6533, pp. 214–223. Springer, Heidelberg (2011)
6. Park, H., Bland, P.H., Hero III, A.O., Meyer, C.R.: Least biased target selection in probabilistic atlas construction. In: Duncan, J.S., Gerig, G. (eds.) MICCAI 2005. LNCS, vol. 3750, pp. 419–426. Springer, Heidelberg (2005)
7. Blezek, D.J., Miller, J.V.: Atlas stratification. MIA **11**(5), 443–457 (2007)
8. Gubern-Mérida, A., Kallenberg, M., Martí, R., Karssemeijer, N.: Segmentation of the pectoral muscle in breast mri using atlas-based approaches. In: Ayache, N., Delingette, H., Golland, P., Mori, K. (eds.) MICCAI 2012, Part II. LNCS, vol. 7511, pp. 371–378. Springer, Heidelberg (2012)
9. Boykov, Y., et al.: Fast approximate energy minimization via graph cuts. IEEE Trans. Pattern Anal. Mach. Intell. **23**(11), 1222–1239 (2001)

Advanced Feature Extraction

Learning Features for Tissue Classification with the Classification Restricted Boltzmann Machine

Gijs van Tulder[1]([✉]) and Marleen de Bruijne[1,2]

[1] Biomedical Imaging Group Rotterdam, Erasmus MC University Medical Center,
Rotterdam, The Netherlands
g.vantulder@erasmusmc.nl
[2] Image Group, Department of Computer Science, University of Copenhagen,
Copenhagen, Denmark

Abstract. Performance of automated tissue classification in medical imaging depends on the choice of descriptive features. In this paper, we show how restricted Boltzmann machines (RBMs) can be used to learn features that are especially suited for texture-based tissue classification. We introduce the convolutional classification RBM, a combination of the existing convolutional RBM and classification RBM, and use it for discriminative feature learning. We evaluate the classification accuracy of convolutional and non-convolutional classification RBMs on two lung CT problems. We find that RBM-learned features outperform conventional RBM-based feature learning, which is unsupervised and uses only a generative learning objective, as well as often-used filter banks. We show that a mixture of generative and discriminative learning can produce filters that give a higher classification accuracy.

1 Introduction

Most machine learning applications – for classification and other tasks, in medical image analysis and elsewhere – do not work directly on the input data, but use a higher-level representation instead. For example, when training a classifier for images, the pixel values are mapped to features that simplify classification. Most conventional approaches used in medical image analysis, such as filter banks of Gaussian derivatives, wavelets or SIFT, are predesigned, general methods that are not tuned for a specific problem or dataset.

Feature learning or representation learning [1] provides an alternative to predesigned filters, because it learns a new representation from the data. Ideally, this data-derived representation discards irrelevant information and preserves only those details that are useful for the intended task. By varying the objective function of the feature learning method, it might be possible to tailor the features to a specific application, such as classification. Because these features have been optimized for a specific classification problem, they may provide a classification result that is better than that of predesigned filter banks.

In this paper, we discuss the restricted Boltzmann machine (RBM), a representation learning method that is popular in computer vision but still little-used

© Springer International Publishing Switzerland 2014
B. Menze et al. (Eds.): MCV 2014, LNCS 8848, pp. 47–58, 2014.
DOI: 10.1007/978-3-319-13972-2_5

in medical image analysis. An RBM is a probabilistic graphical model that learns the probability distribution of the input data and a latent representation of that data. Because the size of this latent representation is limited, the RBM learns a concise representation that still captures most of the important information.

There are two ways to use RBMs in a classification problem. The standard RBM is an unsupervised model without label information. It learns a representation that can be used as the input for an external classifier. This approach has previously been used to model lung CT [2] and brain MR [3] images. The second option is a classification RBM [4], an extension of the standard RBM that includes labels and can be used for classification. Like standard RBMs, classification RBMs can be trained with a purely generative objective that optimizes the joint probability distribution of inputs and labels. Classification RBMs, however, can also be trained with a discriminative objective that optimizes the posterior probability of the label. A discriminative objective can improve classification results, because it helps the RBM to focus on modeling the inter-class variation that is relevant for classification. An RBM trained with only a generative learning objective might waste effort on modeling the intra-class variation in the data, which does not improve the classification. For example, in tissue classification in medical images, the model should represent the subtle differences between tissue types, rather than the more obvious differences between patients.

Specifically designed to model images, convolutional RBMs [5–8] use a weight-sharing approach borrowed from convolutional networks. Convolutional weight-sharing reduces the number of weights and adds some translational invariance to the model. Like standard RBMs, convolutional RBMs are unsupervised models. We introduce the convolutional classification RBM, a combination of the convolutional RBM with a classification RBM. We use this convolutional classification RBM in our texture classification experiments. To our knowledge, the combination of convolution and classification RBMs has not been investigated before, and the application of classification RBMs is new within medical imaging.

In this paper, we evaluate convolutional and non-convolutional RBMs as classifiers and as feature learners, on two lung CT classification problems. In particular, we are interested in the influence of the label information and the learning objective on the classification performance. We test if the classification RBM learns better features than the standard RBM. To do this, we compare the results of the standard RBM and the classification RBM, for different mixtures of discriminative and generative learning.

2   Restricted Boltzmann Machines

Standard RBM. A restricted Boltzmann machine (RBM) models the probability distribution over a set of hidden nodes $\mathbf{h}$ and visible nodes $\mathbf{v}$. We use binary hidden nodes, $h_j \in \{0, 1\}$, and real-valued visible nodes with a Gaussian distribution [9]. The joint probability distribution $P(\mathbf{v}, \mathbf{h})$ is determined by a set of weights and biases. Each visible node v_i has an undirected connection with weight W_{ij} to each hidden node h_j. Each visible node v_i has a bias b_i and each hidden node h_j has a bias c_j. These parameters define the energy function

$$E\left(\mathbf{v},\mathbf{h}\right) = \sum_{j} \frac{(v_i - b_i)^2}{2\sigma_i^2} - \sum_{i,j} \frac{v_i}{\sigma_i} W_{ij} h_j - \sum_{j} c_j h_j , \tag{1}$$

where σ_i is the standard deviation of the Gaussian noise of visible node i. The joint distribution of the input $\mathbf{v}$ and hidden representation $\mathbf{h}$ is defined as

$$P\left(\mathbf{v},\mathbf{h}\right) = \frac{\exp\left(-E\left(\mathbf{v},\mathbf{h}\right)\right)}{Z}, \tag{2}$$

where Z is a normalization constant. The conditional probabilities for the hidden nodes given the visible nodes and vice versa are

$$P\left(h_j \,|\, \mathbf{v}\right) = \mathrm{sigm}(\sum_{i} W_{ij} v_i + c_j) \text{ and} \tag{3}$$

$$P\left(v_i \,|\, \mathbf{h}\right) = \mathcal{N}(\sum_{j} W_{ij} h_j + b_i, \ \sigma_i), \tag{4}$$

where $\mathrm{sigm}\left(x\right) = \frac{1}{1+\exp(-x)}$ is the logistic sigmoid function.

Classification RBM. The classification RBM [4] extends the standard RBM with binary nodes that encode the label of the input. Each label node represents one class, with $y_k = 1$ if the sample belongs to class k and 0 otherwise. Like the visible nodes, the label nodes have a bias d_k and are connected to each of the hidden nodes, with weight U_{kj} connecting label node y_k to hidden node h_j. The energy function of a classification RBM with Gaussian visible nodes is

$$E\left(\mathbf{v},\mathbf{h},\mathbf{y}\right) = \sum_{j} \frac{(v_i - b_i)^2}{2\sigma_i^2} - \sum_{i,j} \frac{v_i}{\sigma_i} W_{ij} h_j - \sum_{j} c_j h_j - \sum_{k,j} y_k U_{kj} h_j - \sum_{k} d_k y_k. \tag{5}$$

The energy function defines the distribution

$$P\left(\mathbf{v},\mathbf{h},\mathbf{y}\right) = \frac{\exp\left(-E\left(\mathbf{v},\mathbf{h},\mathbf{y}\right)\right)}{Z} \tag{6}$$

and the conditional probabilities

$$P\left(h_j \,|\, \mathbf{v},\mathbf{y}\right) = \mathrm{sigm}(\sum_{i} W_{ij} v_i + \sum_{k} U_{kj} y_k + c_j) \text{ and} \tag{7}$$

$$P\left(y_k \,|\, \mathbf{h}\right) = \mathrm{sigm}(\sum_{j} U_{kj} h_j + c_k). \tag{8}$$

The visible and label nodes are not connected, so $P\left(v_i \,|\, \mathbf{h}\right)$ is unchanged from the standard RBM. The posterior probability for classification is

$$P\left(y \,|\, \mathbf{v}\right) = \frac{\exp\left(d_y + \sum_{j} \mathrm{softplus}\left(c_j + U_{jy} + \sum_{i} W_{ij} v_i\right)\right)}{\sum_{y^*} \exp\left(d_{y^*} + \sum_{j} \mathrm{softplus}\left(c_j + U_{y^*j} + \sum_{i} W_{ij} v_i\right)\right)}, \tag{9}$$

where $\mathrm{softplus}\left(x\right) = \log\left(1 + \exp\left(x\right)\right)$.

Learning Objectives. The standard RBM optimizes the generative learning objective $\log P(\mathbf{v}_t)$, the probability distribution of each input image t. The classification RBM can be trained with the generative learning objective $\log P(\mathbf{v}_t, y_t)$, which optimizes the joint probability distribution of the input image and the label. A classification RBM can also be trained with the discriminative objective $\log P(y_t|\mathbf{v}_t)$, which only optimizes the classification and does not optimize the representation of the input image. Larochelle et al. [4] suggest a hybrid objective

$$\beta \log P(\mathbf{v}_t, y_t) + (1-\beta) \log P(y_t|\mathbf{v}_t), \tag{10}$$

where $\beta \in [0, 1]$ is the amount of generative learning. We will use this objective with different values for β in our feature learning experiments.

Learning the Weights. RBMs are probabilistic models, so when given an input, it is necessary to sample the activation of all nodes to find the new state of the model. Gibbs sampling provides a way to make this sampling more efficient. Given the visible and label nodes, the new state of the hidden nodes can be sampled using the distribution $p(\mathbf{h}_t|\mathbf{v}_t, y_t)$. Then, keeping the hidden nodes fixed, the new activation of the visible and label nodes can be sampled from $p(\mathbf{v}_t, y_t|\mathbf{h}_t)$. This can be repeated for several iterations, until the model converges to a stable state. Gibbs sampling forms the basis for contrastive divergence [9], a method that provides an efficient approximation for the gradient-based updates to the weights. We use contrastive divergence and stochastic gradient descent to optimize the weights in our RBMs.

Convolutional RBM. Designed to model images, convolutional RBMs [5–8] use the weight-sharing approach from convolutional neural networks. Unlike convolutional neural networks, convolutional RBMs are generative models and can be trained in the same way as standard RBMs. In a convolutional RBM, the connections share weights in a pattern that resembles convolution, with M convolutional filters $\mathbf{W}_m$ that connect hidden nodes arranged in M feature maps $\mathbf{h}_m$ (Fig. 1). The connections between the visible nodes and the hidden nodes in map m use the weights from convolution filter $\mathbf{W}_m$, such that each hidden node is connected to the visible nodes in its receptive field. The visible nodes share one bias b; all hidden nodes in map m share the bias c_m. With the convolution operator $*$ we define the probabilities

$$P(h_{ij}^m|\mathbf{v}) = \text{sigm}((\tilde{\mathbf{W}}_m * \mathbf{v})_{ij} + c_m) \text{ and} \tag{11}$$

$$P(v_{ij}|\mathbf{h}) = \mathcal{N}\left(\left(\sum_m \mathbf{W}_m * \mathbf{h}_m\right)_{ij} + b, \ 1\right), \tag{12}$$

where $\tilde{\mathbf{W}}_m$ is the horizontally and vertically flipped filter $\mathbf{W}_m$, and $\cdot_{ij}$ denotes the pixel on location (i, j).

Convolutional RBMs can produce unwanted border effects when reconstructing the visible layer, because the visible units near the borders are only connected to a few hidden nodes. We pad our patches with pixels from neighboring patches, and keep the padding pixels fixed during the iterations of Gibbs sampling.

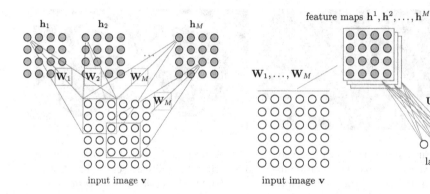

Fig. 1. Schematic view of weight sharing in a convolutional RBM. The hidden nodes are grouped in feature maps $\mathbf{h}_1, \ldots, \mathbf{h}_M$. The weights of the connections are shared using the convolutional filters $\mathbf{W}_1, \ldots, \mathbf{W}_M$.

Fig. 2. Schematic view of a convolutional classification RBM. Convolution of the input image $\mathbf{v}$ with the filter $\mathbf{W}_m$ gives the hidden feature map $\mathbf{h}^m$. The activation of each feature map is summed and connected with the label nodes $\mathbf{y}$ with weights $\mathbf{U}$.

Convolutional Classification RBM. We introduce a convolutional classification RBM that includes visible, hidden and label nodes (Fig. 2) and can be trained in a discriminative way. The visible nodes are connected to the hidden nodes using convolutional weight-sharing, as in the convolutional RBM, and the hidden nodes are connected to the label nodes, as in the classification RBM. In our patch-based texture classification problem, the exact location of a feature inside the patch is not relevant, so we use shared weights to connect the hidden nodes and the label nodes. All connections from a label node y_k to a hidden node h_{ij}^m in map m share the weight U_{km}. The activation probabilities are

$$P\left(y_k \,|\mathbf{h}\right) = \mathrm{sigm}\Big(\sum_m U_{ym} \sum_{i,j} h_{ij}^m + d_k\Big) \text{ and} \tag{13}$$

$$P\left(h_{ij}^m \,|\mathbf{y}\right) = \mathrm{sigm}\big((\tilde{\mathbf{W}}_m * \mathbf{v})_{ij} + \sum_k U_{km} y_k + c_m\big). \tag{14}$$

The probability for the visible nodes is unchanged from the convolutional RBM.

3 Experiments

3.1 Datasets and Problems

Airways. We show results for two classification problems on lung CT images. In the first dataset we classify airway and non-airway patches, to detect airway center points as a preprocessing step for airway extraction algorithms. We use 40 scans of 20 patients from the Danish Lung Cancer Screening Trial [10].

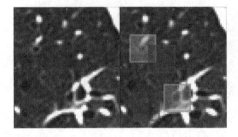 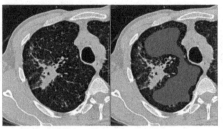

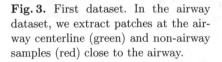

Fig. 3. First dataset. In the airway dataset, we extract patches at the airway centerline (green) and non-airway samples (red) close to the airway.

Fig. 4. Second dataset. Example from the interstitial lung disease scans. The annotation (right) shows an ROI (red) marked as micronodules.

The voxel size is approximately $0.78 \times 0.78 \times 1$ mm. Using the output of an existing segmentation algorithm [11] to find the airways (Fig. 3), we extracted patches of 16×16 pixels at the center point of airways with a diameter of 16 pixels or less. For each airway patch, we create a non-airway sample by extracting a patch at a random point just outside the outer airway wall. We selected a random subset of 500 patches per scan. We use 15 subjects (30 scans, 15 000 patches) as our training set and 5 subjects (10 scans, 5 000 patches) for testing.

Lung Tissue. The second dataset is a larger, publicly available dataset on interstitial lung diseases (see [12] for a description). In this texture classification problem with scans from 73 patients, we do patch-wise classification of five types of lung tissue (healthy tissue: 22 %, emphysema: 3 %, ground glass: 16 %, fibrosis: 15 %, micronodules: 44 %). The resolution varies between 0.4–1 mm, with a slice thickness of 1–2 mm and inter-slice spacing of 10–15 mm. The dataset provides hand-drawn 2D ROIs with labels (Fig. 4) for a subset of slices in each scan. Following other work on this dataset [2,13], we extracted patches of 32×32 pixels along a grid with a 16-pixel overlap. We include a patch if at least 75 % of the pixels belong to the same class. We use 48 patients (8 165 patches) for training and 25 others (4 265 patches) for testing.

3.2 Evaluation Procedure

We trained the RBMs with various learning rates until convergence. We report the test accuracy of the RBM with the best accuracy on the training set. For the airway dataset, the patches are centered at the center point of the airways. This means that the features do not have to be translation-invariant, so we can use a non-convolutional RBM. For the lung tissue classification, translation-invariance is required, so we use convolutional RBMs on this dataset. After learning the filters, we convolve the input patches with the filters and use an adaptive binning method to generate one histogram per filter. We trained support vector machines (SVMs) with linear and radial basis function (RBF) kernels on the concatenated histograms, with 5-fold cross-validation on the training sets to optimize the SVM parameters and number of histogram bins.

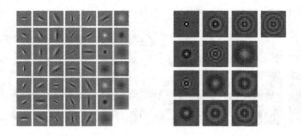

Fig. 5. Two filter banks: Leung-Malik (left) and Schmid (right), generated with the code from http://www.robots.ox.ac.uk/~vgg/research/texclass/filters.html.

3.3 Baselines

We compare the results of RBM-learned filters with several baselines (Table 1). On the airway data, we compare with SVMs trained on the raw input pixels. Raw input pixels do not work for the lung tissue classification problem, because the texture classification needs translation-invariant features. We therefore use convolution with random filters as a baseline for the tissue set. As the second set of baseline results, we use two of the standard filter banks discussed by Varma and Zisserman [14] (Fig. 5). The filter bank of Leung and Malik [15] is a set of Gaussian filters and derivatives, with 48 filters of 16 × 16 pixels. The filter bank of Schmid [16] has 13 filters of 16 × 16 pixels with rotation-invariant Gabor-like patterns. For the airway dataset, we multiply the image patch with each filter to get the feature vector. For the lung tissue data, we apply the filters using the same procedure with convolution and adaptive histograms that we also use for the RBM-learned filters.

Table 1 summarizes the baseline results for both datasets. On the airway dataset, an RBF SVM trained with Leung-Malik filters gives a test accuracy of 90.5 %, against 91.3 % for an RBF SVM trained on the raw intensity values. On the lung tissue dataset, Leung-Malik filters have the best performance at 64.1 %.

For the lung tissue dataset, two earlier publications also give an indication of expected classification results, although the differences in patch extraction and train/test splits make a direct comparison with our results impossible. Depeursinge et al. [13] use a set of near-affine-invariant feature descriptors based on isotropic wavelet filters. Li et al. [2] use unsupervised, non-convolutional RBMs at three scales to learn convolution filters. Both studies show a multi-class classification accuracy of approximately 77 %.

3.4 Results

Airways. Fig. 8 shows the results of the RBM classification and of the SVM classification on airway data, with non-convolutional RBMs with different numbers of hidden nodes (example filters shown in Fig. 6). The best RBM reaches an accuracy on the test set of a little more than 89 %. Discriminative learning improves the RBM classification accuracy, although the difference becomes smaller if the number of hidden nodes is larger.

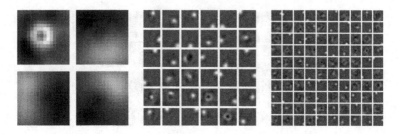

Fig. 6. Three filter sets learned from the airway data: 4, 36 or 100 filters of 16×16 pixels, learned with a mix of discriminative and generative learning ($\beta = 0.01$).

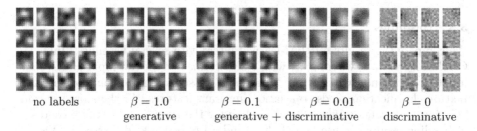

no labels	$\beta = 1.0$	$\beta = 0.1$	$\beta = 0.01$	$\beta = 0$
	generative	generative + discriminative		discriminative

Fig. 7. Filters learned on the lung tissue data. Sets of 16 filters of 10×10 pixels, learned by non-convolutional RBMs on subpatches. RBM without labels (leftmost) and classification RBMs for various mixtures of generative and discriminative learning.

Table 1. SVM classification accuracy on the test set with baseline features.

Features	Raw pixels		Leung-Malik		Schmid	
SVM kernel	Linear	RBF	Linear	RBF	Linear	RBF
Airways	89.30	91.28	90.10	90.50	83.88	85.40
Lung tissue	Not applicable		64.88	64.06	56.90	54.81

The results of SVMs using the RBM-learned features show a similar pattern. At best, an RBF SVM with RBM-learned features achieves an accuracy of 90.3 % (36 filters, pure discriminative learning), comparable to that of the best filter bank. In general, more discriminative learning produces features that give a higher accuracy in the SVM. This difference is strongest if the number of hidden nodes is small, when it is most important to specialize.

Lung Tissue. We trained non-convolutional RBMs and convolutional RBMs on the lung tissue dataset, with different filter sizes and numbers of filters. (Training a large convolutional RBM took up to three days.) On the lung tissue dataset, we found the best SVM classification accuracy (77–78 %) with filters learned with a mixture of generative and discriminative learning (Fig. 9). The best learned filters outperformed both the standard filter banks and the random filters. Adding label information, even with pure generative learning, often improved the results. Filters learned with pure discriminative or pure generative learning generally

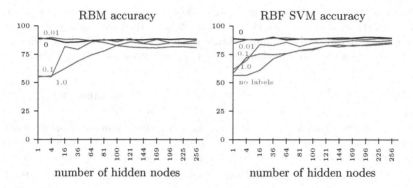

Fig. 8. Airway classification accuracy of the non-convolutional RBM (left) and the RBF SVM (right) trained on the RBM-learned filters. The plot shows the effect of different values for β on the classification accuracy (vertical axis).

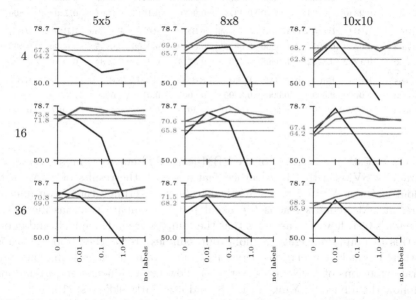

Fig. 9. Lung tissue classification results with the convolutional RBM, for different filter sizes (columns) and numbers of filters (rows). Each subplot shows the RBM classification accuracy (black) and linear SVM accuracy (blue) and RBF SVM accuracy (red) for different β (horizontal axis). Horizontal blue and red lines show the SVM accuracy with random filters.

showed a lower performance than those learned with a mix. In a visual inspection, we found that filters learned with a bit of generative learning seem to have more visible structure (see, for example, the filters in Fig. 7).

We can also evaluate the classification accuracy of the RBM itself. The convolutional RBM had a maximum accuracy on the test set of 77.6 %, with 16 filters of 10×10 pixels. In most cases, pure discriminative learning gave the RBM with the best classification result.

Table 2. Results of McNemar's and Durkalski's tests comparing the classification accuracy on the lung tissue dataset, for linear SVMs with RBM-learned filters versus random filters. 'RBM' and 'random' indicate the method with the highest mean accuracy. The p-values indicate the significance of the difference, according to both tests.

Filter size	5 × 5 pixels			8 × 8 pixels			10 × 10 pixels		
Filters	4	16	36	4	16	36	4	16	36
$\beta = 0$	RBM	Random	RBM	Random	Random	RBM	Random	Random	Random
McNemar	0.0000	0.0000	0.0434	0.0921	0.9202	0.4242	0.0000	0.5826	0.0671
Durkalski	0.1778	0.0867	0.6809	0.6273	0.1614	0.0864	0.2242	0.1848	0.2135
$\beta = 0.01$	RBM	RBM	RBM	RBM	RBM	RBM	RBM	RBM	RBM
McNemar	0.0000	0.0000	0.0000	0.0000	0.0000	0.0000	0.0000	0.0000	0.0000
Durkalski	0.0014	0.2411	0.1680	0.2087	0.4775	0.5432	0.2614	0.6208	0.4958
$\beta = 0.1$	RBM	RBM	RBM	RBM	RBM	RBM	RBM	RBM	RBM
McNemar	0.0000	0.0000	0.0000	0.0000	0.0000	0.0413	0.0000	0.0000	0.0000
Durkalski	0.2340	0.5124	0.3770	0.4374	0.9676	0.1917	0.2661	0.2302	0.8062
$\beta = 1.0$	RBM	Random	RBM	Random	RBM	RBM	Random	RBM	RBM
McNemar	0.0000	0.8027	0.0000	0.0826	0.0049	0.0000	0.0195	0.0000	0.0000
Durkalski	0.1222	0.1732	0.9608	0.7709	0.5714	0.3185	0.7284	0.7086	0.6697
No labels	RBM	Random	RBM	RBM	RBM	RBM	RBM	RBM	RBM
McNemar	0.0000	0.0995	0.0000	0.0000	0.0005	0.0154	0.0000	0.0000	0.0000
Durkalski	0.0576	0.1390	0.5584	0.7621	0.4975	0.0985	0.1520	0.5676	0.5046

For a statistical evaluation of the RBM-learned filters, we compare the mean accuracy of SVMs with RBM-learned features with the results of SVMs with random features. We use two statistical tests to determine the significance of the results. McNemar's test is the usual test to compare two classifiers [17]. McNemar's test, however, assumes that the samples are independent, and in our case this assumption might not hold: our samples are patches from 25 scans, and there might be correlations between samples from the same scan. There are several extensions of McNemar's test that allow for within-cluster correlations. We follow the advice by Yang et al. [18] and use Durkalski's test [19].

Table 2 shows the results of McNemar's test and Durkalski's test for all RBM configurations. In most cases, the average performance with RBM-learned features was higher than the performance of the best-performing baseline, the random filters. According to McNemar's test (which is too optimistic), many of these differences would be significant. In cases where random filters had a higher mean accuracy than RBM-learned filters, the p-value is generally higher and not significant. Durkalski's test is far more conservative: almost none of the differences are significant. But although the individual differences are not significant according to these tests, the differences are mostly in favor of the RBM-learned features. For example, features learned with mixed strategies ($\beta = 0.1$ and $\beta = 0.01$) had the highest mean accuracy for all configurations. This promising result suggests that RBM-based feature learning may provide an advantage.

4   Discussion and Conclusion

We have shown how the classification RBM can be used to learn useful features for medical image analysis, with a mean classification accuracy that is better than or close to that of other methods. Using label information and discriminative learning led to an improved performance. Although no significant differences were found in these relatively small datasets, the results suggest that RBM-learned filters have an advantage over random filters. It is interesting to see that random filters performed better than two standard filter banks. The surprising performance of random filters has been noted in the literature before [20].

Because the lung tissue data that we used in our experiments is highly anisotropic and has 2D annotations only in selected slices, we chose to do feature learning and classification in 2D. However, given the right training data, the methods discussed in this paper could easily be extended to 3D.

The accuracy of the classification RBM in most of our experiments came close to that of an SVM classifier, but the SVMs usually achieved better results. We have two possible explanations for this difference. One, there may be an imbalance in the energy function, because there are many more connections between the visible and hidden nodes than between the hidden and label nodes. This might lead the model to over-optimize the representation at the cost of a higher classification error. Using a discriminative learning objective might help to prevent this. Two, although our results suggest that combining representation and classification can help to learn better features, this combination might make it harder to optimize the classification. Since the representation changes in each update step, the classification weights need to change as well. It might help to add a final training phase that only optimizes the classification weights, while keeping the representation fixed.

Feature learning is usually done with a purely generative learning objective, which favors a representation that gives the most faithful description of the data. But this is not always the representation that is best for the goal of the system. For example, classification may need more features that model inter-class variation than features that model intra-class variation. We therefore argue that it is important to use the right learning objective for feature learning. In this paper, we found that the classification accuracy of SVMs using RBM-learned features can be improved by including label information in the model and by adding discriminative learning to the learning objective of the RBM.

Acknowledgment. This research is financed by the Netherlands Organization for Scientific Research (NWO).

References

1. Bengio, Y., Courville, A., Vincent, P.: Representation learning: a review and new perspectives. Technical report, Université de Montréal (2012)

2. Li, Q., Cai, W., Feng, D.D.: Lung image patch classification with automatic feature learning. In: 35th Annual International Conference on Engineering in Medicine and Biology Society (EMBC) (2013)
3. Brosch, T., Tam, R.: Manifold learning of brain MRIs by deep learning. In: Mori, K., Sakuma, I., Sato, Y., Barillot, C., Navab, N. (eds.) MICCAI 2013, Part II. LNCS, vol. 8150, pp. 633–640. Springer, Heidelberg (2013)
4. Larochelle, H., Mandel, M., Pascanu, R., Bengio, Y.: Learning algorithms for the classification restricted Boltzmann machine. J. Machin. Learn. Res. **13**, 643–669 (2012)
5. Desjardins, G., Bengio, Y.: Empirical evaluation of convolutional RBMs for vision. Technical report, Université de Montréal (2008)
6. Norouzi, M., Ranjbar, M., Mori, G.: Stacks of convolutional restricted Boltzmann machines for shift-invariant feature learning. In: IEEE Computer Society Conference on Computer Vision and Pattern Recognition (CVPR) (2009)
7. Lee, H., Grosse, R., Ranganath, R., Ng, A.Y.: Convolutional deep belief networks for scalable unsupervised learning of hierarchical representations. In: The 26th International Conference on Machine Learning (ICML) (2009)
8. Lee, H., Grosse, R., Ranganath, R., Ng, A.Y.: Unsupervised learning of hierarchical representations with convolutional deep belief networks. Commun. ACM **54**(10), 95–103 (2011)
9. Hinton, G.E.: A practical guide to training restricted Boltzmann machines. Technical report. University of Toronto (2010)
10. Pedersen, J.H., Ashraf, H., Dirksen, A., et al.: The Danish randomized lung cancer CT screening trial—overall design and results of the prevalence round. J. Thorac. Oncol. **4**(5), 608–614 (2009)
11. Petersen, J., Nielsen, M., Lo, P., Saghir, Z., Dirksen, A., de Bruijne, M.: Optimal graph based segmentation using flow lines with application to airway wall segmentation. In: Székely, G., Hahn, H.K. (eds.) IPMI 2011. LNCS, vol. 6801, pp. 49–60. Springer, Heidelberg (2011)
12. Depeursinge, A., Vargas, A., Platon, A., Geissbuhler, A., Poletti, P.A., Müller, H., et al.: Building a reference multimedia database for interstitial lung diseases. Comput. Med. Imaging Graph. **36**(3), 227–238 (2012)
13. Depeursinge, A., Van de Ville, D., Platon, A., Geissbuhler, A., Poletti, P.A., Müller, H.: Near-affine-invariant texture learning for lung tissue analysis using isotropic wavelet frames. Trans. Inf. Technol. Biomed. **16**, 665–675 (2012)
14. Varma, M.: A statistical approach to material classification using image patch exemplars. Trans. Pattern Anal. Mach. Intell. **31**(11), 2032–2047 (2009)
15. Leung, T., Malik, J.: Representing and recognizing the visual appearance of materials using three-dimensional textons. Int. J. Comput. Vis. **43**(1), 29–44 (2001)
16. Schmid, C.: Constructing models for content-based image retrieval. In: IEEE Computer Society Conference on Computer Vision and Pattern Recognition (CVPR) (2001)
17. Dietterich, T.G.: Approximate statistical tests for comparing supervised classification learning algorithms. Neural Comput. **10**(7), 1895–1923 (1998)
18. Yang, Z., Sun, X., Hardin, J.W.: A note on the tests for clustered matched-pair binary data. Biometrical J. **52**(5), 638–652 (2010)
19. Durkalski, V.L., Palesch, Y.Y., Lipsitz, S.R., Rust, P.F.: Analysis of clustered matched-pair data. Stat. Med. **22**(15), 2417–2428 (2003)
20. Saxe, A.M., Koh, P.W., Chen, Z., Bhand, M., Suresh, B., Ng, A.Y.: On random weights and unsupervised feature learning. In: The International Conference on Machine Learning (ICML) (2011)

Dementia-Related Features in Longitudinal MRI: Tracking Keypoints over Time

Elisabeth Stühler$^{(\boxtimes)}$ and Michael R. Berthold

Nycomed Chair for Bioinformatics and Information Mining,
University of Konstanz, Box 712, 78457 Konstanz, Germany
{elisabeth.stuehler,michael.berthold}@uni-konstanz.de

Abstract. We aim at developing new dementia-related features based on longitudinal MRI in order to differentiate various stages of Alzheimer's disease.

Current methods for dementia classification rely heavily on the quality of MRI preprocessing, especially on prior registration. We propose to avoid a possibly unsuccessful and always time-consuming non-rigid registration by employing local invariant features which are independent of image scale and orientation, and can be tracked over time in longitudinal studies. We detect and track such keypoints based on scale-space theory in an automatized image processing workflow, and test it on a standardized MRI collection made available by the Alzheimer's Disease Neuroimaging Initiative (ADNI).

Our approach is very efficient for processing very large datasets collected from different sites and technical devices, and first results show that characteristic scale and movement of keypoints and their tracks differ significantly between controls and diseased subjects.

Keywords: ADNI · Longitudinal MRI · Local-invariant features · Scale-space extrema · Tracking

1 Introduction

Dementia, particularly Alzheimer's disease (AD), is already a widely spread disease in developed countries, and its prevalence is expected to double globally by 2050 [1]. If dementia remains untreated, the economic impact on society will increase dramatically [2], but it is even more important to alleviate the psychological strain on patients and their relatives by improving treatment as well as diagnosis. Notably the availability of newly developed pharmaceuticals

Data used in preparation of this article were obtained from the Alzheimer's Disease Neuroimaging Initiative (ADNI) database (adni.loni.usc.edu). As such, the investigators within the ADNI contributed to the design and implementation of ADNI and/or provided data but did not participate in analysis or writing of this report. A complete listing of ADNI investigators can be found at: http://adni.loni.usc.edu/wp-content/uploads/how_to_apply/ADNI_Acknowledgement_List.pdf.

© Springer International Publishing Switzerland 2014
B. Menze et al. (Eds.): MCV 2014, LNCS 8848, pp. 59–70, 2014.
DOI: 10.1007/978-3-319-13972-2_6

and the research of further treatment, which might delay onset of dementia, has put increasing emphasis on the early detection and prediction of disease progression [3,4].

Neuroimaging is nowadays an essential resource for clinical diagnosis, as it may increase diagnostic confidence in the evaluation of dementia [5]. The neuropathological stages of Alzheimer's are already observed in the preclinical phase, i.e. before clinical symptoms occur [6,7]. These stages include structural changes within the brain, which are observed by magnetic resonance imaging (MRI).

When researching dementia-related features within MRI, there are mainly two approaches for feature extraction:

Voxel-based methods (e.g. by [8,9]), where mostly SVM or variants are employed to differentiate between two or more classes within the dataset, and **ROI-based** methods (e.g. by [10]), where uptakes from previously segmented regions-of-interest (ROIs) are combined in a classifier. A comprehensive overview over state-of-the-art Alzheimer's classification based on MRI is presented by [11]. In general, a classifier with sensitivity of more than $80 - 85\,\%$ and specificity of at least $80\,\%$ is characterized as an ideal biomarker for Alzheimer's classification as discussed in [6,12].

The success of both approaches relies heavily on the quality of prior registration (and segmentation), i.e. the correspondence accuracy of voxels or tissue. Due to high anatomical variance, rigid alignment of brain images is insufficient, and, as discussed in detail by [13], the main obstacles of intersubject brain registration using non-rigid transformations are the computational cost, and the difficulty in validating the results. They claim that a true point-to-point correspondence between different brain images can never be known, and furthermore caution against studies whose results rely on registration techniques of questionable validity. Automatic image segmentation is not only prone to systematic errors [6,14], but also depends on the registration to one or multiple atlases.

In this study, we argue that the possibly unsuccessful and in any case time consuming non-rigid registration can be avoided by employing **local invariant feature detectors** which are independent of image scale and orientation:

We apply such feature detectors to a standardized MRI collection comprising 1915 images of overall 479 subjects. They derive from a longitudinal study conducted over two years by the Alzheimer's Disease Neuroimaging Initiative (ADNI), and contain T1-weighted MRI scans from patients with Alzheimer's Disease (AD) and mild cognitive impairment (MCI), and a control group (CTR).

We use scale-space extrema to efficiently detect keypoints within each image, and subsequently track these keypoints over time. We characterize keypoints by scale, and tracks by length, neighborhood, movement and direction.

These steps are combined into one workflow where image data of one subject at a time is uploaded, processed, and extracted features are collected for each subject. In first statistical evaluations of the extracted features, we find that movement within tracks as well as their neighborhood are most descriptive in differentiating dementia from healthy controls. This result shows the feasibility of such local invariant features for the differentiation of AD, MCI and CTR, and is the first step towards establishing a new classifier independent of inter-subject or atlas-based registration in longitudinal studies.

2   Materials and Methods

2.1   ADNI Data Collection

Data used in the preparation of this article were obtained from the Alzheimers Disease Neuroimaging Initiative (ADNI) database. The ADNI was launched in 2003 by the National Institute on Aging (NIA), the National Institute of Biomedical Imaging and Bioengineering (NIBIB), the Food and Drug Administration (FDA), private pharmaceutical companies and non-profit organizations, as a $60 million, 5-year public-private partnership. Its primary goal has been to test whether serial MRI, positron emission tomography, other biological markers, and clinical and neuropsychological assessment can be combined to measure the progression of MCI and early AD.

For this study we use a standardized MRI collection recently proposed and described in detail by [15] to promote consistency in image data analysis and meaningful comparison of various algorithms. The collection we chose contains 479 subjects, who have baseline and follow-up 1.5T MRI scans, with follow-ups at 6 months, 1 year, 18 months (only MIC patients) and 2 years (with one exception, namely an AD subject where a follow-up at Month 6 was omitted). Overall we downloaded 1915 volumes of the collection, disregarding the 18 months follow-up scans.

All subjects were diagnosed at baseline, and subsequently classified into three groups, i.e. a control group of 168 healthy subjects (CTR, age 76.02 ± 5.11, 83♀), a group of 212 patients affected by mild cognitive impairment (MCI, age 74.85 ± 7.03, 70♀) and a group of 99 patients affected by Alzheimer's disease (AD, age 75.32 ± 7.46, 47♀). At each visit the diagnosis was re-assessed and overall 13 conversions were confirmed by the ADNI conversion committee, i.e. 11 of the MCI patients converted to AD, one CTR subject converted to MCI within three years, and one AD subjects' diagnosis was reset to MCI. An overview over the collection at baseline and more detailed information about all images, assessments and demographics is available on the ADNI website.

2.2   Data Preprocessing

For all MRI scans we use in this study, initial preprocessing is already provided by the ADNI repository, i.e. preprocessing by intensity non-uniformity correction using N3 [16], and scaling for gradient drift using phantom data [17]. Additionally we mask the images by removing the skull and neck area within the volume. We do not perform any other preprocessing, i.e. the images are neither normalized, interpolated or registered.

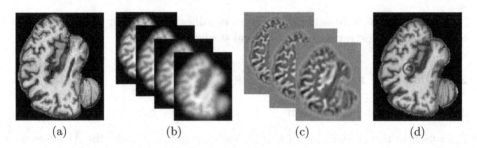

(a)   (b)   (c)   (d)

Fig. 1. Scale-space extrema detection: the original and segmented baseline scan (a) is Gauss-convoluted with increasing σ (b) and a stack of Difference-of-Gaussian (DoG) images is produced. An examplary scale-space maximum corresponding to a local minimum in the original image is depicted in (d).

2.3   Scale-Space Extrema

The first step of our image analysis comprises the efficient detection of keypoints by applying a cascade filtering approach as depicted in Fig. 1, following the implementation of [18].

For each MRI scan we create overall two Gaussian Octaves, with sampling frequencies in the spatial domain of $\sigma = 1.6$ and in scale of $k = 3$ (number of intervals). To keep the implementation efficient, no initial resampling of the images is performed. As discussed in [18], even a low sampling frequency of scales is sufficient to detect stable keypoints; the choice of $\sigma = 1.6$ is a trade-off between repeatability of keypoint detection and efficiency. These values have also been used by [19] on T1-weighted MRI data.

Scale-space extrema are local minima (maxima) within the, in a second step, generated Difference-of-Gaussian (DoG) images. They are also minima (maxima) of the adjacent DoG images, i.e. the value at one keypoint is not only a minimum (maximum) of its 26 neighboring voxels but also a minimum (maximum) of each 27 corresponding neighbors in both adjacent DoG images. Local minima in the DoG image correspond to bright areas in the original MRI scan (and vice versa).

In a third step we refine keypoints which are detected within the second Gaussian octave, i.e. within downsized images, by pushing their position towards the associated local maximum (minimum) of the original MRI scan within a spherical neighborhood. Its radius varies for each keypoint, depending on the associated scale.

2.4   Tracking Keypoints Over Time

In a forth step we track the detected keypoints for each subject over a time of two years, using baseline scans and follow-ups at 6, 12 and 24 months (see Fig. 2).

As described in Sect. 2.3, we generate a set of keypoints representing each image. We now align all point sets of a subject with the object to identify and

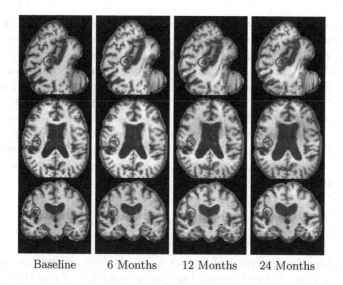

Baseline   6 Months   12 Months   24 Months

Fig. 2. Three views of one exemplary maximum keypoint within an AD subject, which can be tracked over the time of two years. The first view of the baseline image (upper left corner) corresponds to the track depicted in Fig. 1

track recurring keypoints over time. This can be considered as a partial and intra-subject rigid registration of the three follow-up scans to the baseline image: The Iterative Closest Point (ICP, as described by [20,21]) algorithm minimizes locally the mean-square distance metric between the target and source point set, i.e. the keypoints generated from the baseline scan and each follow-up, respectively. As all follow-ups in this dataset were derived using the same technical device and imaging procedure, especially w.r.t. orientation and calibration, the ICP's requirement of rough initial alignment is fulfilled. The algorithm solves a rigid body movement problem by using singular value decomposition of the cross-covariance matrices of the two point clouds, resulting in a rotation matrix and a translation vector. The coordinate system of all follow-up scans and their keypoint sets is subsequently affine transformed to match the baseline scan and point cloud.

We identify keypoint tracks within each subject on all extracted (and transformed) keypoint positions with a maximum object distance of 3.0. This relaxation is based on the assumption that within this neighborhood a keypoint describes the same feature within a subject along time. As our sample of image data across time is very restricted, we do not account for splitting or merging of tracks and do not allow gap closing within tracks.

2.5   Characterization of Keypoints and Their Tracks

In a last step, keypoints $k_i = (x_i, y_i, z_i)$ and their tracks $t = \{k_i\}|_{i \in \{1,...,tl\}}$ are characterized:

We determine the scale on which a keypoint is found, and if it is a local maximum or minimum. If a keypoint is a local maximum, we measure how many of its neighboring voxels within the original image are smaller than the 0.25-quantile of the whole-brain area, i.e. we measure the radius r of the maximal spherical neighborhood below this threshold. We differentiate between recurring keypoints being part of a track with tracklength $tl > 1$, and keypoints which appear only once over time ($tl = 1$). If $tl > 1$, we also describe the track's onset t_{start} and end t_{end} (at timepoints $\{1, ..., 4\}$), its scale variation along time (increasing, decreasing, mixed or constant) and compute the amount of spatial variation sv by summing up the steplengths of the jitter within all three dimensions, and normalizing it by tracklength (see Fig. 3, on the left):

$$sv = \frac{1}{tl} \sum_{i=2}^{tl} (|x_i - x_{i-1}| + |y_i - y_{i-1}| + |z_i - z_{i-1}|) \tag{1}$$

We also analyze the directions of a track w.r.t. the brain center, i.e. how much a track moves along the orthogonal direction to the centroid c of the brainmask we created for skull and neck-removal by

$$d_{orth} = sin(\gamma)||k_{tl} - c||, \tag{2}$$

with γ being the angle (in radians) between $\overline{k_1 c}$ and $\overline{k_{tl} c}$, and we compute analogously, how much it moves towards (or away from) c by:

$$d_{center} = s\sqrt{|k_1 - k_{tl}|^2 - d_{orth}^2}, \tag{3}$$

where $s = sign(||\overline{k_{tl}c}|| - ||\overline{k_1 c}||)$ denotes the orientation of the direction vector, i.e. $s = -1$ indicates a track moving towards and $s = 1$ a movement away from the brain center as illustrated in Fig. 3 (on the right).

We combine these characteristics in a feature vector f for each subject by overall 32 measures, where the set of all tracks T found within all four MRI scans of one subject is partitioned into T_{max} and T_{min}, i.e. into sets containing only maxima and minima tracks, respectively. We measure the ratio of single and recurring keypoints by

$$f(1) = \frac{|\{t_i | tl = 1, t_i \in T_{min}\}|}{|\{t_i | tl > 1, t_i \in T_{min}\}|}, \tag{4}$$

the ratio of starting and ending tracks within the follow-up scan after 6 months (and analogously $f(3)$ within the 1 year follow-up) by

$$f(2) = \frac{|\{t_i | t_{start} = 2, t_i \in T_{min}\}|}{|\{t_i | t_{end} = 2, t_i \in T_{min}\}|}, \tag{5}$$

the ratio of tracks with spatial variance by

$$f(4) = \frac{|\{t_i | sv > 0.5, t_i \in T_{min}\}|}{|\{t_i | sv \leq 0.5, t_i \in T_{min}\}|}, \tag{6}$$

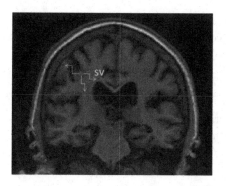 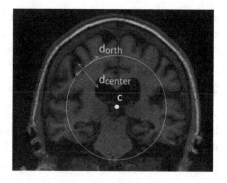

Fig. 3. Schematic representation of spatial variation sv (left), and of track movements w.r.t. brain center c (right) as described in Sect. 2.5. The red arrows depict possible future paths of the track along the time axis, and in both cases the length of the arrow characterizes the track which contains the keypoint k and its successors. Note that in this representation only one slice of the 3D scan is depicted, however all measurements are conducted in three dimensions (Color figure online).

the ratio of tracks moving towards the brain center by

$$f(5) = \frac{|\{t_i | d_{center} < -0.5, t_i \in T_{min}\}|}{|\{t_i | -0.5 \leq d_{center} < 0.5, t_i \in T_{min}\}|}, \tag{7}$$

analogously $f(6)$ by the ratio of tracks moving away from the brain center (for $d_{center} > 0.5$), and the ratio of tracks moving orthogonal to the brain center by

$$f(7) = \frac{|\{t_i | d_{orth} > 0.5, t_i \in T_{min}\}|}{|\{t_i | d_{orth} \leq 0.5, t_i \in T_{min}\}|}. \tag{8}$$

We also compute the mean spatial variation of tracks $t_i \in T_{min}, tl > 1$ ($f(8)$, with $sv > 0.5$), their mean movement towards the brain center ($f(9)$, with $d_{center} < -0.5$), away from the brain center ($f(10)$, with $d_{center} > 0.5$) and orthogonal to the brain center ($f(11)$, with $d_{orth} > 0.5$), and the percentage of minima tracks on constant, increasing or decreasing scale ($f(12)$ to $f(14)$). The features $f(15)$ to $f(28)$ are computed analogously for maxima tracks $t_i \in T_{max}$, where we additionally measure the percentage of tracks with increasing, decreasing and constant maximal neighborhood radius ($f(29)$ to $f(31)$).

Finally we measure the ratio of maxima and minima tracks by

$$f(32) = \frac{|\{t_i | tl > 1, t_i \in T_{max}\}|}{|\{t_i | tl > 1, t_i \in T_{min}\}|}. \tag{9}$$

2.6 Statistical Evaluation

As we aim at developing features for the classification of all groups within the data collection (disregarding diagnosis conversions for now), we evaluate if they are suited for discriminating between CTR and AD or MCI via an independent groups t-test on each feature $f(i)$. We use a confidence interval of 95 % ($p < 0.05$) and do not assume equality of variance.

2.7   Software

All image processing and analysis as described in Sects. 2.2–2.6 is performed by creating a new workflow using the open-source platform KNIME [22] and its extension for Image Processing (http://tech.knime.org/community/image-processing).

3   Results and Discussion

On average, 6678 keypoints are detected for each subject, i.e. within 4 images at baseline and follow-ups in months 6, 12, and 24, and it takes on average about 10 min to extract them on a regular computer (Intel(R) Core(TM) i7-2620M CPU, 8 GB RAM). Around 70 % of these keypoints are recurring over time, i.e. are part of a track with length $tl > 1$. This number constitutes a lower bound for recurring keypoints, as we are not counting the (unknown) part of ending tracks at baseline, and starting tracks at month 24, respectively.

In absolute quantification, we find slightly more scale-space minima than maxima per subject (on average 57, 3 %), i.e. there are more keypoints corresponding to bright areas within the original MRI scan. However when considering the amount of white and grey matter, which cover most of the whole-brain area, we find that relatively there is a higher density of scale-space minima describing the small dark structures within the volume, formed (mostly) between cerebral gyri and ventricles.

3.1   Statistical Evaluation of AD vs. CTR

Overall, 14 of 32 features are significant when differentiating between AD and CTR (listed in Table 1):

Occurrence. The ratio of single and recurring minima keypoints $f(1)$ is significantly higher for AD than for CTR, i.e. we find relatively more keypoints within the bright areas (white and grey matter) of the image which can't be tracked over time. This implies the increased amount of structural and textural change within this area, whereas all other quantifications of tracklength, start and ending ($f(2$–$3,15$–$17)$) do not correlate with disease progression from CTR to AD. Also the ratio $f(32)$ of maxima and minima tracks is independent from class membership.

Scale. The percentage of tracks containing keypoints on constant scale differs significantly for both minima and maxima tracks ($f(12,26)$), whereas the percentage of tracks with increasing scale $f(27)$ is only significant for maxima tracks, and analogously the percentage of minima tracks $f(14)$ is significant only for

Table 1. List of significant (top) and insignificant features (bottom) when differentiation between AD and CTR, sorted by p-value (2-tailed).

Feature	Description	t-value	p-value
f(31)	Constant radius (max, in %)	−3.75	0
f(30)	Decreasing radius (max, in %)	3.36	0.001
f(27)	Increasing scale (max, in %)	3.35	0.001
f(14)	Decreasing scale (min, in %)	3.01	0.003
f(20)	Movement away from center (max, ratio)	2.77	0.006
f(6)	Movement away from center (min, ratio)	2.68	0.008
f(9)	Movement towards center (min, mean)	−2.41	0.017
f(12)	Constant scale (min, in %)	−2.35	0.02
f(24)	Movement away from center (max, mean)	2.11	0.036
f(1)	Single vs. recurring keypoints (min, ratio)	2.10	0.037
f(26)	Constant scale (max, in %)	−2.10	0.037
f(11)	Movement orthogonal to center (min, mean)	2.03	0.044
f(10)	Movement away from center (min, mean)	2.01	0.046
f(19)	Movement towards center (max, ratio)	2.01	0.047
f(13)	Increasing scale (min, in%)	1.95	0.053
f(29)	Increasing radius (max, in %)	1.95	0.053
f(2)	Onsetting vs. ending tracks in month 6 (min, ratio)	−1.90	0.059
f(16)	Onsetting vs. ending tracks in month 6 (max, ratio)	−1.69	0.091
f(5)	Movement towards center (min, ratio)	1.50	0.136
f(15)	Single vs. recurring keypoints (max, ratio)	1.50	0.137
f(17)	Onsetting vs. ending tracks in month 12 (max, ratio)	1.43	0.157
f(25)	Movement orthogonal to center (max, mean)	1.34	0.183
f(3)	Onsetting vs. ending tracks in month 12 (min, ratio)	1.33	0.185
f(23)	Movement towards center (max, mean)	−1.25	0.214
f(28)	Decreasing scale (max, in %)	1.25	0.215
f(7)	Movement orthogonal to center (min, ratio)	1.14	0.255
f(21)	Movement orthogonal to center (max, ratio)	0.91	0.366
f(22)	Spatial variation (max, mean)	0.79	0.43
f(8)	Spatial variation (min, mean)	0.59	0.56
f(4)	Spatial variation (min, ratio)	−0.53	0.59
f(32)	Maxima tracks vs. minima tracks (ratio)	−0.31	0.757
f(18)	Spatial variation (max, ratio)	−0.10	0.92

decreasing scale. This is a very consistent result and closely linked to atrophy: For both AD and CTR we do not find a significant amount f(13) of bright areas (i.e. minima tracks) on increasing scale, or f(28) dark areas on decreasing scale, as both groups are affected by atrophy over time. The difference between normal aging and an increased amount of atrophy however is reflected in f(14) and f(27).

Maximal radius of neighborhood. In the dark structures of the image, AD subjects have on average more increasing as well as decreasing spherical neighborhoods within a predefined threshold (f(29), although it is not significant at $p < 0.05$, and f(30)), and less neighborhoods with constant radius f(31) across time. This underlines the fact that an increased amount of such changes between the cerebral gyri and within ventricles is linked to an increased amount of atrophy within a brain affected by dementia.

Track movement and direction. All quantification of spatial variation, i.e. the amount of jittering within the tracks is insignificant (f(4,8,18,22)), however as soon as the direction of tracks is accounted for, the movement of tracks becomes very descriptive. Especially a movement towards f(9,19) and away from the brain center f(6,10,20) is significant, i.e. in an AD brain are more keypoints between the cerebral gyri wandering into the brain f(19) and they go significantly deeper f(9), indicating the degeneration of grey matter. Analogously there are more keypoints following a bright spot wandering away from the brain center f(20) in an AD brain. The movement of tracks orthogonal to the brain center is only significant for minima tracks f(11), as there is more movement in an AD brain corresponding to the increased amount of atrophy.

3.2   Differentiating MCI

None of the features developed in this study are significant when differentiating MCI from CTR, indicating that they are not yet sensitive enough to discover early stages of dementia. When evaluating the changes from MCI to AD, eight of the features discussed above are also significant (f(6,11,14,20,26,27,30,31)), and furthermore two containing information about movement orthogonal to center (f(7,25)). However, there is no significant difference between the amount of single and recurring scale-space minima anymore, nor is the movement of minima and maxima tracks towards the brain center anymore significant, suggesting that these are the changes most likely to indicate a conversion of MCI to AD.

4   Summary and Future Work

The focus of this study lies on unsupervised feature extraction from structural image data, which can be performed fast and efficient without the necessity of time-consuming and, w.r.t. point-to-point correspondence, unratable preprocessing steps. Main challenges were the large data collection of 1915 MRI volumes, and the robust and efficient implementation of a processing workflow. We used scale-space theory to extract scale- and orientation invariant features from all images and tracked them over a time of 2 years. We successfully linked track characteristics to disease progression from CTR and MCI to AD in longitudinal

MRI, and thereby took a first step towards a classifier independent of registration quality.

Our future work comprises the building of such a classifier, its comparison to voxel- and ROI-based state-of-the-art classifiers as well as the development of more sensitive features for the detection of MCI.

Acknowledgements. Data collection and sharing for this project was funded by the Alzheimer's Disease Neuroimaging Initiative (ADNI) (National Institutes of Health Grant U01 AG024904) and DOD ADNI (Department of Defense award number W81XWH-12-2-0012). ADNI is funded by the National Institute on Aging, the National Institute of Biomedical Imaging and Bioengineering, and through generous contributions from the following: Alzheimers Association; Alzheimers Drug Discovery Foundation; Araclon Biotech; BioClinica, Inc.; Biogen Idec Inc.; Bristol-Myers Squibb Company; Eisai Inc.; Elan Pharmaceuticals, Inc.; Eli Lilly and Company; EuroImmun; F. Hoffmann-La Roche Ltd and its affiliated company Genentech, Inc.; Fujirebio; GE Healthcare; IXICO Ltd.; Janssen Alzheimer Immunotherapy Research & Development, LLC.; Johnson & Johnson Pharmaceutical Research & Development LLC.; Medpace, Inc.; Merck & Co., Inc.; Meso Scale Diagnostics, LLC.; NeuroRx Research; Neurotrack Technologies; Novartis Pharmaceuticals Corporation; Pfizer Inc.; Piramal Imaging; Servier; Synarc Inc.; and Takeda Pharmaceutical Company. The Canadian Institutes of Health Research is providing funds to support ADNI clinical sites in Canada. Private sector contributions are facilitated by the Foundation for the National Institutes of Health (www.fnih.org). The grantee organization is the Northern California Institute for Research and Education, and the study is coordinated by the Alzheimer's Disease Cooperative Study at the University of California, San Diego. ADNI data are disseminated by the Laboratory for Neuro Imaging at the University of Southern California.

References

1. Thies, W., Bleiler, L.: 2013 Alzheimer's disease facts and figures. Alzheimer's Dement. J. Alzheimer's Assoc. **9**(2), 208–245 (2013)
2. Mueller, S.G., Weiner, M.W., Thal, L.J., Petersen, R.C., Jack, C., Jagust, W., Trojanowski, J.Q., Toga, A.W., Beckett, L.: The Alzheimer's disease neuroimaging initiative. Neuroimaging Clin. North Am. **15**(4), 869–877 (2005)
3. Cramer, P.E., Cirrito, J.R., Wesson, D.W., Lee, C.Y.D., Karlo, J.C., Zinn, A.E., Casali, B.T., Restivo, J.L., Goebel, W.D., James, M.J., Brunden, K.R., Wilson, D.A., Landreth, G.E.: ApoE-directed therapeutics rapidly clear β-amyloid and reverse deficits in AD mouse models. Science **335**(6075), 1503–1506 (2012)
4. Petrella, J.R., Coleman, R.E., Doraiswamy, P.M.: Neuroimaging and early diagnosis of Alzheimer disease: a look to the future. Radiology **226**(2), 315–336 (2003)
5. Hort, J., O'Brien, J.T., Gainotti, G., Pirttila, T., Popescu, B.O., Rektorova, I., Sorbi, S., Scheltens, P.: On behalf of the EFNS scientist panel on dementia: EFNS guidelines for the diagnosis and management of Alzheimer's disease. Eur. J. Neurol. **17**(10), 1236–1248 (2010)
6. Weiner, M.W., Veitch, D.P., Aisen, P.S., Beckett, L.A., Cairns, N.J., Green, R.C., Harvey, D., Jack, C.R., Jagust, W., Liu, E., et al.: The Alzheimer's disease neuroimaging initiative: a review of papers published since its inception. Alzheimer's Dement. **9**(5), e111–e194 (2013)

7. Braak, H., Braak, E.: Neuropathological stageing of Alzheimer-related changes. Acta Neuropathol. **82**, 239–259 (1991)
8. Klöppel, S., Stonnington, C.M., Chu, C., Draganski, B., Scahill, R.I., Rohrer, J.D., Fox, N.C., Jack, C.R., Ashburner, J., Frackowiak, R.S.J.: Automatic classification of MR scans in Alzheimer's disease. Brain **131**(3), 681–689 (2008)
9. Ashburner, J., Friston, K.J.: Voxel-based morphometry–the methods. Neuroimage **11**(6), 805–821 (2000)
10. Duchesne, S., Caroli, A., Geroldi, C., Barillot, C., Frisoni, G.B., Collins, D.L.: MRI-based automated computer classification of probable AD versus normal controls. IEEE Trans. Med. Imaging **27**(4), 509–520 (2008)
11. Cuingnet, R., Gerardin, E., Tessieras, J., Auzias, G., Lehèricy, S., Habert, M.O., Chupin, M., Benali, H., Colliot, O.: Automatic classification of patients with Alzheimer's disease from structural MRI: a comparison of ten methods using the ADNI database. NeuroImage **56**(2), 766–781 (2011)
12. Shaw, L.M., Korecka, M., Clark, C.M., Lee, V.M.Y., Trojanowski, J.Q.: Biomarkers of neurodegeneration for diagnosis and monitoring therapeutics. Nat. Rev. Drug Discov. **6**(4), 295–303 (2007)
13. Crum, W.R., Hartkens, T., Hill, D.L.G.: Non-rigid image registration: theory and practice. Br. J. Radiol. **77**(supp. 2), S140–S153 (2004)
14. Wang, H., Das, S.R., Suh, J.W., Altinay, M., Pluta, J., Craige, C., Avants, B., Yushkevich, P.A.: A learning-based wrapper method to correct systematic errors in automatic image segmentation: consistently improved performance in hippocampus, cortex and brain segmentation. NeuroImage **55**(3), 968–985 (2011)
15. Wyman, B.T., Harvey, D.J., Crawford, K., Bernstein, M.A., Carmichael, O., Cole, P.E., Crane, P.K., DeCarli, C., Fox, N.C., Gunter, J.L., Hill, D., Killiany, R.J., Pachai, C., Schwarz, A.J., Schuff, N., Senjem, M.L., Suhy, J., Thompson, P.M., Weiner, M., Jack Jr., C.R.: Standardization of analysis sets for reporting results from ADNI MRI data. Alzheimer's Dement. **9**(3), 332–337 (2013)
16. Boyes, R.G., Gunter, J.L., Frost, C., Janke, A.L., Yeatman, T., Hill, D.L., Bernstein, M.A., Thompson, P.M., Weiner, M.W., Schuff, N., et al.: Intensity non-uniformity correction using N3 on 3-T scanners with multichannel phased array coils. Neuroimage **39**(4), 1752–1762 (2008)
17. Clarkson, M.J., Ourselin, S., Nielsen, C., Leung, K.K., Barnes, J., Whitwell, J.L., Gunter, J.L., Hill, D.L., Weiner Jr., M.W., Jack Jr., C.R., Fox, N.C.: Comparison of phantom and registration scaling corrections using the ADNI cohort. NeuroImage **47**(4), 1506–1513 (2009)
18. Lowe, D.G.: Distinctive image features from scale-invariant keypoints. Int. J. Comput. Vision **60**(2), 91–110 (2004)
19. Toews, M., Wells III, W.M.: Efficient and robust model-to-image alignment using 3D scale-invariant features. Med. Image Anal. **17**(3), 271–282 (2013)
20. Besl, P., McKay, N.D.: A method for registration of 3-D shapes. IEEE Trans. Pattern Anal. Mach. Intell. **14**(2), 239–256 (1992)
21. Bergström, P.: Computational methods for shape verification of free-form surfaces. Doctoral thesis/Luleå University of Technology. Luleå tekniska universitet (2011)
22. Berthold, M.R., Cebron, N., Dill, F., Gabriel, T.R., Kötter, T., Meinl, T., Ohl, P., Sieb, C., Thiel, K., Wiswedel, B.: KNIME: the konstanz information miner. In: Preisach, C., Burkhardt, H., Schmidt-Thieme, L., Decker, R. (eds.) Data Analysis, Machine Learning and Applications. Studies in Classification, Data Analysis, and Knowledge Organization, pp. 319–326. Springer, Heidelberg (2008)

Object Classification in an Ultrasound Video Using LP-SIFT Features

Mohammad Ali Maraci[1]([⊠]), Raffaele Napolitano[2], Aris Papageorghiou[2], and J. Allison Noble[1]

[1] Department of Engineering Science, Center for Doctoral Training, Institute of Biomedical Engineering, University of Oxford, Oxford, UK
mohammad.maraci@eng.ox.ac.uk
[2] Nuffield Department of Obstetrics and Gynaecology, University of Oxford, Oxford, UK

Abstract. The advantages of ultrasound (US) over other medical imaging modalities have provided a platform for its wide use in many medical fields, both for diagnostic and therapeutic purposes. However one of the limiting factors which has affected wide adoption of this cost-effective technology is requiring highly skilled sonographers and operators. We consider this problem in this paper which is motivated by advancements within the computer vision community. Our approach combines simple and standardized clinical ultrasound procedures with machine learning driven imaging solutions to provide users who have limited clinical experience, to perform simple diagnostic decisions (such as detection of a fetal breech presentation). We introduce LP-SIFT features constructed using the well-known SIFT features, utilizing a set of feature symmetry filters. We also illustrate how such features can be used in a bag of visual words representation on ultrasound images for classification of anatomical structures that have significant clinical implications in fetal health such as the fetal head, heart and abdomen, despite the high presence of speckle, shadows and other imaging artifacts in ultrasound images.

1 Introduction

Ultrasound imaging is perceived to be advantageous compared to other imaging modalities for its real-time acquisition capabilities, portability, absence of adverse effects and the lower costs associated with its use for diagnostic and therapeutic purposes. Although such advantages have helped the uptake of this technology, it requires well-trained and expert sonographers to perform diagnostics tasks. This is mainly due to the fact that guiding the transducer to the correct diagnostic plane as well as interpreting the data is often complex and requires understanding intricate sonographic patterns. Although 3D ultrasound helps by simplifying the data acquisition stage to some extent, it shifts the burden of finding the diagnostic plane to finding a plane in an ultrasound volume. This problem has also been looked at recently e.g. in [1,2]. To simplify acquisition and interpretation of data we have, with the help of our clinical partners,

© Springer International Publishing Switzerland 2014
B. Menze et al. (Eds.): MCV 2014, LNCS 8848, pp. 71–81, 2014.
DOI: 10.1007/978-3-319-13972-2_7

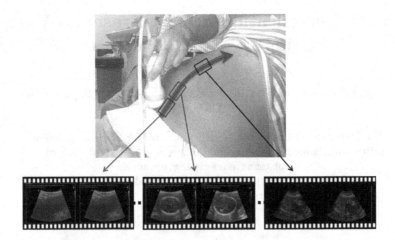

Fig. 1. A simplified scanning protocol. A straight ultrasound video sweep is obtained from the cervix upwards. Two sample frames are shown from various points in the ultrasound video sweep illustrating "Other Structures" (left), "Fetal Skull" (center) and "Fetal Abdomen" (right). Such structures can provide vital information about the health of the fetus.

introduced simple standardised scanning protocols where an ultrasound video sweep is obtained from a region of interest and processed such that structures of interest within the video are automatically identified for the less experienced users. This not only enables such users to make diagnostic decisions for certain conditions, but potentially can also be used as a means of training to enhance data acquisition skills over time.

Although the problem of object detection in ultrasound videos has been recently looked at e.g. in [3,4], they considered a different technical approach. The technical contributions of this paper are to introduce the LP-SIFT (Local Phase SIFT) features and illustrate their efficacy on a set of ultrasound images compared to standard SIFT features. We demonstrate how a pre-processing step can effectively be utilized to allow classification of ultrasound images using a bag of visual words representation [5] of such images. We further illustrate the performance of the proposed features on clinical data.

2   Method

The steps in our approach are illustrated schematically in Fig. 2. Once an ultrasound video is acquired following a simple and repeatable protocol, such as in Fig. 1, the frames within the sequence are extracted and are initially fed into a pre-processing step as explained in Sect. 2.1 to enhance acoustically significant structures in images. This step is vital to ensure discriminative Local Phase-based SIFT features can be extracted from the frames. Once LP-SIFT features are extracted from the enhanced video frames, a subsection of this data is used to construct a vocabulary of visual words using the well known dense SIFT feature.

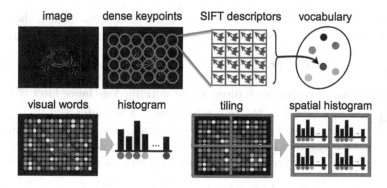

Fig. 2. Initially SIFT features are calculated from the local phase filtered images on a dense grid and vectorised into visual words. The frequency of each visual word is represented in a histogram for each tile of the spacial filter. LP-SIFT features are then created from these histograms.

Each frame (2D image) is then encoded as a spatial histogram using the learnt vocabulary of visual words. An SVM classifier with a homogeneous χ^2 kernel map as defined in [6] is then trained and evaluated on unseen data. Details of each step are given below.

2.1 Pre-processing

The 2D ultrasound slices contain textual information on the top left and right corners of each frame including the acquisition date and subject's ID. Therefore the extracted ultrasound frames are initially masked to remove this, followed by downsampling using a Gaussian pyramid reduction method for computational efficiency. Furthermore in order to construct LP-SIFT features, local-phase based filters are used for detecting intensity invariant features [7]. Pre-processing is an important step in this process as some of the inherent characteristics of ultrasound images such as presence of speckle patterns and shadows can cause simple interest point detectors such as SIFT (Scale Invariant Feature transform) [8] to perform poorly in detecting meaningful features, depending on the image quality.

2.2 Local Phase and Intensity Invariant Features

Due to the potential shortcomings of the intensity based feature detection approaches on ultrasound images and as the local phase filters encode local structural information in an image, it is a natural first step to utilize them when dealing with such images as they have also been successfully used in previous studies e.g. [9,10].

2D local phase is typically implemented (as here) using a monogenic signal framework [11]. The spatial representations of these 2D filters are: $h_1(x,y) = -x/(2\pi(x^2 + y^2)^{\frac{3}{2}})$ and $h_2(x,y) = -y/(2\pi(x^2 + y^2)^{\frac{3}{2}})$. Therefore in order to construct the even (symmetric) component of the monogenic signal, the image $I(x,y)$ is initially convolved with an even isotropic band-pass filter $b(x,y)$

$$even(x,y) = I_b(x,y) = b(x,y) * I(x,y) \tag{1}$$

One of the commonly used such filters is the isotropic log-Gabor filter $G^{lg}(\omega) = exp(-\frac{log^2(\omega/k)}{2log^2(\sigma_\omega)}))$ where k is the centre frequency of the filter and $0 < \sigma_\omega < 1$ is related to the spread of the frequency spectrum in the logarithmic function. Furthermore to construct the two odd (anti-symmetric) components, the band-passed images are convolved with the Riesz filter to produce the following

$$\begin{aligned} odd_1(x,y) &= h_1(x,y) * I_b(x,y) \\ odd_2(x,y) &= h_2(x,y) * I_b(x,y) \end{aligned} \tag{2}$$

and therefore the monogenic signal $I_m(x,y)$ of image $I(x,y)$ can be expressed as

$$I_m(x,y) = \left[I_b(x,y), h_1(x,y) * I_b(x,y), h_2(x,y) * I_b(x,y) \right] \tag{3}$$

As fetal ultrasound images typically exhibit non-uniform intensities and shadows (highly dependant on the presence of fatty tissues/bones) which can affect the visual appearance of the same anatomical structures in different scans (e.g. the fetal skull, heart or abdomen), we use the multi-scale feature symmetry map which is defined as

$$FS(x,y) = \sum_s \frac{\lfloor [|even_s(x,y)| - |odd_s(x,y)|] - T_s \rfloor}{\sqrt{even_s(x,y)^2 + odd_s(x,y)^2} + \epsilon}, \tag{4}$$

where s is the scale of the band-pass filter, ϵ is a small positive constant to avoid division by zero, $\lfloor . \rfloor$ denotes replacing negative values with zeros, $T_s = \exp\left(mean(log(\sqrt{even_s(x,y)^2 + odd_s(x,y)^2})) \right)$ is a scale specific noise compensation term corresponding to the maximum response generated from noise only in the signal.

Here by utilizing the local feature symmetry and the local energy (amplitude) filters, a feature symmetry map of locations with high amplitude is produced. For the clinical application considered in this paper, this combination can nicely discriminate between the fetal skull and the soft tissue objects as indicated in Fig. 3 (please refer to the electronic copy for color encoding). For the band-pass filtering with the log-Gabor filter it was empirically shown that the following parameters produced the best results where $\sigma_\omega = 0.05$ and the three scales of the filter wavelength used are [28 30 32] pixels. It is important to note that these scales were chosen to correspond to the size of the features of interest, in pixels, and may require tuning for other applications.

2.3   LP-SIFT Features and Training

Gradient based features such as SIFT have shown to provide a simple and powerful set of descriptors for a variety of applications. SIFT transforms an image into a large collection of local feature vectors where they are invariant to rotation, scaling or translation of the image. However these features can be susceptible to imaging noise and the presence of speckle patterns and attenuation and shadows in ultrasound images can affect their performance. Generally, to compute SIFT features, a histogram of local oriented gradients is calculated, either around some predefined interest points or on a dense grid, where this description from the training image can then be used to locate the object of interest in a test image.

To increase generality, mid-level representations of temporally segmented video clips have been utilized here. Whereas low-level features are based on the raw training images, mid-level features are usually created after carrying out some intermediate operation on the features with the aim of creating more descriptive and discriminative feature descriptors. Hence here initially the images are preprocessed as explained in Sect. 2.1 using the feature symmetry and local energy filters, and then SIFT features are created on a regular dense grid and vectorised into visual words, forming the LP-SIFT features.

The frequency of each visual word is represented in a histogram for each tile of a spatial filter which represents the features on the image. A homogeneous kernel map representation of the χ^2 kernel, $k_{\chi^2}(x,y) = 2\frac{(x-y)^2}{x+y}$ where $x,y \in \mathbb{R}$ are non-negative scalars, is used as they have shown to be particularly suitable for comparing histograms [6], which is the format of the visual descriptors described in this paper. The mid-level feature vectors are then created from these histograms and used to train an SVM classifier.

3   Experiments

3.1   Data Acquisition

The clinical data generated for this paper consists of 60 fetal ultrasound videos (two 2D videos acquired from 30 participants). Clinical data acquisition was carried out using a mid-range US machine (Philips HD9 with a V7-3 transducer) by an experienced obstetrician who was asked to follow a simple scanning protocol of moving the ultrasound probe from bottom to top of the abdomen in approximately 6–8 s. Four classes of video frames were created from these video sweeps of the fetal abdomen, heart, skull and other structures. Other structures class includes any video frame that does not fall into the other three classes. All the subjects included in this study are healthy volunteers of 26 weeks of gestation and over.

3.2   Two-Class Classification

Here a number of experiments have been designed to allow a systematic comparison between the classification results obtained when using the proposed LP-SIFT features introduced in this paper versus the dense SIFT features on the

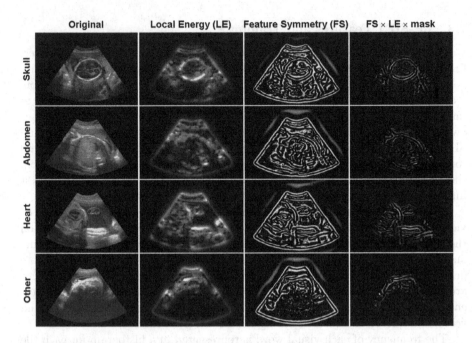

Fig. 3. Sample images from each of the four classes. From top to bottom, an example of fetal skull, abdomen, heart and other structures are shown. The Local Energy (amplitude), Feature Symmetry and the masked product of the two filters are illustrated for each image class. (Hot color coding has been used for illustration purposes and a clearer visual appearance)

raw pixel intensities. Three binary classification experiments have been designed. The first test was carried out to measure how well the frames that exhibit the fetal skull were separated from the ones which did not. For the second test the same procedure was repeated but for fetal heart class. The third test was to compare classification accuracy between the frames which exhibit the fetal skull and those which exhibit the abdominal structures. This is because the fetal skull and abdominal structures exhibit similar oval geometric characteristics and thus it was felt to be interesting to investigate how well they can be distinguished using the two features.

All experiments were performed using a 5-fold cross-validation where the data has been trained on 4/5 of the data and accuracy is evaluated on 1/5 of the data. The results are summarised in the next section in Table 1 and are reported using the minimum, maximum and the mean classification accuracy over a 5-fold cross validation.

3.3 Four-Class Classification

A similar experimental protocol to the Two-Class classification experiment was followed with the difference being the inclusion of the four image classes.

Clinically it is important to know where the fetal heart is and whether it beats as expected or not. The size and position of the fetal skull and abdominal structures are also indicative of the growth of the fetus as well as presence or absence of certain complications and risks. A 5-fold cross-validation was conducted using a multi-class SVM classifier and the results are summarised in Table 1.

4 Results

Two-Class Classification: Results from this experiment are summarised in Table 1a for fetal skull verses other structures, Table 1b for fetal skull versus abdominal structures and Table 1c for fetal heart versus other structures. Generally a higher classification accuracy is achieved when using the proposed LP-SIFT features and a higher performance is obtained as the number of codewords increase.

For the fetal skull versus other structures, the highest mean accuracy obtained using the LP-SIFT features is 95.87 % (200 codewords) compared to 86.51 % (300 codewords) using the SIFT features. Similarly for the fetal skull versus the abdomen, the highest mean accuracy was obtained using the LP-SIFT features of 97.90 % (100 codewords). For the SIFT features it was 90.53 % using 50 codewords. The fetal heart is the exception here where the best result is achieved using the SIFT features and 200 codewords with an accuracy of 92.36 % compared to 90.00 % with 300 codewords for the LP-SIFT features.

Four-Class Classification: Table 1d summarises classification results for the four class classification of fetal skull, abdomen, heart and other structure classes. As can be seen the highest mean classification has been achieved using the LP-SIFT features (78.95 %) using 200 codewords. For the SIFT features, the best results have been achieved using 100 codewords with a mean accuracy of 66.05 %.

Classifier Performance: In order to visually assess the classification performance for the different classes on the test data, the classifier scores for each image have been ranked in descending order, where the classifier confidence is highest for the first item in this list and lowest for the last image. Figures 4 and 5 illustrate the top nine images with the highest scores in each class for classification results using a codebook of 50 and 100 visual words respectively, where figures (a) and (b) correspond to a binary classification for fetal skull versus other structures, (c) and (d) for the fetal abdominal structures versus other structures and (e) and (f) show classification results for fetal heart versus other structures, using the two features discussed in this paper.

As it can be seen in Fig. 4a, standard SIFT features fail to capture a full representation of the fetal skull as the second, third, fourth and sixth top items in the list are not fetal skull. However the LP-SIFT features have a better representation where only the fifth and the ninth images are misclassified. For the abdomen the results are better using the SIFT features as shown in Fig. 4c compared to Fig. 4d where the second image, a fetal skull, is incorrectly classified as

Table 1. Classification Results. Skull versus Other Structures (a), Skull versus Abdomen (b), Heart versus Other Structures (c) and four class classification (Fetal Abdomen, Heart, Skull and Other structures) (d). Minimum, maximum and mean accuracy are reported over a 5 fold cross validation for codebooks of various sizes.

(a) Fetal Skull Vs Other Structures

Codewords	Features	min/max (%) Ave. Accuracy	Mean (%) Ave. Accuracy
30	LP-SIFT	91.0/95.0	93.10
	SIFT	75.9/80.4	78.15
50	LP-SIFT	93.9/94.2	93.87
	SIFT	81.0/84.9	83.01
100	LP-SIFT	95.0/96.3	95.82
	SIFT	82.8/86.5	84.97
200	LP-SIFT	95.2/97.4	**95.87**
	SIFT	83.1/86.0	84.60
300	LP-SIFT	94.2/97.4	95.61
	SIFT	85.0/88.6	**86.51**

(b) Fetal Skull Vs Abdomen

Features	min/max (%) Ave. Accuracy	Mean (%) Ave. Accuracy
LP-SIFT	92.1/100.0	94.98
SIFT	73.7/86.6	77.89
LP-SIFT	92.1/100.0	96.84
SIFT	89.5/92.1	**90.53**
LP-SIFT	94.7/100.0	**97.90**
SIFT	79.0/97.4	89.47
LP-SIFT	94.7/100.0	97.37
SIFT	84.2/92.1	86.84
LP-SIFT	94.7/100.0	96.84
SIFT	84.2/92.1	88.42

(c) Fetal Heart Vs Other Structures

Codewords	Features	min/max (%) Ave. Accuracy	Mean (%) Ave. Accuracy
30	LP-SIFT	85.3/92.7	89.61
	SIFT	88.2/92.7	90.87
50	LP-SIFT	88.2/92.7	89.71
	SIFT	72.1/92.7	87.35
100	LP-SIFT	85.3/92.7	89.70
	SIFT	85.3/92.7	89.41
200	LP-SIFT	83.8/92.7	89.41
	SIFT	91.2/92.7	**92.36**
300	LP-SIFT	83.8/92.7	**90.00**
	SIFT	88.2/92.7	91.77

(d) Fetal Four-Class Classification

Features	min/max (%) Ave. Accuracy	Mean (%) Ave. Accuracy
LP-SIFT	54.0/86.8	72.63
SIFT	54.0/73.7	64.74
LP-SIFT	64.5/80.3	70.51
SIFT	58.0/65.8	62.10
LP-SIFT	71.1/81.6	77.37
SIFT	51.3/75.0	**66.05**
LP-SIFT	72.4/85.5	**78.95**
SIFT	56.6/71.1	65.00
LP-SIFT	65.9/81.6	73.10
SIFT	51.3/79.0	64.74

a fetal abdomen. An improvement can be noticed when a codebook of 100 words is used as shown in Fig. 5. For the fetal skull the LP-SIFT features have illustrated a higher confidence in capturing a wider set of fetal skulls in comparison to the SIFT features as demonstrated in Figs. 5a and b, where again there are five incorrectly classified images in the top nine classifications.

It is interesting to note that using a larger codebook of visual words using the LP-SIFT features has allowed for a diverse set of images to be selected. For example the top nine fetal skulls selected using LP-SIFT with 50 codewords are all of similar structures as shown in Fig. 4b whereas the same setting with 100 visual words has allowed for a wide variety of head structures to be selected as show in Fig. 5b. Furthermore although generally increasing the number of visual words has resulted in a higher classification accuracy, the performance gain is

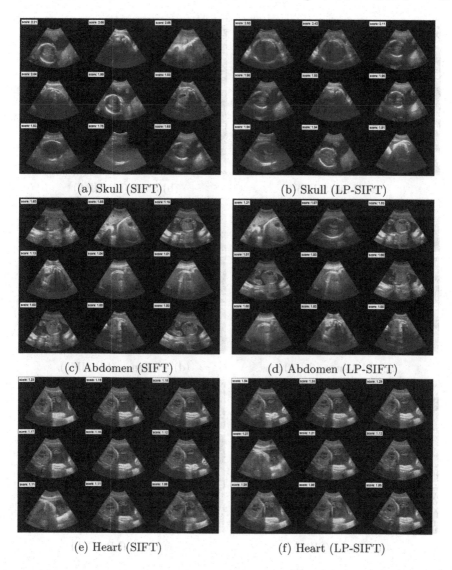

(a) Skull (SIFT)   (b) Skull (LP-SIFT)

(c) Abdomen (SIFT)   (d) Abdomen (LP-SIFT)

(e) Heart (SIFT)   (f) Heart (LP-SIFT)

Fig. 4. Top nine ranked images based on the classifier scores on test data for Skull Vs not Skull (a,b), Abdomen Vs not Abdomen (c,d) and Heart Vs not Heart (e,f). SIFT features are used in (a) & (c) & (e) and LP-SIFT in (b) & (d) & (f) with a codebook of 50 words.

only marginal after 100 words. It is also important to note that classification results for the fetal heart are better using the SIFT features. This may be due to the fact that fetal heart is relatively small compared to the skull and abdomen and the pre-processing filters might have removed necessary data.

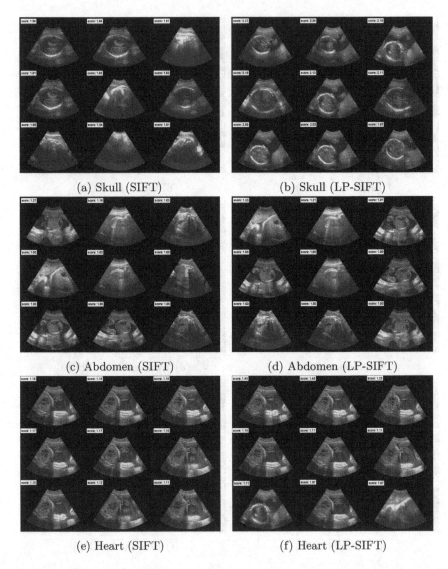

(a) Skull (SIFT)   (b) Skull (LP-SIFT)

(c) Abdomen (SIFT)   (d) Abdomen (LP-SIFT)

(e) Heart (SIFT)   (f) Heart (LP-SIFT)

Fig. 5. Top nine ranked images based on the classifier scores on test data for Skull Vs not Skull (a,b), Abdomen Vs not Abdomen (c,d) and Heart Vs not Heart (e,f). SIFT features are used in (a) & (c) & (e) and LP-SIFT in (b) & (d) & (f) with a codebook of 100 words.

5   Discussion and Conclusion

Ultrasound image acquisition and interpretation can be a challenging task for non-experts. We have tackled this obstacle and as the results in Sect. 4 demonstrate the new proposed features allow for a good classification of structures in ultrasound images. In summary, we have proposed a general framework for ultrasound video analysis, motivated by our interest in ultrasound in pregnancy and perinatal care, which couples standardised, and possibly non-conventional scanning protocols, with image analysis methods designed to extract useful information from ultrasound videos which can be used for making simple diagnostic decision.

Our technical interest is extending this work to other structures on larger databases of images. In collaboration with clinicians in the UK and Africa, we are exploring the role of methodology of this kind in supporting medical training and roll out of ultrasound services in rural areas and we thank them for posing the challenge to us to look at the clinical need outlined in the experiments which motivated this paper.

Acknowledgments. Mohammad Ali Maraci acknowledges the support of RCUK Digital Economy Programme grant number EP/G036861/1 (Oxford Centre for Doctoral Training in Healthcare Innovation). The authors also acknowledges that the data was acquired as part of the Intergrowth-21st study.

References

1. Lu, X., Georgescu, B., Zheng, Y., Otsuki, J., Comaniciu, D.: Autompr: automatic detection of standard planes in 3d echocardiography. In: 5th IEEE International Symposium on ISBI 2008, pp. 1279–1282 (2008)
2. Chykeyuk, K., Yaqub, M., Noble, J.: Class-specific regression random forest for accurate extraction of standard planes from 3d echocardiography. In: MICCAI International Workshop on Machine Learning in Medical Imaging (2013)
3. Kwitt, R., Vasconcelos, N., Razzaque, S., Aylward, S.: Localizing target structures in ultrasound video - a phantom study. Med. Image Anal. **17**(7), 712–722 (2013)
4. Maraci, M.A., Napolitano, R., Papageorghiou, A., Noble, J.A.: Searching for structures of interest in an ultrasound video sequence. In: Wu, G., Zhang, D., Zhou, L. (eds.) MLMI 2014. LNCS, vol. 8679, pp. 133–140. Springer, Heidelberg (2014)
5. Sivic, J., Zisserman, A.: Video google: a text retrieval approach to object matching in videos. In: Ninth IEEE International Conference on Computer Vision, Proceedings, pp. 1470–1477. IEEE (2003)
6. Vedaldi, A., Zisserman, A.: Efficient additive kernels via explicit feature maps. IEEE Trans. Pattern Anal. Mach. Intell. **34**(3), 480–492 (2012)
7. Kovesi, P.: Symmetry and asymmetry from local phase. In: Tenth Australian Joint Conference on Artificial Intelligence, pp. 185–190. Citeseer (1997)
8. Lowe, D.G.: Distinctive image features from scale-invariant keypoints. Int. J. Comput. Vis. **60**(2), 91–110 (2004)
9. Rajpoot, K., Noble, A., Grau, V., Rajpoot, N.M.: Feature detection from echocardiography images using local phase information. In: Medical Image Understanding and Analysis (MIUA), Dundee, UK (2008)
10. Rahmatullah, B., Papageorghiou, A.T., Noble, J.A.: Integration of local and global features for anatomical object detection in ultrasound. In: Ayache, N., Delingette, H., Golland, P., Mori, K. (eds.) MICCAI 2012, Part III. LNCS, vol. 7512, pp. 402–409. Springer, Heidelberg (2012)
11. Felsberg, M., Sommer, G.: The monogenic signal. IEEE Trans. Signal Process. **49**(12), 3136–3144 (2001)

Unsupervised Pre-training Across Image Domains Improves Lung Tissue Classification

Thomas Schlegl$^{(\boxtimes)}$, Joachim Ofner, and Georg Langs

Computational Imaging Research Lab, Department of Biomedical Imaging
and Image-guided Therapy, Medical University Vienna, Vienna, Austria
{thomas.schlegl,joachim.ofner,georg.langs}@meduniwien.ac.at

Abstract. The detection and classification of anomalies relevant for disease diagnosis or treatment monitoring is important during computational medical image analysis. Often, obtaining sufficient annotated training data to represent natural variability well is unfeasible. At the same time, data is frequently collected across multiple sites with heterogeneous medical imaging equipment. In this paper we propose and evaluate a semi-supervised learning approach that uses data from multiple sites (domains). Only for one small site annotations are available. We use convolutional neural networks to capture spatial appearance patterns and classify lung tissue in high-resolution computed tomography data. We perform domain adaptation via unsupervised pre-training of convolutional neural networks to inject information from sites or image classes for which no annotations are available. Results show that across site pre-training as well as pre-training on different image classes improves classification accuracy compared to random initialisation of the model parameters.

1 Introduction

Computer aided diagnosis often relies on automatic classification of observations made in medical imaging data. When constructing classifiers we face challenges such as limited annotated training data, the need to collect training data across multiple sites with potentially heterogeneous imaging hardware, and the choice of visual features that represent the data well, and are at the same time suited for discriminative learning. Existing methods often use handcrafted features. Manual feature engineering and feature selection requires appropriate expert knowledge. Apart from this, hand-crafted features are very domain-specific, thus applicable to other tasks or domains only to a limited extend. In contrast, shallow

Thomas Schlegl: This work has received funding from the European Union FP7 (KHRESMOI FP7-257528, VISCERAL FP7-318068), from the Austrian Science Fund (FWF P22578-B19, PULMARCH) and from the Austrian Federal Ministry of Science, Research and Economy and the National Foundation for Research, Technology and Development (OPTIMA).

© Springer International Publishing Switzerland 2014
B. Menze et al. (Eds.): MCV 2014, LNCS 8848, pp. 82–93, 2014.
DOI: 10.1007/978-3-319-13972-2_8

convolutional neural networks (CNN) [1] tend to learn low-level features, which are less domain-specific and thus yield better generalization to different domains. Before training of a CNN on annotated data starts, the model parameters have to be initialized with random values, or alternatively, with parameters pre-learned on non-annotated data. Random initialization is an appropriate approach only if large amounts of annotated data is available. In this paper we explore CNN as a means to learn low-level imaging features, to integrate non-annotated data, and to use data from multiple sites (*domains*) in the training process. A clinically highly relevant example where accurate classification of anomalies is crucial for treatment decisions are interstitial lung diseases. *Computed tomography (CT)* of the lung is an invaluable tool in the diagnostic process of interstitial lung diseases, which comprise a broad heterogeneous group of parenchymal lung disorders [2]. A wide range of anomalous patterns can be identified in high resolution CT scans of the lung, which correspond to specific lung diseases. Some of them show only subtly different appearance. Furthermore, the diagnosis of interstitial lung disease is a challenging task for computer-aided diagnosis systems as well as for human specialists, because various types of the disease occur with only low frequency (cf. [3]). In this paper, we study how CNN can be used to classify pathologies of the lung in CT imaging data and evaluate the ability of CNN to adapt across sites and image classes during unsupervised pre-training of feature extractors. We classify anomalous lung tissue (ground glass opacity, reticular interstitial pattern, honeycombing, emphysema) and normal lung parenchyma. Here, CNN allow to perform three tasks that are central to learning from partially annotated data obtained from different sites or different image classes. The algorithm learns representative and discriminative feature extractors based on the available partially annotated imaging data. It uses a substantial amount of non-annotated data to pre-train the network, and can inject data from different sites or different image classes to improve classification accuracy even if only data acquired on a single target site is annotated.

Related work. CNN were introduced in 1980 [1]. Since then, different variants of CNN were used to solve classification problems. The areas of successful application range from classification of handwritten digits (MNIST dataset) [4,5] to NORB [5] and ImageNet [6] datasets. Due to its ability to capture abstract representations deep learning applied successfully to unsupervised learning, transfer learning, domain adaptation and self-taught learning (cf. [4,7]). Lee et al. presented in [4] an approach of self-taught learning for object recognition using CNN on non-medical images. But contrary to our proposed work, the target images were not taken from the medical domain. *Deep Belief Networks (DBN)* in general, and in particular CNN were successfully applied in detection tasks, such as mitosis detection in breast cancer histology images by means of supervised CNN [8]. In contrast to conventional DBN, CNN also use convolutional layers in the first few layers in addition to fully-connected layers. The beneficial effect of layer-wise unsupervised pre-training has been shown in [9]. *Convolutional Restricted Boltzmann Machines (CRBM)* [10] were used for manifold learning by reducing the dimensionality of 3D brain *magnetic resonance (MR)* images [11].

There, parameter learning in the frequency domain of the first CRBM layers was used to reduce the high dimensionality of the input images. Typically, DBN have been successfully applied in tasks processing relatively small images. Their application to image sizes characteristic for medical imaging (e.g., 256×256 or 512×512 for CT) remains challenging (cf. [4]).

Contribution. We use CNN to perform pixel-wise classification of lung tissue in 2D CT slices (images). Layer-wise unsupervised pre-training to initialize the parameters of a CNN is a well-known concept in deep learning theory. In the proposed work we aim to evaluate the beneficial effect on classification accuracy when this concept is applied to train a classifier on medical target images. The contributions of the paper are the data driven learning of spatial low-level features for lung tissue classification, the integration of unlabeled data in a pre-training phase, and the domain adaptation that allows the use of unlabeled data from different sites or different image classes to improve classification accuracy on medical images. The proposed approach focuses on classification tasks where only few labeled data from the target domain but large amounts of unlabeled data from different domains are available. We evaluate the algorithm on CT data of the lung and brain collected at the Vienna General Hospital, the STL-10 dataset [12] and the *Lung Tissue Research Consortium (LTRC)* dataset [13], and study the effect of unsupervised pre-training and supervised fine-tuning on different sites or image classes in detail.

2   Restricted Boltzmann Machines

A *Restricted Boltzmann Machine (RBM)* is an undirected graphical model with two layers. The first layer consists of a set of binary or real-valued input units v - also referred to as visible units - of dimension C and the second layer consists of a set of binary hidden units h of dimension B. The units of both layers are fully-connected by a weight matrix $W \in \mathbb{R}^{C \times B}$, i.e. every visible unit is connected with every hidden unit. The model parameteres of an RBM are trained to perform some kind of (non-linear) transformation between visible and hidden units. A DBN is a generative model that is constructed by stacking RBM on top of each other. Adjacent RBM within a DBN are in turn fully connected. Hinton et al. [14] showed that deep models can be efficiently trained by greedily training each layer as an RBM. The first RBM is trained with input samples. The single RBM from the second RBM upwards are trained by using the activations of the previous layer as inputs. RBM and DBN have an important limitation in common when using images as inputs. Both ignore the 2D structure of the input image. A CNN is a feature extractor that preserves the 2D structure of the input. The architecture of CNNs is motivated by biological vision [15].

A CNN is a feed-forward network that is hierarchically structured with one or more pairs of convolutional and max-pooling layers followed by one or more *fully-connected layers*. The *convolutional layers* act as detection layers. Each convolutional layer maps the input to Γ groups. Thus every convolution layer

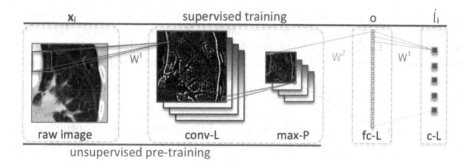

Fig. 1. Illustration of the architecture of our shallow CNN with one convolution (*conv-L*) and max-pooling layer (*max-P*), one fully-connected layer (*fc-L*) and a classification layer (*c-L*).

learns Γ different feature detectors. Because the weights of every group are shared across the whole input image, the number of parameters to be learned is massively reduced so that CNNs scale well to full images. *Max-pooling* layers are stacked on top of every convolution layer. A pooling layer shrinks the size of the matrix of activations of the preceding detection layer by a constant factor by only taking the maximum activation within small non-overlapping regions. The pooling layer has no parameters that have to be trained. For classification tasks, a terminal *classification layer* is needed. We use softmax regression as classifier which enables our model to perform multi-class classification. Figure 1 illustrates the architecture of the CNN used in our experiments.

3   Domain Adaptation in Lung Tissue Classification

We are given two different datasets. The first dataset comprises pairs of 2D medical imaging data and corresponding pixel-wise class labels $\langle \mathbf{I}_m, \mathbf{L}_m \rangle$, with $m = 1, 2, \ldots, M$, where $\mathbf{I}_m \in \mathbb{R}^{n \times n}$ is an image of size $n \times n$ of pixel intensities, and $\mathbf{L}_m \in \{1, ..., K\}^{n \times n}$ is an array of the same size containing the corresponding class labels. The second dataset comprises only 2D image data $\mathbf{J}_u$, with $u = 1, 2, \ldots, U$ without corresponding class labels. We extract small input image patches $\mathbf{x}_i^I \in \mathbb{R}^{s \times s}$ with $s < n$ from image $\mathbf{I}_m$, corresponding patches of ground truth class labels $\mathbf{l}_i \in \{1, ..., K\}^{s \times s}$ from $\mathbf{L}_m$ and input image patches $\mathbf{x}_i^J \in \mathbb{R}^{s \times s}$ from $\mathbf{J}_u$ respectively, where s is the width and height and i the index of the centroid of the patch. The true class label l_i, for patch $\mathbf{x}_i^I$ corresponds to the mode of given ground truth class labels in $\mathbf{l}_i$. The class label l_i is assigned to the whole image patch $\mathbf{x}_i^I$ centered at pixel position i. We use $\langle \mathbf{x}_i^I, l_i \rangle$ pairs for supervised training of our model. Our objective is to learn a mapping $f :$ $\mathbf{x}_i^I \longmapsto l_i$ from image patches $\mathbf{x}_i^I$ to corresponding class labels l_i in a semi-supervised fashion. During testing we apply the mapping to new image patches in the test set.

During classification, an unseen image patch $\mathbf{x}_i$ causes an activation o of the fully-connected layer (fc-L) of the CNN (Fig. 1). The activation o of the fully-connected layer is the input of the classification layer. The classification layer t has as its parameters a weight matrix W^t and a bias term a^t. We apply the softmax function on activations of the classification layer which gives us predictions $\hat{l}_i$ for the class k having the highest class membership probability:

$$\hat{l}_i = \underset{k}{\mathrm{argmax}}\, P(\hat{l}_i = k | o, W^t, a^t). \tag{1}$$

During training, all weights and bias terms of the whole model are optimized by minimizing the misclassification error on image patches of the training set.

3.1 Unsupervised Pre-training

We can pre-train convolutional neural networks on unlabeled data to improve the training procedure [4]. Before supervised training starts, we use CRBM layers as a means for unsupervised pre-training of the CNN parameters of the convolutional layers. CRBM consist of an input layer and $\gamma = 1, ..., \Gamma$ groups of hidden units. Its parameters are learned via block Gibbs sampling [4] using the conditional distributions for the hidden units h in group γ

$$P(h_\gamma = 1 | v) = \sigma\left((\tilde{W}_\gamma * v) + b\right) \tag{2}$$

and for the visible units v

$$P(v | h) = \sum_\gamma (W_\gamma * h_\gamma) + c. \tag{3}$$

Here, $*$ is the convolution operation, b is the bias term of the hidden units in group γ, c is the bias term of the visible units and $\sigma(q) = \frac{1}{1+e^{-q}}$ is the sigmoid function. The tilde above the weight matrix $\tilde{W}$ denotes the usage of a horizontally and vertically flipped version of matrix W. Lee et al. [4] proposed a technique, also referred to as probabilistic max-pooling, which allows to stack CRBM into a multilayer model that is referred to as *Convolutional Deep Belief Network (CDBN)*. This model integrates the information whether a pooling unit is on or off. The random variables for the hidden units h are sampled from a multinomial distribution including this information.

Nair et al. [16] showed that the hidden units of a Restricted Boltzmann machine can be approximated efficiently by noisy rectified linear units. Thus, instead of sampling the hidden units based on the conditional distribution given in Eq. (2) we use the noisy rectified activation $A(h)$ of hidden units h which is given by

$$A(h_\gamma) = max\left(0, x + N(0, \sigma(x))\right), \tag{4}$$

where $N(0, V)$ is the added Gaussian noise with zero mean and variance V. The variance V is the sigmoid activation function σ applied to the convolved input

$$x = (\tilde{W}_\gamma * v) + b. \tag{5}$$

At this point, instead of using unsupervised pre-training exclusively from the same samples $\mathbf{x}_i^I$ as used for supervised training, we evaluate the accuracy of the classifier f by using additional unlabeled samples $\mathbf{x}_i^J$ of either the same, or other domains during pre-training of the CRBM.

4   Experiments

Data. We perform experiments on two clinical CT datasets of the lung, on a clinical CT dataset of the brain and on a natural image dataset (see Fig. 2).

The clinical lung datasets comprise clinical high-resolution lung CT scans of different patients from two different sites. The first lung dataset (V) comprises unlabeled clinical data from the Vienna General Hospital. The second lung dataset (L) comprises a subset of data from the LTRC dataset [13].

Dataset-L contains 20,000 2D image patches extracted from axial slices of 380 scans from the LTRC dataset provided by the Lung Tissue Research Consortium of the National Heart Lung and Blood Institute (NHLBI). It contains data of patients predominantly suffering from Chronic Obstructive Pulmonary Disease (COPD) or Interstitial Lung Disease (ILD).

Dataset-LL contains 1000 labeled 2D image patches extracted from axial slices of a randomly selected subset of the 380 scans of the LTRC dataset. These image patches are used for unsupervised pre-training (without using the corresponding labels) and for supervised fine-tuning (including the corresponding patch labels). This dataset contains pixel-wise annotations of all patterns listed above. There is no overlap between samples of dataset-L and dataset-LL regarding pixel locations of image patch centers.

Dataset-V consists of 20,000 unlabeled 2D image patches extracted from axial slices of 65 randomly selected clinical lung CT scans, not restricted to the labeled pathologies in L but containing a large variation of different pathologies such as chronic obstructive pulmonary disease, cyst, pneumonia, bronchiectasis or space-occupying lesions.

The brain dataset, ***Dataset-B***, contains 20,000 unlabeled 2D image patches extracted from axial slices of 427 randomly selected clinical high-resolution head CT scans.

Finally, we also use non-medical unlabeled natural images. ***Dataset-S*** contains 20,000 unlabeled image patches extracted from the STL-10 dataset [12].

Data selection and preprocessing. We use 2D axial slices from the clinical datasets and grayscale versions of the STL-10 dataset for pre-training or supervised fine-tuning of the classifier. Images of CT scans have typically image resolutions of 512×512 pixels. From these images we extract 40×40 pixel patches x_i centered at pixel positions i. The positions of the patch centers as well as the slice positions within the CT scan (in the case of clinical datasets) are sampled randomly. The image patches are preprocessed by transforming the data to zero-mean and unit variance. Standardization of real valued data is a common requirement in deep learning.

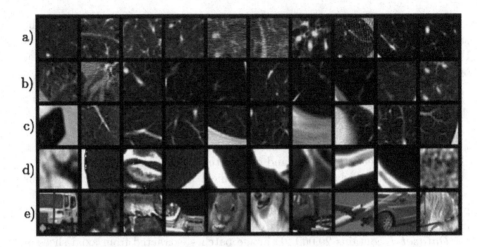

Fig. 2. Datasets used in the experiments: a) dataset-LL, b) dataset-L, c) dataset-V, d) dataset-B, e) dataset-S. The labels which correspond to the patches from left to right of dataset-LL (a) are as follows: 'normal', 'normal', 'ground glass', 'ground glass', 'reticular', 'reticular', 'honeycomb', 'honeycomb', 'emphysema', 'emphysema'.

Evaluation. We train a classifier to differentiate between five tissue classes (ground glass opacity, reticular interstitial pattern, honeycombing, emphysema and healthy lung tissue). We perform two experiments.

(1) In our first experiment we perform supervised training using dataset-LL (the target domain) and evaluate the classification accuracy when pre-training is performed on different unlabeled datasets. Supervised fine-tuning is performed on 50, 100, 150 or 200 samples of dataset-LL, which corresponds to 0.25 %, 0.5 %, 0.75 % and 1 % of the samples used for unsupervised pre-training (in experiments 1b–e) respectively. These samples are always already included in the pre-training phase of all scenarios without using the class labels. We evaluate the minimum classification error over the fine-tuning epochs. We use a random split of these samples to perform 5-fold-cross-validation. The performance measure of the classifier is the average of misclassification errors over the 5-fold-cross-validation runs. The images in the test set of the supervised fine-tuning step are also excluded from the training set of the pre-training phase. We evaluate the following pre-training scenarios. (1a) We evaluate the classification accuracy when pre-training is only performed on samples (LL) that are used for fine-tuning. (1b) Unsupervised pre-training on dataset-L evaluates the classification accuracy when a larger unlabeled image set of the target site is available. (1c) By including dataset-V in the pre-training we evaluated if the unsupervised pre-training across different sites yields comparable classification accuracy. (1d) Instead of pre-training on images of the same type (lung CT scans) we perform pre-training on brain CT scans (B) and (1e) on natural images (S) to evaluate if the learning of image feature extractors generalizes across image types. The last two scenarios simulate cases where only very little

imaging data of a specific anatomical site is available. **(1f)** The classification accuracy is also evaluated for training the classifier without performing any pre-training.

(2) In the second experiment we vary the training set size for supervised fine-tuning from 10 patches to 20,000 patches, to understand how even with minimal sets of annotated images, we can train classifiers with reasonable accuracy, if pre-training has been performed. Furthermore, we evaluate the performance of the classifier using all patches for supervised fine-tuning that are used for unsupervised pre-training. In this experiment we use all samples of dataset-L for unsupervised pre-training and samples of dataset-LL for supervised fine-tuning. Where necessary we also use additional samples of dataset-L and corresponding class labels in the supervised fine-tuning phase.

All experiments are implemented in Python 2.7 using the Theano [17] library and run on a graphics processing unit (GPU).

4.1 Model Parameters

We use gaussian visible units to model real valued data with the CRBM. Each CRBM pre-training is performed for 200 epochs. We choose a simple CNN architecture, intentionally. The shallowness of the network allows to focus on the extraction of low-level features, learned on different datasets. The *CNN* (see Fig. 1) is hierarchically structured with 1 convolution layer, 1 fully-connected layer and a classification layer with 5 classification units. The convolution layer contains 32 groups of hidden units and is followed by a max-pooling layer. The filter size of the convolution layer is set to 5×5. The fully connected layer consists of 1000 neurons. For all classification experiments there is no overlap between the training set and the test set regarding pixel locations of image patch centers. But some patches share few pixels. The pre-training with different datasets results in corresponding parameter sets of learned weights W and bias terms b of the hidden units of the CRBMs. Before fine-tuning starts, we initialize the convolution layer of different CNNs with the pre-learned parameters. Because of normalizing the input data to zero mean and unit variance the bias terms c of the visible units have not to be learned. Fine-tuning of each CNN is performed for 400 epochs.

4.2 Classification Results

In experiment **(1)** we evaluate domain adaptation on dataset-V, dataset-B and dataset-S. Pre-training only on dataset-LL serves as the most restricted case, where no additional training samples are available or simply not used. We evaluate also the performance of the CNN without performing prior pre-training. This scenario also serves as reference scenario. Pre-training on dataset-L involves no domain adaptation of model parameters between unsupervised pre-training and supervised fine-tuning but this is an obvious approach when only a restricted amount of labeled data and a larger amount of unlabeled data of the same domain is available. Results are shown in Table 1.

Table 1. Misclassification errors of the CNN pre-trained on different datasets and the corresponding sample sizes of dataset-LL used for supervised fine-tuning. The results of pre-training datasets with overall minimum misclassification errors are highlighted.

	No pre-training	Dataset-LL	Dataset-L	Dataset-V	Dataset-B	Dataset-S
50	0.2853	0.2709	0.2600	0.2737	0.3008	**0.2499**
100	0.2076	0.1929	**0.1724**	0.1924	0.2242	0.1736
150	0.2057	0.1901	0.1656	0.1792	0.2148	**0.1628**
200	0.1977	0.1893	0.1633	0.1773	0.2138	**0.1604**

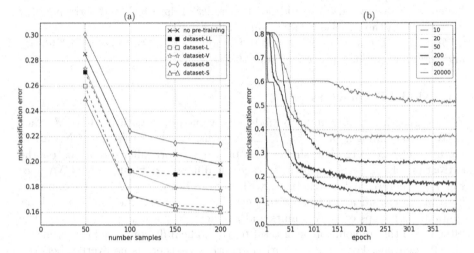

Fig. 3. (a) Misclassification error as a function of number of samples used for supervised fine-tuning using unsupervised pre-training on different datasets. (b) Misclassification error of a single run of the 5-fold-cross-validation setup as a function of training epochs using different sample sizes for supervised fine-tuning after pre-training on dataset-L.

Results show that the beneficial effect of unsupervised pre-training depends on the domain of the data used for pre-training. Pre-training on datasets of similar domains, both clinical CT datasets of the lung, result in similar performance. Dataset-L and dataset-V improve classification accuracy over only supervised training on dataset-LL. The performance of the fine-tuned CNN after pre-training on dataset-LL is slightly better than the performance of the CNN with no prior pre-training. Unsurprisingly, pre-training on dataset-B does not improve the performance of the classifier. The performance of the CNN initialized with random weights (*no pre-training*) is even better than the performance of the CNN that is pre-trained on dataset-B. All the more surprising, pre-training on dataset-S, a domain of natural images, performs comparably or even slightly better than the pre-training on medical images of the lung (dataset-L) in the classification of visual lung tissue patterns. A summary of the results of experiment **(1)** is given in Table 1.

Table 2. Misclassification error of the CNN for different numbers of annotated images used for supervised fine-tuning after pre-training on dataset-L.

Sample size	Error
10	0.5048
20	0.4145
50	0.2600
200	0.1633
300	0.1190
600	0.1130
1000	0.1094
1500	0.1029
3000	0.0878
10000	0.0674
20000	0.0531

Figure 3(a) shows the misclassification errors as a function of the number of samples used for supervised fine-tuning and different pre-training datasets. Increasing the number of annotated data in the fine-tuning phase reduces the misclassification error. This holds true for all datasets used for pre-training. The choice of the dataset used for pre-training as well as the number of samples of the target site used for fine-tuning influence the classification accuracy.

(2) We investigate to what extend the sample size of labeled data of the target domain can be reduced when pre-training is performed. Unsupervised pre-training is always performed on the entire dataset-L. Results show that a model that is fine-tuned with only 10 randomly chosen image patches from the dataset-LL already performs better than chance. Fine-tuning the model with all samples of dataset-LL and dataset-L (20,000 patches) results in a minimum misclassification error of 5.3 % on the 5 class classification task. The number of lung image patches used for supervised fine-tuning and the corresponding misclassification errors are summarized in Table 2. Figure 3(b) shows the misclassification error of the CNN as a function of training epochs for different sample sizes of lung images used for supervised fine-tuning. Again, the performance measure corresponds to the results of the 5-class classification task.

5   Discussion

We propose methodology for improving lung tissue classification by unsupervised pre-training of CNN with samples drawn from different data and clinical sites. In contrast to previous work, we perform unsupervised pre-training of a CNN not (only) on medical images sampled from the distribution which is also used for fine-tuning the model. The overall classification performance can be improved via unsupervised pre-training by using large amounts of additional data, that is similar to the target domain. This is relevant in cases where only part of the training data is annotated, and data has to be collected across different sites to obtain sufficient training set size. It indicates that injecting data from different sites during pre-training can improve results, even if their characteristics are slightly different from the target site. The proposed classification outperforms previous approaches on the LTRC data. Zavaletta et al. [18] presented an approach for 5-class classification on the LTRC dataset using canonical signatures based on an adaptive histogram binning algorithm. Their classification of cubic image patches ($15 \times 15 \times 15$ voxels) of the lung into the same classes we use in our experiments yielded an overall misclassification error of 27.33 %. Pre-training results in good classifier performance, even if only very small numbers of annotated data are available for supervised fine-tuning. Surprisingly, we observe that a domain of natural images outperforms the pre-training on clinical CT scans of the lung in the classification of visual lung tissue patterns. This can be explained due to the fact that pre-training of a single convolution layer leads to learning of low-level features which are not as domain-specific as for example features learned by pre-training and stacking more than one convolution layer on top of each other. Furthermore, natural images show fine textures which are advantageous for the learning of low-level features. In contrast, pre-training on clinical CT datasets of the brain lead to a worse performance of the CNN on the lung tissue classification task. Contrary to natural images and CT images of the lung as well, CT images of the brain comprise large regions of homogeneous gray values and less texture information. Thus they are not as beneficial for pre-training of a low-level feature extractor. The proposed domain adaptation is relevant in cases where only few labeled training data but large amounts of unlabeled data from a similar domain is available. We conclude, that unsupervised pre-training using additional data from a slightly different domain can lead to better generalization from the training data set, and improves classification performance.

References

1. Fukushima, K.: Neocognitron: a self-organizing neural network model for a mechanism of pattern recognition unaffected by shift in position. Biol. Cybern. **36**(4), 193–202 (1980)
2. Ryu, J.H., Daniels, C.E., Hartman, T.E., Yi, E.S.: Diagnosis of interstitial lung diseases. In: Mayo Clinic Proceedings, vol. 82, pp. 976–986. Elsevier (2007)
3. Depeursinge, A., Sage, D., Hidki, A., Platon, A., Poletti, P.A., Unser, M., Muller, H.: Lung tissue classification using wavelet frames. In: 29th Annual International Conference of the IEEE Engineering in Medicine and Biology Society, pp. 6259–6262 (2007)
4. Lee, H., Grosse, R., Ranganath, R., Ng, A.Y.: Unsupervised learning of hierarchical representations with convolutional deep belief networks. Commun. ACM **54**(10), 95–103 (2011)
5. Ciresan, D., Meier, U., Schmidhuber, J.: Multi-column deep neural networks for image classification. In: Conference on Computer Vision and Pattern Recognition, pp. 3642–3649. IEEE (2012)

6. Krizhevsky, A., Sutskever, I., Hinton, G.E.: Imagenet classification with deep convolutional neural networks. In: Advances in Neural Information Processing Systems, vol. 1, p. 4 (2012)
7. Bengio, Y.: Deep learning of representations for unsupervised and transfer learning. J. Mach. Learn. Res. Proc. Track **27**, 17–36 (2012)
8. Cireşan, D.C., Giusti, A., Gambardella, L.M., Schmidhuber, J.: Mitosis detection in breast cancer histology images with deep neural networks. In: Mori, K., Sakuma, I., Sato, Y., Barillot, C., Navab, N. (eds.) MICCAI 2013, Part II. LNCS, vol. 8150, pp. 411–418. Springer, Heidelberg (2013)
9. Erhan, D., Bengio, Y., Courville, A., Manzagol, P.A., Vincent, P., Bengio, S.: Why does unsupervised pre-training help deep learning? J. Mach. Learn. Res. **11**, 625–660 (2010)
10. Lee, H., Grosse, R., Ranganath, R., Ng, A.Y.: Convolutional deep belief networks for scalable unsupervised learning of hierarchical representations. In: Proceedings of the 26th Annual International Conference on Machine Learning, pp. 609–616 (2009)
11. Brosch, T., Tam, R.: Manifold learning of brain MRIs by deep learning. In: Mori, K., Sakuma, I., Sato, Y., Barillot, C., Navab, N. (eds.) MICCAI 2013, Part II. LNCS, vol. 8150, pp. 633–640. Springer, Heidelberg (2013)
12. Coates, A., Ng, A.Y., Lee, H.: An analysis of single-layer networks in unsupervised feature learning. In: International Conference on Artificial Intelligence and Statistics, pp. 215–223 (2011)
13. Holmes III, D., Bartholmai, B., Karwoski, R., Zavaletta, V., Robb, R.: The lung tissue research consortium: an extensive open database containing histological, clinical, and radiological data to study chronic lung disease. In: The Insight Journal MICCAI Open Science Workshop (2006)
14. Hinton, G.E., Osindero, S., Teh, Y.W.: A fast learning algorithm for deep belief nets. Neural Comput. **18**(7), 1527–1554 (2006)
15. LeCun, Y., Bottou, L., Bengio, Y., Haffner, P.: Gradient-based learning applied to document recognition. Proc. IEEE **86**(11), 2278–2324 (1998)
16. Nair, V., Hinton, G.E.: Rectified linear units improve restricted boltzmann machines. In: Proceedings of the 27th International Conference on Machine Learning, pp. 807–814 (2010)
17. Bergstra, J., Breuleux, O., Bastien, F., Lamblin, P., Pascanu, R., Desjardins, G., Turian, J., Warde-Farley, D., Bengio, Y.: Theano: a CPU and GPU math expression compiler. In: Proceedings of the Python for Scientific Computing Conference (SciPy), vol. 4 (2010)
18. Zavaletta, V.A., Bartholmai, B.J., Robb, R.A.: High resolution multidetector CT-aided tissue analysis and quantification of lung fibrosis. Acad. Radiol. **14**(7), 772–787 (2007)

Multi-atlas and Beyond

Atlas-Guided Multi-channel Forest Learning for Human Brain Labeling

Guangkai Ma[1,2], Yaozong Gao[2], Guorong Wu[2], Ligang Wu[1],
and Dinggang Shen[2(✉)]

[1] Space Control and Inertial Technology Research Center,
Harbin Institute of Technology, Harbin, China
[2] Department of Radiology and BRIC,
University of North Carolina at Chapel Hill, Chapel Hill, NC, USA
dgshen@med.unc.edu

Abstract. Labeling MR brain images into anatomically meaningful regions is important in quantitative brain researches. Previous works can be roughly categorized into two classes: multi-atlas and learning based labeling methods. These methods all suffer from their own limitations. For multi-atlas based methods, the label fusion step is often handcrafted based on the predefined similarity metrics between voxels in the target and atlas images. For learning based methods, the spatial correspondence information encoded in the atlases is lost since they often use only the target image appearance for classification. In this paper, we propose a novel atlas-guided multi-channel forest learning, which could effectively address the aforementioned limitations. Instead of handcrafting the label fusion step, we learn a non-linear classification forest for automatically fusing both image appearance and label information of the atlas with the image appearance of the target image. Validated on LONI-LBPA40 dataset, our method outperforms several traditional labeling approaches.

1 Introduction

Automatic anatomical labeling of the brain MR images has become a hot topic in the field of medical image analysis. Quantitative brain image analysis often relies on the reliable labeling of brain images. Due to huge work burden of manual brain labeling, developing an automatic and reliable brain labeling method is imperative. However, due to the highly complexity of brain structures, the overlap of intensity distributions between different brain structures, blurred boundaries, as well as large anatomical variations across individual subjects, it is still a challenging task for the automatic labeling of brain MR images.

Among existing brain image labeling techniques, **multi-atlas based labeling methods** have achieved a great success recently. In those methods, the already labeled brain MR images, namely atlases, are used to guide the labeling of new target images [3]. Specifically, given a target image to be labeled, multiple atlas images can be registered onto the target image space, and then the estimated transformations can be used to warp the corresponding label maps of

© Springer International Publishing Switzerland 2014
B. Menze et al. (Eds.): MCV 2014, LNCS 8848, pp. 97–104, 2014.
DOI: 10.1007/978-3-319-13972-2_9

atlases, which will be further combined by a label fusion step for labeling the target image. The performance of multi-atlas based labeling methods depends on both the accuracy of registration and the effectiveness of the label fusion step. Since image registration is still a challenging problem in medical image area, recently more researchers focus on improving the performance of multi-atlas based labeling methods by proposing more effective label fusion techniques. For example, Coupé et al. [7] proposed a non-local patch-based label fusion technique by using patch-wise similarity as weight to propagate the neighboring labels from aligned atlases to the target image for overcoming the potential registration error. Instead of pair-wisely estimating the patch-based similarity for label fusion, Wu et al. [8] proposed to use sparse representation to jointly estimate all patch-based similarities between a to-be-labeled target voxel and its neighboring voxels in the atlases. In general, the traditional multi-atlas based labeling techniques suffer from **two limitations**: (1) the patch-wise similarity is often globally handcrafted based on the predefined features (e.g., intensity patch), which might be not effective for labeling all types of brain structures; (2) only linear prediction model is used for propagating the atlas labels to the target image, thus potentially limiting the labeling accuracy.

On the other hand, **learning-based labeling methods** have also attracted much attention recently. In the learning-based methods, a strong classifier (e.g., Adaboost, SVM, random forest) is typically trained for each label/ROI (region of interest) in the brain image based on local appearance features. During the testing stage, the learned classifiers are applied to voxel-wisely classify the target image, by determining the label of each voxel by the class with the largest classification response on that voxel. For example, Zikic et al. [2] proposed atlas forest, which encodes an atlas by learning a classification forest on it. The final labeling of a target image is achieved by averaging the labeling results from all selected atlas forests. Tu et al. [5] adopted the probabilistic boosting tree (PBT) with Haar features and texture features for labeling the MR brain images. To further boost the labeling performance, an auto-context model (ACM) was proposed to iteratively refine the labeling results. **The major concern** with the learning-based labeling methods is that the spatial correspondence information encoded in the registered atlases are not fully utilized. In contrast to the multi-atlas based labeling methods described above, the learning-based labeling method often determines a target voxel's label solely based on the local image appearance without getting the assistance from the aligned atlases, thus potentially limiting their labeling accuracy since similar local image appearances might appear in different brain locations but with different labels. Although Zikic et al. [2] utilizes the population mean atlas in learning atlas forests, due to the large inter-subject variations, many details of brain structures are lost in the construction of the mean atlas, thus hindering the accurate brain labeling. Moreover, the risk of overfitting is largely increased by learning one strong classifier from a single brain image. Specially, if the target brain image is anatomically different from any single atlas in the library, the classification forest trained on the single atlas will degrade the final labeling result.

In this paper, we propose a novel atlas-guided learning method for multiple-ROI (regions of interest) labeling. Instead of labeling each voxel in the target image based on only local image appearance, we also utilize both appearance and label information from the aligned atlas. Specifically, **during the training stage**, to label one ROI, we will learn one multi-channel classifier for each atlas, along with the (training) target image. The multi-channel classifier of one atlas determines the label of a target voxel by combining information from three different channels: **(1)** local image appearance of this voxel in the (training) target image, **(2)** local image appearance of corresponding voxel in the aligned atlas, and **(3)** local label information of corresponding voxel in the aligned atlas. Different from the previous multi-atlas based methods [7,8], which handcrafted a similarity metric between voxels in the target and atlas images for label propagation, our method uses a non-linear classification forest as multi-channel classifier to automatically fuse information from both target and atlas images for brain labeling. This could effectively overcome the aforementioned two limitations of the previous multi-atlas based methods (i.e., using only the handcrafted similarity and linear model). **In the testing stage**, all learned multi-channel classifiers can be independently applied to label the new target image. The final labeling result is obtained by averaging the individual labeling results from all multi-channel classifiers. Validated on the public LONI-LBPA40 dataset, our proposed atlas-guided random forest learning outperforms both traditional multi-atlas based methods and learning-based methods in human brain labeling.

2   Method

In this section, we will first present the notations used in our descriptions. Then, we will explain the learning procedure of our atlas-guided multi-channel forest. Finally, the application of the learned forests to single-ROI and multi-ROI labeling will be described.

2.1   Notations

An atlas libarary **A** consists of multiple atlases $\{A_i = (I_i, L_i) \mid i = 1, \ldots, N\}$, where I_i and L_i are the intensity image and the label image of the i-th atlas, and N is the total number of atlases in the library **A**. For each atlas label map, the labels for M brain ROIs are encoded as $\{1, \ldots, M\}$. In addition, $A_i^j = \{I_i^j, L_i^j\}$, $j \neq i$, $j = 1, \ldots, N$, denotes the intensity (I_i^j) and label (L_i^j) images of the i-th atlas after warping it onto the j-th atlas space.

2.2   Atlas-Guided Multi-channel Forests Learning

To increase the flexibility of our learning procedure, we will train one multi-channel random forest (i.e., multi-channel forest) for each ROI and each atlas. In this way, when a new atlas is added into the atlas library **A**, only one multi-channel forest needs to be trained with the new atlas while all previously trained

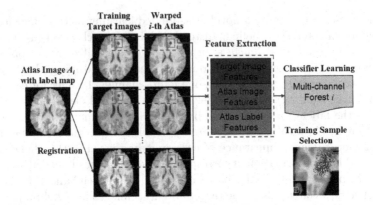

Fig. 1. The flowchart of our method for learning one multi-channel forest with the i-th atlas. An example for sample selection during the training stage is given in the right-bottom corner, where samples belonging to the ROI are highlighted by blue points and samples belonging to the non-ROI are highlighted by green points. Here, more samples are drawn around the ROI boundaries (Colour figure online).

forests could be reused. To label a single ROI, N multi-channel forests (corresponding to N atlas) will be learned, with each trained with one specific atlas. Section 2.3 will show how the multi-channel forests of different ROIs could be combined effectively together for multiple-ROI labeling. In this section, we focus on the learning part of our method.

To label one ROI, i.e., the k-th ROI, during the training stage, we will learn one multi-channel forest for each atlas. Specifically, to learn a multi-channel forest for the i-th atlas, all other atlases are treated as the training target images. Since our learning-based labeling method utilizes information from both the to-be-labeled target image and the aligned atlas, before multi-channel forest learning, we need to nonrigidly register the i-th atlas to each training target image, thus forming $N - 1$ training image pairs $\{A_j, A_i^j\}$, $j \neq i$, $j = 1, \ldots, N$. Afterwards, the positive and negative samples are taken inside and outside of the k-th ROI from every training image for multi-channel forest learning, which combines the apparance features from both target and atlas images along with the label features from the atlas image for infering a correct label for each voxel in the training target image. After training, N multi-channel forests (corresponding to N atlases) will be learned for each ROI. In total, $M \times N$ multi-channel forests will be obtained for all M ROIs to be labeled. The flowchart shown in Fig. 1 gives an illustration for learning one multi-channel forest.

Sampling Strategy: The positive and negative samples used in training multi-channel forests for the k-th ROI are the voxels randomly sampled inside and outside the k-th ROI, respectively. To effectively classify voxels near the ROI boundary and also to avoid data imbalance between positive and negative samples, we select only positive and negative samples near the boundary of target ROI, as shown in Fig. 1. Intuitively, pixels around the ROI boundary are more difficult to be correctly classified than other voxels. Therefore, more samples should be drawn around the ROI boundary during the sampling stage. In particular, voxels that lie in the areas within 2 voxels from the ROI boundary account for 80 % of total training samples in our implementation. In addition, the numbers of positive and negative samples are kept the same in our implementation.

Feature Extraction: To train the multi-channel forest for the i-th atlas, every training target image I_j, $j \neq i$, $j = 1, \ldots, N$ will be associated with the aligned i-th atlas (on the j-th atlas space) $A_i^j = \{I_i^j, L_i^j\}$, as mentioned above. The features of any sampled voxel that are input to our multi-channel forest come from both training target image and the aligned atlas image. More specifically, they consist of three different channels: **(1)** local image appearance features of this voxel extracted from the training target image (e.g., I_j), **(2)** local image appearance features of corresponding voxel extracted from the aligned atlas image (e.g., I_i^j), and **(3)** local label information of corresponding voxel extracted from the aligned atlas image (e.g. L_i^j).

The local image appearance features used in our implementation include: patch intensities within a $7 \times 7 \times 7$ neighborhood, the outputs from first-order difference filters, second-order difference filters, 3D Hyperplan filters, 3D Sobel filters, Laplacian filters and range difference filters [4], and the random 3D Haar features computed from a $11 \times 11 \times 11$ neighborhood. These appearance features could capture the rich texture information embedded in both training target image and atlas images, which could be utilized in the multi-channel forest learning for selecting the informative features for voxel-wise labeling. For the 3D Haar features, the number of Haar cubes, and the size and the position of each Haar cube are randomly selected.

Motivated by the traditional multi-atlas based labeling methods, the label map of aligned atlas can provide valuable information for estimating the correct labels in the target image. Thus, we also extracted features from the label map of the aligned atlas (e.g., L_i^j). Specifically, to extract the label features for one ROI, we first convert the multi-ROI label map into a binary image for each ROI, where only voxels belonging to this specific ROI are with label 1 (positive) while all other voxels are with label 0 (negative). To overcome the limitation of potential registration errors, we first smooth this binary image with a Gaussian kernel ($\sigma = 2$), and then uniformly and sparsely select 125 voxels from a neighborhood of size $11 \times 11 \times 11$. Their smoothed (label) values (ranging from 0 to 1) are served as local label features in our work.

By integrating the appearance and label information from three different channels into a supervised learning framework, the random forest learning could identify the most informative features as well as a non-linear mapping that can connect them with the target label. In this way, our method can more effectively exploit the information in both (training) target and atlas images than the traditional multi-atlas and learning based labeling methods.

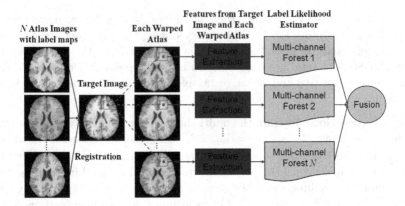

Fig. 2. A diagram for single-ROI labeling with our proposed atlas-guided multi-channel forest learning.

2.3 Single-ROI and Multi-ROI Labeling

Once multi-channel forests have been learned for each atlas and each ROI, they can be used for labeling a new target image. In this section, we will first explain how the learned forests could be used for single-ROI labeling, and then we will extend our method to multiple-ROI labeling.

Single-ROI Labeling: To label a single ROI in a new target image, all the altases are first non-rigidly registered onto the target image space, which is similar to the traditional multi-atlas based methods. Then, each aligned atlas can use its corresponding trained multi-channel forest for brain labeling. Specifically, we can apply the trained multi-channel forest to obtain a likelihood of each target image voxel belonging to this ROI by using the image and label features extracted from both the target and aligned atlas images. Finally, the predicted label maps from all aligned atlases are averaged to obtain the final labeling result. To increase the efficiency of the voxel-wise labeling, we can use the label map from the majority voting of all aligned atlas label maps as an initial label map, based on which our method can be applied only to label voxels near that initial labeling map. Figure 2 gives an illustration of our single-ROI labeling method.

Multi-ROI Labeling: The extension from single-ROI labeling to multi-ROI labeling is quite straightforward. With the single-ROI labeling technique described above, we can obtain a labeling map for each ROI, where the value of each image voxel indicates the likelihood of this voxel belonging to a specific ROI. The fusion of multiple single-ROI labeling maps into one multi-ROI labeling map is simply to assign each image voxel with the label that has the maximum value at this voxel location across all different single-ROI label maps.

3   Experimental Results

All experiments are conducted on the LONI-LPBA40 dataset [1]. The dataset consists of 40 T1-weighted MRI brain images from 40 healthy volunteers, each with 54 manually labeled ROIs (excluding cerebrum and brainstem). Most of these ROIs are within the cortex. The intensity normalization of each brain image is performed by using histogram matching before labeling. We use two-fold cross-validation to evaluate the performance of our method by using 20 images for training and 20 images for testing in each round. The average DSC ratio of all 54 ROIs achieved by our method is 81.35 % ± 4.35 %.

Parameters: In the training stage, we train 10 trees for each multi-channel forest. The maximum tree depth is set to 25, and the minimum number of samples in the tree leaf node is set as 8. For each tree node training, about 1000 random Haar features are adopted.

Comparison with multi-atlas based methods: Figure 3 compares our method with two state-of-the-art multi-atlas based labeling methods: the non-local patch-based label propagation (Nonlocal PBL) [7] and sparse patch-based label propagation (Sparse PBL) [9]. We can clearly see that our method significantly outperforms these two methods in all ROIs. The average Dice ratios achieved by "Nonlocal PBL" and "Sparse PBL" for all ROIs are 75.31 %±5.06 % and 77.65 %±4.72 %, respectively, which are lower than 81.35 %±4.35 % achieved by our method. This indicates the importance of learning a non-linear classifier for fusing the information from both target and atlas images, instead of hand-crafting it.

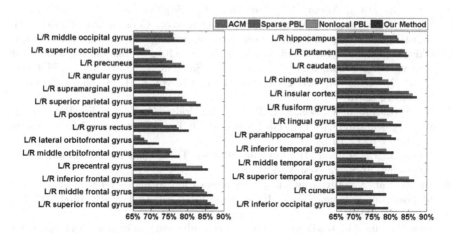

Fig. 3. The average Dice ratios of 54 ROIs obtained by four different methods.

Comparison with learning based methods: We also compared our method with two learning-based methods in the same LONI dataset. The average Dice ratios achieved by atlas forest [2] and ACM [5,6] for all ROIs are 77.46 % and 79.21 %, respectively. It is worth noting that the performance of atlas forest [2] is obtained by using leave-one-out cross-validation, which generally achieves better performance than the two-fold cross validation (as used in our method).

Our method outperforms these two learning-based methods, which indicates the effectiveness of incorporating the atlas guidance into the learning-based labeling procedure in our method. We respectively perform the paired t-test on our proposed method with other three labeling methods (ACM, Nonlocal PBL and Sparse PBL) on all 54 ROIs. Our method obtains statistically significant ($p < 0.05$) improvement on 53 ROIs over ACM, 54 ROIs over non-local PBL, and 52 ROIs over sparse PBL, respectively.

4   Conclusion

In this paper, we propose a novel atlas-guided multi-channel forest learning to effectively combine the advantages of both multi-atlas based and learning-based labeling methods together. Instead of labeling a target voxel based on its own local image appearance, we also utilize both image appearance and label information from the aligned atlas. By learning a non-linear multi-channel forest for automatically fusing these information, our method shows more accurate labeling results than both traditional multi-atlas based and learning-based labeling methods on the public LONI-LBPA40 dataset.

References

1. Shattuck, D.W., Mirza, M., Adisetiyo, V., Hojatkashani, C., Salamon, G., Narr, K.L., Poldrack, R.A., Bilder, R.M., Toga, A.W.: Construction of a 3D probabilistic atlas of human cortical structures. Neuroimage **39**(3), 1064–1080 (2007)
2. Zikic, D., Glocker, B., Criminisi, A.: Atlas encoding by randomized forests for efficient label propagation. In: Mori, K., Sakuma, I., Sato, Y., Barillot, C., Navab, N. (eds.) MICCAI 2013, Part III. LNCS, vol. 8151, pp. 66–73. Springer, Heidelberg (2013)
3. Wang, H., Sub, J.W., Das, S.R., Pluta, J.B., Craige, C., Yushkevich, P.A.: Multi-atlas segmentation with joint label fusion. IEEE Trans. Pattern Anal. Mach. Intell. **35**(3), 611–623 (2013)
4. Toriwaki, J., Yoshida, H.: Fundamentals of Three-Dimensional Digital Image Processing. Springer, New York (2009)
5. Tu, Z., Bai, X.: Auto-context and its application to high-level vision tasks and 3d brain image segmentation. IEEE Trans. Pattern Anal. Mach. Intell. **32**(10), 1744–1757 (2010)
6. Seyedhosseini, M., Tasdizen, T.: Multi-class multi-scale series contextual model for image segmentation. IEEE Trans. Image Process. **22**, 4486–4496 (2013)
7. Coupé, P., Manjón, J.V., Fonov, V., Pruessner, J., Robles, M., Collins, D.L.: Patch-based segmentation using expert priors: application to hippocampus and ventricle segmentation. NeuroImage **54**(2), 940–954 (2011)
8. Wu, G., Wang, Q., Zhang, D., Shen, D.: Robust patch-based multi-atlas labeling by joint sparsity regularization. In: MICCAI Workshop on Sparsity Techniques in Medical Imaging (STMI) (2012)
9. Tong, T., Wolz, R., Coupé, P., Hajnal, J.V., Rueckert, D.: Segmentation of MR images via discriminative dictionary learning and sparse coding: application to hippocampus labeling. NeuroImage **76**, 11–23 (2013)

Fast Multiatlas Selection Using Composition of Transformations for Radiation Therapy Planning

David Rivest-Hénault[1]([✉]), Soumya Ghose[1], Josien P.W. Pluim[2],
Peter B. Greer[3,4], Jurgen Fripp[1], and Jason A. Dowling[1,4]

[1] CSIRO The Australian e-Health Research Centre, Herston, QLD, Australia
`david.rivest-henault@csiro.au`
[2] Image Sciences Institute, University Medical Center Utrecht,
Utrecht, The Netherlands
[3] Calvary Mater Newcastle Hospital, Newcastle, NSW, Australia
[4] University of Newcastle, Newcastle, NSW, Australia

Abstract. In radiation therapy, multiatlas segmentation is recognized as being accurate, but is generally not considered scalable since the highest accuracy is achieved only when using a large atlas database. The fundamental problem is to use such a large database, to accurately represent the population variability, while conserving a relatively small computational cost. A method based on the composition of transformations is proposed to address this issue. The main novelties and key contributions of this paper are the definition of a transitivity error function and the presentation of an image clustering scheme that is based solely on the computed registration transformations. Leave-one-out experiments conducted on a database of $N = 50$ MR prostate scans demonstrate that a reduction of $(N - 1) = 49$x in the number of pre-alignment registrations, and of 3.2x in term of total registration effort, is possible without significant impact on segmentation quality.

1 Introduction

Multiatlas segmentation techniques are currently considered state of the art for the automatic delineation of many important tissues [12,16]. Atlas-based methods propagate the information associated with the atlases to a target image following registration. In a multiatlas scheme, the information of many atlases is aggregated together using various selection and fusion techniques. It has been demonstrated [2,11] that, by fusing the information contained in the 10–20 best matching atlases, a multiatlas method is able to generate results that are of higher quality than when just the best reference atlas is used, an average atlas is used, or when all the atlases are used indiscriminately. Multiatlas methods are especially useful in image guided radiation therapy (IGRT) and other fields where it is difficult to create a reference atlas capable of representing the whole population [5,8], and [12]. The best performing automatic multiatlas segmentation techniques require nonrigid registration of all atlas images to the target image,

B. Menze et al. (Eds.): MCV 2014, LNCS 8848, pp. 105–115, 2014.
DOI: 10.1007/978-3-319-13972-2_10

and therefore these methods incur a high computational cost which increases linearly with the number of atlases in the database. This is one of the main drawbacks of multiatlas methods.

Various strategies have been proposed to attempt to decrease the computational cost associated with multiatlas methods. In certain cases, simple methods such as the use of a simpler image similarity metric [15], or the stratification of the database according to demographic information [2], can result in substantial improvements. A different technique consists in using different registration algorithms: a fast method for the selection of the best matching atlas, and a slower, more accurate, one for propagation of the atlas segmentation information [14–16].

Another popular strategy is to pre-register all atlases from the database to a common reference point that can be either an average image or a central image [2,6,7]. In this case, a target image only needs to be registered to the reference point before continuing with the atlas selection step. For example, a high quality BrainWeb image was used in [2] to define the reference space. For certain types of application, however, the population might present too much variability to be correctly represented by a single reference point [3], which potentially limits the performance of this approach. More specifically, to the best of our knowledge, the use of a single reference point for atlas selection has never been demonstrated in the context of pelvis radiation therapy planning. Moreover, due to the large anatomical variability of the pelvis area across the population, defining a reference space does not appear trivial.

Other authors have proposed to use manifold learning techniques allowing selection of atlas images which are most similar to the target image in a lower dimensional space [10,20], which is computationally less expensive. For the estimation of the manifold, such methods rely on a certain image similarity metric that is as much an indicator of the performance of the registration algorithm as a true indicator of image similarity. For example, in [10] a high similarity might be an indication that the registration algorithm stalled in a poor quality local minimum, which might limit the performance of one certain dataset.

Langerak et al. [13] proposed to cluster the images based on how well the associated labels overlap. One limitation of this approach is that even if transitivity is tacitly assumed, it is not guaranteed nor sought by the process. For example, if the labels of A overlap well with those of K, and if a target image T register well with K, there is still no guarantee that A is correctly aligned with B and the relation is always indirect.

The method presented in this paper also uses a clustering algorithm, but in contrast to the above, it seeks to identify the best proxy images $P_i \in \mathcal{P}$ such that $\mathbf{T}_{A \to B} \approx \mathbf{T}_{A \to P} \circ \mathbf{T}_{P \to B}$, where $\mathbf{T}_{X \to Y}$ is an invertible transformation obtained using any registration method, and $\circ$ is the composition operator. While most existing fast multiatlas methods tend to group the atlas images based on a similarity criterion, the presented method only uses the geometric transformation estimated by a registration algorithm to identify the proxies introducing the minimal amount of geometrical distortion in the process. This is in direct opposition to existing methods where large differences in pose or deformation are penalized. Also, the proposed method is *not* dependant on the requirement to align all the atlases in a common reference point beforehand, which is important in the context of radiation therapy.

This paper presents a new fast multiatlas methodology that uses compositions of transformations to reduce the number of registrations needed at the atlas selection step. Background information about multiatlas segmentation and transitive registration are presented in Sects. 2 and 3. Section 4 describes the proposed fast multiatlas framework. The results of 49 leave-one-out experiments conducted on a 50 patients dataset are reported in Sect. 5. Finally, Sect. 6 holds a discussion and the conclusion.

2   Multiatlas Segmentation

Let I_i and L_i be respectively the image and labelling composing the atlas A_i from the atlas database $\mathcal{A}$. In atlas based segmentation (Fig. 1 *top*), an atlas image I_i is first registered with a target image I_T, which allows to estimate a transformation $\mathbf{T}_{I_i \to T}$. Then, the labelling L_i is propagated to the space of I_T using the same transform to obtain an estimate $\hat{L}_T$ of the labelling of I_T. Since it is unlikely that this labelling is a good estimate of the true labelling L_T^*, it as been suggested to combine the estimations found with many atlases in what is know as multiatlas segmentation [18]. Subsequently, it has been empirically found that the results were often better if only the best matching atlases were retained for the final label fusion step [2,11] (Fig. 1 *bottom*).

The performance of a multiatlas segmentation method generally improves with the size of $\mathcal{A}$ since the variability of the population is better represented. However, a large $\mathcal{A}$ also results in a large computational cost, which is one of the main drawback of multiatlas methods, as discussed in the introduction. Since the main computational bottleneck is the multiple image registrations required during the process, one would like to compute as few registrations as possible. Unfortunately, image registration is generally not transitive ($\mathbf{T}_{A \to B} \neq \mathbf{T}_{A \to P} \circ \mathbf{T}_{P \to B}$), which limits the possibility to propage a registration result obtained with one image to another one. The objective of the presented method is to minimize this issue.

3   Transitive Registration Using an Image Proxy

Any diffeomorphic registration algorithm can be incorporated in a scheme that assures the symmetry and the transitivity of the transformations. This is done by redefining all registration transforms so that they use an image proxy such as $\bar{\mathbf{T}}_{A \to B} \equiv \mathbf{T}_{A \to P} \circ \mathbf{T}_{B \to P}^{-1}$, see Fig. 2 *left* (*Please note the difference between $\bar{\mathbf{T}}_i$ and $\mathbf{T}_i$*). It is trivial to show that for a given proxy, all $\bar{\mathbf{T}}_i$ are indeed symmetric and transitive, regardless of the registration method used [19]. This scheme however does not provide any guarantee about the quality of the registration or about how close $\bar{\mathbf{T}}_i$ would be from $\mathbf{T}_i$, the transformation computed directly by the selected registration method. In the most extreme case, using just a blank

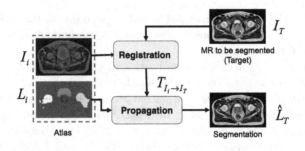

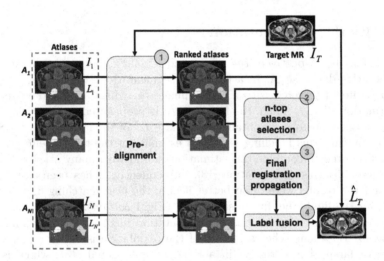

Fig. 1. Atlas (*top*) and multiatlas (*bottom*) segmentation. Adapted from [1].

proxy image, the registration method is likely to always return identity, leading to $\bar{\mathbf{T}}_i$ that are both symmetric and transitive, but very different from $\mathbf{T}_i$. Hence, a key factor is the selection of appropriate proxy images.

4   Atlas Selection Using Composition of Transformations

4.1   Image Affinity and Clustering

The proposed method for the selection of the best image proxy is based on the hypothesis that if P is a suitable proxy for the estimation of the transitive transformations $\bar{\mathbf{T}}_{A \to B}, \bar{\mathbf{T}}_{A \to C} \ldots \bar{\mathbf{T}}_{A \to N}$, then it is probable that P is also suitable for the transformation $\bar{\mathbf{T}}_{A \to T}$, the transformation from A to an unseen image T. The suitability of an image P to act as a proxy in the transformation $\bar{\mathbf{T}}_{A \to B}$ can be evaluated as follows:

$$E_{A \to B}^{P} = \left| (\mathbf{T}_{A \to P} \circ \mathbf{T}_{B \to P}^{-1}) - \mathbf{T}_{A \to B} \right|, \tag{1}$$

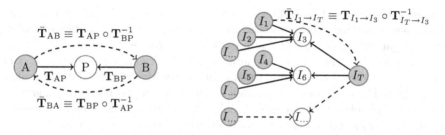

Fig. 2. (*Left*) Symmetric and transitive transformation scheme. (*Right*) Approximately transitive transformation scheme for fast atlas selection.

where $|.|$ is some geometric norm. That is: the error involved in using P to define the transform from A to B is the norm of the difference $\bar{\mathbf{T}}_{A \to B} - \mathbf{T}_{A \to B}$. If that norm is close to zero, then $\bar{\mathbf{T}}_{A \to B}$ is a good estimate of $\mathbf{T}_{A \to B}$. In this work, we use rigid transformations at the atlas selection step. These can readily be mapped to a linear (s, t) representation, where s and t are rotation and translation vectors, respectively, using Rodrigue's rotation formula. Thus, a suitable error function is [4]:

$$E^P_{A \to B} = |s_{\bar{\mathbf{T}}} - s_{\mathbf{T}}|_{L2} + \lambda |t_{\bar{\mathbf{T}}} - t_{\mathbf{T}}|_{L2}, \tag{2}$$

where λ is set to 0.05 following the recommendation in [4]. We now expand this definition to the case where the suitability of having the proxy P in the transformations from A to *any other images in the database*. First the vector $\boldsymbol{E}_{\text{sorted}}(A, P) = [E^P_{A \to B}, \ldots, E^P_{A \to X}]$, $X \in \mathcal{A}, X \notin \{A, P\}$ is computed, and sorted in increasing order. Then, the suitability function is define as follows:

$$S(A, P) = - \sum_{i=1}^{K} \boldsymbol{E}_{\text{sorted}}(A, P)[i]. \tag{3}$$

The suitability thus decreases with the accumulation of geometric error. We propose to sum only the first K elements of the vector since it is assume that more than one proxy will be identified for the database. Thus, it is not necessary to find the best proxy for all the atlases simultaneously, but only for a reasonable subset. In this paper, $K = N/2$ was used. For an atlas of size N, $N(N-1)$ suitability functions need to be evaluated. In turn, those depends on the result of $N(N-1)$ pairwise registration, but these can be computed off line, during the creation of the atlas, and not before the segmentation of a new image.

Once all suitability functions have been evaluated, the problem is to identify the atlas images that best serve as proxies, globally for all other atlas images in the database. This problem can be represented as a graph where the N atlas images are nodes, and where the suitability functions $S(X, Y)$ define the edges. Note that in general $S(X, Y) \neq S(Y, X)$, which means that the edges are directed, and that two opposite edges link each pair of nodes. Affinity propagation has been proposed [9] to tackle this kind of problem using an efficient message passing algorithm (affinity propagation is also used in [13], but the clustering metric and hypothesis and the atlas selection method are different). Affinity propagation was designed to automatically determine the number of clusters given a preference value that can be adjusted. A target number of clusters, C, can therefore be attained by running the algorithm iteratively, with different preference values. The result of the algorithm is a list of exemplar nodes together with the nodes that relate to them. In our multiatlas technique, the exemplar become the proxy images that allows to rapidly propagate the transformation from any atlas in the database to an unseen target image, as it is depicted in Fig. 2 *right*.

4.2   Summary of the Algorithm

The proposed fast multiatlas segmentation method comprises four main steps, as shown on Fig. 1 *right*. *Step1 – pre-alignment*: the target image T is registered to all proxy images using a robust rigid registration algorithm [17], the transformation is then propagated to all other atlases using the approximately transitive scheme described above. *Step 2 – atlases selection*: the best matching atlases are selected using a normalized mutual information (NMI) metric. Either a relative confidence parameter α [12] or a set number γ controls the number of atlases that are selected. We denote by *PROPOSED*$^{\alpha}$ the presented method when using former alternative, and by *PROPOSED*$^{\gamma}$ when using the later. *Step 3 – final registration and propagation*: The selected atlases are nonrigidly registered to the target image [12], and the atlas label propagated to the target image space. *Step 4 – Label fusion*: The propagated labels are fused together using the majority voting method [18].

5   Experiments

A dataset consisting of $N = 50$ clinical MR scans with manual segmentations of the prostate from University Medical Center Utrecht [12] was used to assess the performance of the proposed method. The results were validated against a combined contour obtained by fusing the manual contouring of three observers. All experiments reported in this section were performed in a leave one out manner.

5.1   Suitability of the Selected Proxies

Ideally, the proxies should introduce minimal distortion in the system. To test that hypothesis, we computed the segmentation performance of majority voting after: (1) the transitive transform scheme, and (2) the regular pairwise rigid transform. In those experiments, nonrigid registration and atlas selection were omitted to highlight the performance of the pre-alignment step. The Dice similarity coefficient (DSC) [12] was used to evaluate segmentation accuracy. Results shown in Fig. 3-(*Left*) indicate that the approximately transitive scheme effectively results in only very small reduction in performance (min/max/mean absolute difference = 0.001/0.059/0.017 DSC).

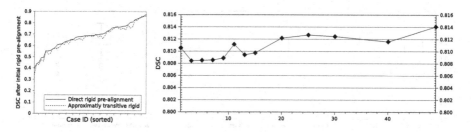

Fig. 3. (*Left*) Comparison of the direct and approximately transitive pre-alignment. (*Right*) Performance of the proposed method with $\gamma = 15$ in function of the number of proxies C

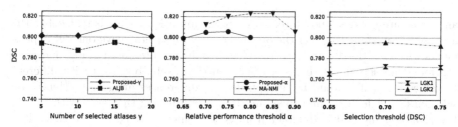

Fig. 4. Behaviour of the multiatlas segmentation algorithms in function of their respective parameter: (*left*) *PROPOSED*$^\gamma$ and *ALJB*, (*middle*) *PROPOSED*$^\alpha$ and *MA-NMI*, (*right*) *LGK1* and *LGK2*. See Sect. 5.2 for the definition of the acronyms.

5.2   Evaluation of the Segmentation Performance

The proposed fast methods (*PROPOSED*$^\alpha$ and *PROPOSED*$^\gamma$, defined in Sect. 4.2) were evaluated on the dataset mentioned above, and compared with other related multiatlas methods: (1) *LGK1* a reimplementation of the clustering method in [13] (using VOTE instead of SIMPLE at the atlas selection step), (2) *LGK2* same as *LGK1*, but without the clustering step, (3) *MA-NMI* the multiatlas method in [5], (4) *ALJB* a reimplementation of the method in [2] (this method depends on a reference image, and since a widely recognized reference pelvis image is not available, a random atlas was selected to serve as the reference in each leave-one-out experiment), (5) *VOTE* label fusion of the 49 atlases with VOTE, and (6) *STAPLE* label fusion of the 49 atlases with STAPLE. For *VOTE* and *STAPLE*, the atlas images were first registered to the target image using a rigid algorithm followed by the nonrigid diffeomorphic demons (ITK) method. Of the competing methods, only method *LGK1*, *ALJB*, and the proposed are *fast methods* requiring less than N-1 registration operations at the atlas selection step.

Number of Image Proxies. With the proposed method, the target number of clusters C can be adjusted to select the optimal number of proxies that will be used. A small C is associated with low computational burden since C registrations are needed at the atlas selection step. Conversely, at the limit if $C = (N - 1)$,

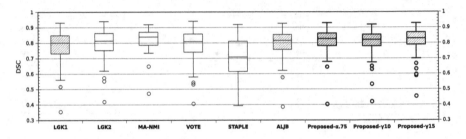

Fig. 5. Comparison of the segmentation results for the 7 tested methods. See Sect. 5.2 for the definition of the acronyms.

all atlases are proxies, and no reduction in computational time is realized at the atlas selection step. To select the optimal C, we ran several leave-one-out experiments with $C \in [1-49]$ and $\gamma = 15$. Those results are presented in Fig. 3($Right$). We found no significant difference between the results obtained with different C values (even if a trend is perceptible, the differences are small). Hence, we selected $C = 1$ for maximal speed-up. It is worth noting that even with $C = 1$, the proposed method is different from $ALJB$ since: (1) the presented method offer a criterion to select the reference proxie(s), and (2) the atlas selection step is performed in the target space, instead of the reference space, which might be more accurate. Furthermore, it is possible that the parameter C would be more influential with a larger or more complex dataset.

Parameters. All algorithms except $VOTE$ and $STAPLE$ have an adjustable parameter influencing the atlas selection step. This parameter can correspond to a DSC threshold, in the cases of $LGK1$ and $LGK2$, to a metric ratio $\alpha \in [0,1]$ [12], in the cases of MA-NMI and $PROPOSED^\alpha$, or to the number of best atlases, in the cases of $ALJB$ and $PROPOSED^\gamma$. The behaviours of the algorithms while varying their respective atlas selection parameter are illustration in Fig. 4. In what concerns the presented method, we found that fixing the number of selected atlas γ, instead of using the relative threshold α, allowed to achieve slightly superior results with that dataset.

Results. The final results, considering the best performances of each algorithms, are presented in Fig. 5. The fast method $PROPOSED^{C=1,\gamma=15}$ performs slightly worst, but not significantly so, than the best performing method MA-NMI (mean DSC smaller by 0.012 DSC, $p > .01$), but better that $ALJB$, $LGK1$, $VOTE$, and $STAPLE$ ($p < \{.01, .001, .001, .001\}$), and equivalent to $LGK2$ ($p > .01$), which is not a fast method. It can be noted that $PROPOSED^{C=49,\gamma=15}$ achieve lower score than MA-NMI, even if direct registrations of all the atlases with the target are performed. This is probably caused by the fact that atlas selection is performed after nonrigid registration in MA-NMI, where as only rigid registration is considered at this stage with the proposed method. However, because many nonrigid registration are avoided, $PROPOSED^{C=49,\gamma=15}$ is still 1.5x faster than MA-NMI. This is consistent with the finding in [2].

It is also worth nothing that the $PROPOSED^{C=1,\alpha=.75}$ and $PROPOSED$-$^{C=1,\gamma=10}$ methods allows to achieve results that are almost as good as that of $PROPOSED^{C=1,\gamma=15}$ (see Fig. 5), but with significantly higher speed-ups, 4.5x and 4.7x, respectively, instead of 3.2x (see Table 1).

5.3 Computational Effort

When setting the number of clusters to 1, the proposed method leads to a reduction of $(N-1) = 49$x in the number of pre-alignment registrations required before the atlas selection step by design. Nonetheless, the ~10–15 selected atlases need to be registered directly, rigidly and nonrigidly, with the target. The overall numbers of registration operations required with each method are presented in Table 1, and show a reduction of 4.5x of the registration effort. The overall computational effort, in term of real time, is dominated by registration, and thus depends mostly on the performance of selected rigid and nonrigid registration algorithms. In the presented experiments, we selected a relatively slow but accurate block matching rigid algorithm [17], and a relatively fast ITK diffeomorphic demons nonrigid implementation. On average, they take 130 s and 84 s, respectively, to register a pair of images.

Table 1. Computational effort required to segment one image. Number of rigid, nonrigid and total registrations operation required (mean±std), and relative effort.

Method	Number of			Relative	
	Rigid reg.	Nonrigid reg.	Total reg.	Effort	Reduction
LGK1	28 ± 4	28 ± 4	56 ± 8	0.57	1.8x
LGK2	49 ± 0	49 ± 0	98 ± 0	1.00	1.0x
MA-NMI	49 ± 0	49 ± 0	98 ± 0	1.00	1.0x
VOTE	49 ± 0	49 ± 0	98 ± 0	1.00	1.0x
STAPLE	49 ± 0	49 ± 0	98 ± 0	1.00	1.0x
ALJB	16 ± 0	15 ± 0	31 ± 0	0.32	3.2x
Proposed$^{C=1,\alpha=.75}$	11.2 ± 5.9	10.5 ± 6	21.7 ± 8.5	0.22	4.5x
Proposed$^{C=1,\gamma=10}$	10.7 ± 0.5	10 ± 0	20.7 ± 0.5	0.21	4.7x
Proposed$^{C=1,\gamma=15}$	15.7 ± 0.5	15 ± 0	30.7 ± 0.5	0.31	3.2x
Proposed$^{C=49,\gamma=15}$	49 ± 0	15 ± 0	64 ± 0	0.65	1.5x

6 Discussion and Conclusion

The main contribution of the paper is in the definition of a fast atlas selection method. It uses an approximately transitive transformation scheme via image proxies. Those proxies are identified by minimizing an error function accounting for geometric distortion associated with the transitive transformation definition.

Unlike previous fast methods, no image similarity metric is involved in the selection of clusters, which simplifies the methodology. Also, no hard decision is made at the atlas construction stage since the approximately transitive transforms allows the mapping of all available atlas images to the target image space. The method has been demonstrated on a well known database comprising 50 clinical prostate scans, and it was found that a reduction of $(N-1) = 49$x in the number of pre-alignment registrations, and of 3.2x in term of total registration effort, is possible without significant impact on segmentation quality. It was also demonstrated that further speed-up (up to 4.7x in this study) is possible if a small reduction in segmentation quality is acceptable. This is important in situations where computational time limits exist, such as automatic adaptive radiation therapy planning. The method proposed in this paper enables the processing of a larger atlas collection, with a corresponding increase in robustness to anatomical variability. This provides an advantage over a full multiatlas segmentation method run on a reduced database in the same amount of time. As a final note, we would like to stress that the computational time of the proposed method is *not* directly proportional on the size of the database, and in the presented situation is approximately constant. Hence, the proposed method is extensible, efficient and highly scalable.

Acknowledgments. This research was supported by the Cancer Council NSW (RG 11-05), the Prostate Cancer Foundation of Australia (YI2011), Movember and Cure Cancer Australia.

References

1. Acosta, O., Dowling, J., Drean, G., Simon, A., Crevoisier, R.D., Haigron, P.: Multi-atlas-based segmentation of pelvic structures from CT scans for planning in prostate cancer radiotherapy. In: El-Baz, A.S., Saba, L., Suri, J. (eds.) Abdomen and Thoracic Imaging, pp. 623–656. Springer, New york (2014)
2. Aljabar, P., Heckemann, R.A., Hammers, A., Hajnal, J.V., Rueckert, D.: Multi-atlas based segmentation of brain images: atlas selection and its effect on accuracy. NeuroImage **46**(3), 726–738 (2009)
3. Blezek, D.J., Miller, J.V.: Atlas stratification. Med. Image Anal. **11**(5), 443–457 (2007)
4. Boisvert, J., Cheriet, F., Pennec, X., Labelle, H., Ayache, N.: Geometric variability of the scoliotic spine using statistics on articulated shape models. IEEE Trans. Med. Imaging **27**(4), 557–568 (2008)
5. Chandra, S.S., Dowling, J.A., Shen, K.K., Raniga, P., Pluim, J.P.W., Greer, P.B., Salvado, O., Fripp, J.: Patient specific prostate segmentation in 3-D magnetic resonance images. IEEE Trans. Med. Imaging **31**(10), 1955–1964 (2012)
6. Commowick, O., Warfield, S.K., Malandain, G.: Using frankenstein's creature paradigm to build a patient specific atlas. In: Yang, G.-Z., Hawkes, D., Rueckert, D., Noble, A., Taylor, C. (eds.) MICCAI 2009, Part II. LNCS, vol. 5762, pp. 993–1000. Springer, Heidelberg (2009)
7. Depa, M., Holmvang, G., Schmidt, E.J., Golland, P., Sabuncu, M.R.: Towards efficient label fusion by pre-alignment of training data. In: Proceedings of the 2011 MICCAI Workshop on Multi-Atlas Labeling and Statistical Fusion, pp. 38–46 (2011)

8. Dowling, J., Lambert, J., Parker, J., Salvado, O., Fripp, J., Capp, A., Wratten, C., Denham, J.W., Greer, P.B.: An atlas-based electron density mapping method for magnetic resonance imaging MRI-alone Treatment Planning and Adaptive MRI-based prostate radiation therapy. Int. J. Radiat. Oncol. Biol. Phys. **83**(1), e5–e11 (2012)

9. Frey, B.J., Dueck, D.: Clustering by passing messages between data points. Science **315**(5814), 972–976 (2007)

10. Hoang Duc, A.K., Modat, M., Leung, K.K., Cardoso, M.J., Barnes, J., Kadir, T., Ourselin, S.: Using manifold learning for atlas selection in multi-atlas segmentation. PloS One **8**(8), e70059 (2013)

11. Isgum, I., Staring, M., Rutten, A., Prokop, M., Viergever, M.A., van Ginneken, B.: Multi-atlas-based segmentation with local decision fusion-application to cardiac and aortic segmentation in CT scans. IEEE TMI **28**(7), 1000–1010 (2009)

12. Klein, S., van der Heide, U.A., Lips, I.M., van Vulpen, M., Staring, M., Pluim, J.P.W.: Automatic segmentation of the prostate in 3D MR images by atlas matching using localized mutual information. Med. Phys. **35**(4), 1407 (2008)

13. Langerak, T.R., Berendsen, F.F., van der Heide, U.A., Kotte, A.N.T.J., Pluim, J.P.W.: Multiatlas-based segmentation with preregistration atlas selection. Med. Phys. **40**(9), 091701 (2013)

14. Leung, K.K., Barnes, J., Ridgway, G.R., Bartlett, J.W., Clarkson, M.J., Macdonald, K., Schuff, N., Fox, N.C., Ourselin, S.: Automated cross-sectional and longitudinal hippocampal volume measurement in mild cognitive impairment and Alzheimer's disease. NeuroImage **51**(4), 1345–1359 (2010)

15. Lötjönen, J.M., Wolz, R., Koikkalainen, J.R., Thurfjell, L., Waldemar, G., Soininen, H., Rueckert, D.: Fast and robust multi-atlas segmentation of brain magnetic resonance images. NeuroImage **49**(3), 2352–2365 (2010)

16. van Rikxoort, E.M., Isgum, I., Arzhaeva, Y., Staring, M., Klein, S., Viergever, M.A., Pluim, J.P.W., van Ginneken, B.: Adaptive local multi-atlas segmentation: application to the heart and the caudate nucleus. Med. Image Anal. **14**(1), 39–49 (2010)

17. Rivest-Hénault, D., Dowson, N., Greer, P., Dowling, J.: Inverse-consistent rigid registration of CT and MR for MR-based planning and adaptive prostate radiation therapy. J. Phys: Conf. Ser. **489**, 012039 (2014)

18. Rohlfing, T., Brandt, R., Menzel, R., Maurer, C.R.: Evaluation of atlas selection strategies for atlas-based image segmentation with application to confocal microscopy images of bee brains. NeuroImage **21**(4), 1428–1442 (2004)

19. Skrinjar, O., Bistoquet, A., Tagare, H.: Symmetric and transitive registration of image sequences. Int. J. Biomed. Imaging **2008**, 686875 (2008)

20. Wolz, R., Aljabar, P., Hajnal, J.V., Hammers, A., Rueckert, D.: LEAP: learning embeddings for atlas propagation. NeuroImage **49**(2), 1316–1325 (2010)

Classifier-Based Multi-atlas Label Propagation with Test-Specific Atlas Weighting for Correspondence-Free Scenarios

Darko Zikic[1]([✉]), Ben Glocker[2], and Antonio Criminisi[1]

[1] Microsoft Research, Cambridge, UK
darko@microsoft.com
[2] Biomedical Image Analysis Group,
Imperial College London, London, UK

Abstract. We propose a segmentation method which transfers the advantages of multi-atlas label propagation (MALP) to correspondence-free scenarios. MALP is a branch of segmentation approaches with attractive properties, which is currently applicable only in correspondence-based regimes such as brain labeling, which assume correspondence between atlases and test image. This precludes its use for the large class of tasks without this property, such as tumor segmentation. In this work, we propose a method which circumvents the correspondence assumption by using a classifier-based atlas representation in the spirit of the recently proposed Atlas Forests (AF). To counteract the negative effects of the over-training property of AF for applications with highly heterogeneous examples, we employ test-specific atlas weighting by the STAPLE approach. The main idea is that over-training ceases to be a problem if the prediction is based only on training atlases which are "similar" to the test image. Here, the "similarity" is based on the estimated ability of an atlas-based classifier to perform a correct labeling. We show a successful use of the proposed method for segmentation of brain tumors on data from the BraTS 2013 Challenge, which presents a correspondence-free scenario in which standard MALP cannot be expected to operate.

1 Introduction

Multi-atlas label propagation (MALP) is a popular branch of segmentation approaches. Given an atlas as a training image and the corresponding label map, the essence of MALP approaches is to perform individual atlas-based predictions, followed by a fusion step to form the final estimate. While MALP-based methods are extremely successful in certain settings such as brain labeling [1,2] or segmentation of abdominal organs [3], they are restricted to the *correspondence-based scenario*, where the assumption of correspondence between points in test and atlas images is made. In this work, we aim to transfer the advantages of the MALP framework to *correspondence-free scenarios*. Such regimes are an important class of problems in medical image analysis - they occur for example when highly heterogeneous pathologies such as tumors develop at different locations,

© Springer International Publishing Switzerland 2014
B. Menze et al. (Eds.): MCV 2014, LNCS 8848, pp. 116–124, 2014.
DOI: 10.1007/978-3-319-13972-2_11

or their shapes strongly vary. Our model problem for such a setting is multi-class segmentation of brain tumors in the BraTS 2013 challenge, which presents a challenging problem with a database of highly heterogeneous atlases [4].

Our work is motivated by two properties of the MALP framework which we aim to transfer to correspondence-free settings: (1) ability for atlas selection, and (2) computational efficiency. In the following we discuss these properties and why current MALP approaches are not applicable to correspondence-free scenarios, outline the main idea of our approach, and relate it to previous work.

A central characteristic of the MALP framework is that individual predictions are made based on each atlas, which are then fused into a final estimate. The first advantageous property resulting from the *per-atlas* characteristic is the ability for atlas selection [5]. Prediction based only on those training images which are similar to the test image has the potential to improve results, especially for underrepresented cases. This property is of increased importance for settings with highly heterogeneous atlases, and its potential can be expected to rise with the growing size of available labeled databases. The second advantageous property is the high efficiency. Recently, classifier-based MALP (CB-MALP) approaches have been introduced, which explicitly encode each atlas by an individual classifier [6,7], and significantly increase efficiency for training and experimentation compared to standard learning schemes which pool data from all atlases. The training efficiency comes from the smaller amount of samples for training of a single classifier, and the experimentation efficiency is given by the ability for cross-validation without retraining [6].

The combination of the ability for atlas selection and high efficiency makes MALP an attractive framework for general purpose segmentation, however, current MALP methods are applicable only in correspondence-based settings.

Most current MALP methods are registration-based [1,2], and thus explicitly operate in correspondence-based regimes. This holds for both, approaches based on non-linear registration which make the one-to-one correspondence assumption (e.g. [5,8,9]), as well as for patch-based approaches which use the relaxed one-to-many assumption [10,11]. The recently proposed classifier-based MALP methods [6,7] are in principle applicable to correspondence-free scenarios. However, approaches which train a classifier on a single atlas suffer from over-training, and can be expected not to generalize well to examples very different from the training dataset. While this property is not an issue in relatively homogeneous settings such as brain labeling where above methods were shown to perform well, it becomes problematic in highly heterogeneous correspondence-free settings such as brain tumor segmentation, as our experiments confirm for the atlas forests scheme from [6]. So, despite the potential of MALP-based approaches, they are currently not used in correspondence-free scenarios. More specifically, for our model problem of brain tumor segmentation, none of the proposed methods at the BraTS challenges 2012 and 2013 [4] was set within the MALP framework.

The main idea of this work is to base the segmentation on a classifier-based MALP method, thus keeping the advantages of the MALP framework, and to counteract the over-training issues of CB-MALP schemes by using classifiers according to their ability to correctly label the test image. The rationale is that over-training becomes a smaller issue with increasing "similarity" of testing and training data. Since the classifiers are atlas-based, such test-specific classifier weighting corresponds to weighting of training atlases based on their "similarity" to the test image. Here, the "similarity" between atlas and test image is determined by the accuracy performance of the associated atlas-based classifier, i.e. its ability to accurately label the test image. In this work, our CB-MALP method is based on the Atlas Forests (AF) framework [6], which operates by training an individual randomized forest classifier for each atlas. Originally, AF fuses the predictions by averaging the individual probabilistic classifier estimates. Instead, we propose to perform implicit atlas weighting by using the Simultaneous Truth and Performance[1] Level Estimation (STAPLE) method [12]. At test time, AF generates a set of candidate segmentations, for which STAPLE subsequently estimates the performance level, and uses these estimates as weights to combine the candidates into the final segmentation. Effectively, this means that for each test image, each of the atlases is used for prediction according to its estimated ability to perform a correct labeling. This way, our approach preserves the advantages of computational efficiency of the CB-MALP framework, while eliminating its negative effects of over-training, thus making it applicable to correspondence-free scenarios.

1.1   Relation to Prior Work

Our work is closely related to the recently proposed classifier-based MALP schemes from [6,7]. Our method is based on the atlas forest scheme from [6], which is an instance of CB-MALP without atlas weighting. More details of AF are discussed in Sect. 2. The focus of [7] is a generalization of STAPLE to operate on probabilistic estimates, which are in that work generated by a Gaussian Mixture Model of intensity patches, which are trained per atlas. Thus, this method is an instance of CB-MALP with implicit atlas weighting, similar to the approach proposed in this work. The studied setting in [7] is brain labeling, and application in correspondence-free scenarios is not considered.

While we are not aware of any work using a MALP-based approach for brain tumor segmentation, an interesting strategy to fuse multiple segmentations is considered in [4], where the majority vote strategy is used to fuse the results of methods which were *a priori* determined to achieve high accuracy. Since the candidate segmentations are not associated with individual atlases, this approach does not retain the MALP properties, and does not perform atlas weighting.

There are many strategies for atlas weighting for MALP. One is the use of heuristics such as intensity-based similarity of images [3,5], or subject age [5]. Heuristics are usually used to perform atlas selection (i.e. binary weighting) *prior* to testing. Alternatively, STAPLE [12] performs an implicit weighting of

---

[1] In the context of STAPLE, 'performance' stands for 'accuracy', and we use the term in the same sense in this paper.

atlas estimates. It operates *a posteriori* on computed candidate segmentations. Its generality makes it applicable also in highly heterogeneous correspondence-free settings, for which heuristic design is difficult.

2   Method

The proposed framework consists of two steps: (1) use a classifier-based MALP method, i.e. represent an individual atlas A_i by a classifier trained only on the data from A_i, and at test, use each classifier to generate a candidate segmentation $\hat{L}_i$, and (2) perform test-specific atlas weighting based on $\{\hat{L}_i\}$. In this work, we use randomized forests (RF) for (1), and the STAPLE method [12] for (2). We briefly describe these two components below.

2.1   Atlas-Based Estimates by Randomized Classification Forests

We use the general idea of the atlas forest framework [6], but modify the actual RF classifier according to [13] for the task of brain tumor segmentation. In contrast to [6], we do not incorporate any location-based features since we aim for the correspondence-free setting. Instead, as discussed in [13], we augment the multi-channel input data with class-probability estimates, and train an RF with context-aware features on this augmented data.

Given a set of N training atlases $\{A_i\}_{i=1:N}$, consisting of an intensity image I_i and the corresponding labelmap L_i, the task is to estimate a labelmap L for the test image I. As described in detail in Sect. 3.1, the original intensity images are multi-channel 3D images, with 4 different MR-contrasts as channels, and the labelmap encodes 5 different label classes, i.e. $L(x) \in \{0, \dots, 4\}$.

In the first step, an initial test-specific probabilitiy $p_{\mathrm{GMM}}^c(I)$ is created for each class c, by testing with a Gaussian Mixture Model of local multi-channel intensity for the class c, which is trained on all training data. These probabilities are then used to augment the original input data as additional channels. This can be seen as pre-processing for each image I, and we redefine $I = [I, p_{\mathrm{GMM}}(I)]$ to denote the resulting 9-channel 3D image for the following.

Based on the augmented input, we train randomized classification trees with context-aware features. Following the atlas forest scheme, each tree is trained only on an individual atlas A_i. A set of n such trees forms an atlas forest $a_i = \{T_i^k\}_{k=1:n}$. The training uses axis-aligned features and information gain as splitting criterion. Randomization is introduced via random sampling of the feature space by uniformly drawing feature types and parameters for the 3 randomized feature types: (1) Intensity difference between location of interest x in channel I_{j_1} and an offset point $x+v$ in channel I_{j_2}; (2) Difference between intensity means of a cuboid around x in I_{j_1} and a cuboid around $x+v$ in I_{j_2}; (3) Intensity range along a 3D line between x and $x+v$ in I_j. For cross-channel features (1) and (2), both I_{j_1} and I_{j_2} are drawn either from intensity or probability channels.

At test time, the image I is labeled by each atlas forest a_i, resulting in N candidate labelmaps $\hat{L}_i(x) = \arg\max_c \sum_j p_{T_i^j}(c|x, I)$. This is in contrast to the original atlas forests [6], which averages the probabilistic estimates of the AFs into a single prediction $\hat{L}(x) = \arg\max_c \sum_i \sum_j p_{T_i^j}(c|x, I)$.

2.2   Implicit Atlas Weighting by STAPLE

Given the set of candidate estimates $\hat{L}_i$, STAPLE [12] performs an Expectation-Maximization (EM) algorithm to estimate the conditional probability of the hidden true segmentation $p(L(x) = c|\{\hat{L}_i\}, \{\theta_i\})$, as well as the corresponding performances θ_i of the individual segmentations, modeled as confusion matrices. Starting from initial estimates for $\{\theta_i\}$, STAPLE iterates in standard EM manner until convergence, with the final segmentation estimate being $\hat{L}_S(x) = \arg\max_c p(L(x) = c|\{\hat{L}_i\}, \{\theta_i\})$, with

$$p\left(L(x) = c \mid \{\hat{L}_i\}, \{\theta_i\}\right) = \frac{p\left(L(x) = c\right) \prod_i p\left(\hat{L}_i(x) \mid L(x) = c, \theta_i\right)}{\sum_{c'} p\left(L(x) = c'\right) \prod_i p\left(\hat{L}_i(x) \mid L(x) = c', \theta_i\right)} \quad (1)$$

In the numerator, the prior $p(L(x) = c)$ is weighted by the probability of correct prediction of c by the candidate segmentation $\hat{L}_i(x)$, according to its estimated performance θ_i. Since the estimates $\hat{L}_i$ are directly associated to the atlases A_i via the atlas-forest classifiers a_i, this results in an implicit weighting of the training atlas images according to their estimated relevance. Please note that the performance for a_i is in general not the same for different classes.

3   Evaluation

After providing details about data and setup, we present two experiments: In Sect. 3.3 we evaluate the quality of STAPLE performance estimation, and in Sect. 3.4 we compare the results of a standard forest (Std. Forest) approach as in [13], AFs with probabilistic averaging as fusion (AF-PrAvg) as in [6], and the proposed AFs with atlas weighting by STAPLE (AF-STAPLE).

3.1   Data

The evaluation is performed on the real data from the NCI-MICCAI BraTS 2013 Challenge [4], which consists of 3 datasets: training, leaderboard and challenge. The training data, for which the reference manual segmentations are available, consists of 20 high-grade (HG) and 10 low-grade (LG) cases. Leaderboard has 21 HG and 4 LG cases, and challenge has 10 HG cases. We refer to the leaderboard and challenge data, for which the reference labelmaps are not known, as evaluation data. The actual labelmaps contain 5 classes, however, the challenge evaluation is performed on three "regions", which combine the classes to: *complete tumor*, *tumor core*, and *enhancing tumor*. For each case, 4 different MR contrasts are given as input data: contrast enhanced T1, T1, T2 and FLAIR. As additional pre-processing, we perform inhomogeneity correction by [14], set the median of each channel to a fixed value (1000), and downsample the images by factor of two with nearest-neighbor interpolation. Quantitative evaluation for all experiments is performed by submitting to the BraTS challenge system.

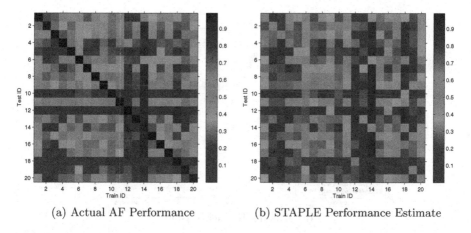

(a) Actual AF Performance   (b) STAPLE Performance Estimate

Fig. 1. Quality of STAPLE performance estimate on high-grade training data: (a) Actual Dice scores (**D**) (average over all classes) resulting from testing on individual AFs (diagonal: testing on training images, note the over-training effect). (b) Dice scores *estimated* by STAPLE (**D**$_E$). Rows show performance of different AFs for a given test image, which is relevant for atlas weighting: e.g. AF-14 seldom performs well. The similarity between (a) and (b) shows that STAPLE performance estimates have high-quality: excluding the diagonal, average correlation of corresponding rows of **D** and **D**$_E$ is 0.87.

Table 1. Quantative summary of results on complete BraTS 2013 data, including *training* (leave-1-out validation), and *evaluation*. Please see also Fig. 2.

Method	Training all			Evaluation all		
	Complete	Core	Enhancing	Complete	Core	Enhancing
Std. Forest	75.0±15.2	63.8±29.1	44.9±36.8	74.3±16.4	62.7±28.0	51.6±32.5
AF Pr.Avg	64.2±30.2	50.0±33.8	40.1±36.9	64.3±29.4	46.9±32.7	43.1±33.2
AF STAPLE	76.6±17.3	62.6±23.8	47.0±35.4	76.5±18.0	62.9±25.2	52.1±31.5

3.2   Implementation and Parameter Settings

For the basic tree training, we use the method as described in Sect. 2.1 with the same settings as in [13]. To replicate the results from [13] for Std. Forest, we train 60 trees per forest for HG and LG. For Std. Forest, we perform random subsampling of the background class with a sampling rate of 0.2. For Atlas Forests, we train 3 trees per AF, resulting in 60 trees for HG and 30 for LG. To perform STAPLE, we use the implementation from http://www.crl.med.harvard.edu/software/STAPLE/index.php with the default settings.

3.3   Quantifying the Quality of Performance Estimates by STAPLE

This experiment evaluates the ability of STAPLE to predict the performance of individual AFs for brain tumor data, with results summarized in Fig. 1. In this

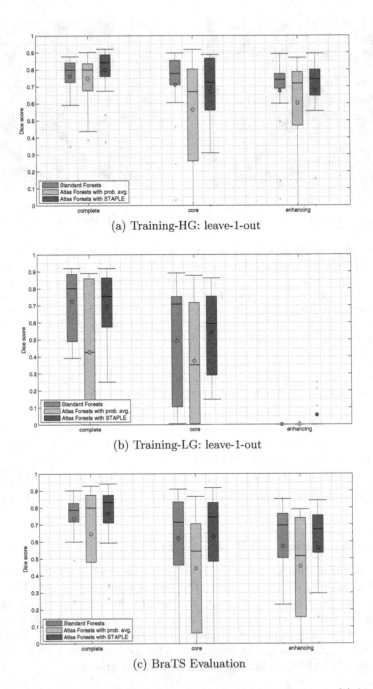

(a) Training-HG: leave-1-out

(b) Training-LG: leave-1-out

(c) BraTS Evaluation

Fig. 2. Evaluation on BraTS 2013 data: Leave-1-out experiment on (a) high-grade (HG) and (b) low-grade (LG) cases on the training data. (c) results on the evaluation data (*leaderboard* and *challenge*). Please see also Table 1.

context, performance describes the accuracy of the prediction by an individual classifier. For this task, we use the HG training dataset, and train an AF a_i for each case. Then with each a_i we generate a set of segmentations $\{\hat{L}_i^k\}$ for each image I_k.

First, we measure the actual performance of the individual AFs in this scenario by computing the average Dice score per class for each $\hat{L}_i^k$ compared to the reference manual segmentation L_i (Fig. 1a). The rows of the matrix in Fig. 1a show the performance of different AFs for a given test image, which is relevant for atlas weighting. For example, one can observe that AF-14 seldom performs well. We observe a high variance of performance for the individual AFs, which was the initial motivation for this work. Please note the high values on the diagonal (training and testing on the same image), which shows the over-training property of AFs.

Second, we measure the ability of STAPLE to *estimate* the performance of the individual AFs, *without access to reference labels or any prior information* (Fig. 1b). For each test case k we apply STAPLE to candidate segmentations $\{\hat{L}_i^k\}_{i \neq k}$, which yields performance estimates for each AF a_i. These are quantified by computing (excluding the diagonal) the correlation of the actual and estimated performance matrix (0.91), and the average correlation of corresponding rows (0.87), showing the high accuracy of STAPLE for this task.

3.4 Evaluation on BraTS 2013

We use same settings for all experiments, but two different protocols for training and evaluation data. For training data, we perform a leave-1-out experiment to simulate a realistic scenario. For the evaluation data, we use all available training atlases. For each method, we separately train and test for HG and LG.

The results are summarized in Fig. 2 and Table 1, and seem consistent across the different data subsets. We observe that as expected, the original AF method with probabilistic averaging (AF-PrAvg) [6] has significantly reduced accuracy compared to the baseline (Std. Forest) which uses the same basic classifier. The proposed AF-STAPLE which performs atlas weighting has the desired effect of recovering the performance to the level of the original classifier, cf. Table 1, while keeping the computational efficiency advantages of the MALP framework.

4   Discussion and Summary

We propose a segmentation method which retains the advantages of CB-MALP (increased efficiency, ability for atlas selection) but can be applied to general scenarios, such as brain tumor segmentation. The results show that even in such settings, in which other CB-MALP methods are shown to fail, the proposed approach is capable of the same accuracy as the standard learning scheme, while using the same basic classifier method. As future work, it would be interesting to consider alternative classifiers, which are potentially more tuned towards specific problems, and evaluate the effect of the proposed framework. Also, different alternative weighting methods could be used, e.g. the probabilistic version of STAPLE from [7], which might be more suitable for classifier-based predictions. We believe that in the light of growing annotated databases, the ability to learn from more similar data has the potential to provide increased accuracy, especially for under-represented outlier cases.

References

1. Landman, B., Warfield, S. (eds.): MICCAI Workshop on Multi-Atlas Labeling (2012)
2. Asman, A., Akhondi-Asl, A., Wang, H., Tustison, N., Avants, B., Warfield, S.K., Landman, B.: MICCAI 2013 segmentation algorithms, theory and applications (SATA) challenge results summary. In: MICCAI Challenge Workshop on Segmentation: Algorithms, Theory and Applications (SATA) (2013)
3. Wolz, R., Chu, C., Misawa, K., Mori, K., Rueckert, D.: Multi-organ abdominal CT segmentation using hierarchically weighted subject-specific atlases. In: Ayache, N., Delingette, H., Golland, P., Mori, K. (eds.) MICCAI 2012, Part I. LNCS, vol. 7510, pp. 10–17. Springer, Heidelberg (2012)
4. Menze, B., et al.: The Multimodal Brain Tumor Image Segmentation Benchmark (BRATS) (2014). http://hal.inria.fr/hal-00935640
5. Aljabar, P., Heckemann, R., Hammers, A., Hajnal, J., Rueckert, D.: Multi-atlas based segmentation of brain images: atlas selection and its effect on accuracy. NeuroImage 46(3), 726–738 (2009)
6. Zikic, D., Glocker, B., Criminisi, A.: Atlas encoding by randomized forests for efficient label propagation. In: Mori, K., Sakuma, I., Sato, Y., Barillot, C., Navab, N. (eds.) MICCAI 2013, Part III. LNCS, vol. 8151, pp. 66–73. Springer, Heidelberg (2013)
7. Akhondi-Asl, A., Warfield, S.: Simultaneous truth and performance level estimation through fusion of probabilistic segmentations. IEEE TMI 32, 1840–1852 (2013)
8. Rohlfing, T., Brandt, R., Menzel, R., Maurer, C.: Evaluation of atlas selection strategies for atlas-based image segmentation with application to confocal microscopy images of bee brains. NeuroImage 21(4), 1428–1442 (2004)
9. Heckemann, R., Hajnal, J., Aljabar, P., Rueckert, D., Hammers, A., et al.: Automatic anatomical brain MRI segmentation combining label propagation and decision fusion. NeuroImage 33(1), 115–126 (2006)
10. Rousseau, F., Habas, P., Studholme, C.: A supervised patch-based approach for human brain labeling. IEEE TMI 30(10), 1852–1862 (2011)
11. Coupé, P., Manjón, J., Fonov, V., Pruessner, J., Robles, M., Collins, D.: Patch-based segmentation using expert priors: application to hippocampus and ventricle segmentation. NeuroImage 54(2), 940–954 (2011)
12. Warfield, S., Zou, K., Wells, W.: Simultaneous truth and performance level estimation (STAPLE): an algorithm for the validation of image segmentation. IEEE TMI 23(7), 903–921 (2004)
13. Zikic, D., Glocker, B., Konukoglu, E., Shotton, J., Criminisi, A., Ye, D., Demiralp, C., Thomas, O.M., Das, T., Jena, R., Price, S.J.: Context-sensitive classification forests for segmentation of brain tumor tissues. In: MICCAI 2012 Challenge on Multimodal Brain Tumor Segmentation (BraTS) (2012)
14. Tustison, N., Gee, J.: N4ITK: Nick's N3 ITK implementation for MRI bias field correction. Insight J. (2010)

Translational Medical Computer Vision

CT Prostate Deformable Segmentation by Boundary Regression

Yeqin Shao[1,2], Yaozong Gao[2,3], Xin Yang[1], and Dinggang Shen[2(✉)]

[1] Institute of Image Processing and Pattern Recognition,
Shanghai Jiao Tong University, Shanghai 200240, China
[2] Department of Radiology and BRIC, University of North Carolina,
Chapel Hill, NC 27599, USA
dgshen@med.unc.edu
[3] Department of Computer Science, University of North Carolina,
Chapel Hill, NC 27599, USA

Abstract. Automatic and accurate prostate segmentation from CT images is challenging due to low image contrast, uncertain organ motion, and variable organ appearance in different patient images. To deal with these challenges, we propose a new prostate boundary detection method with a boundary regression strategy for prostate deformable segmentation. Different from the previous regression-based segmentation methods, which train one regression forest for each specific point (e.g., each point on a shape model), our method learns a single global regression forest to predict the nearest boundary points from each voxel for enhancing the entire prostate boundary. The experimental results show that our proposed boundary regression method outperforms the conventional prostate classification method. Compared with other state-of-the-art methods, our method also shows a competitive performance.

1 Introduction

Prostate cancer is the second leading cause of male cancer death in USA [1]. As one of the major treatments to the prostate cancer, image-guided radiation treatment (IGRT) aims to deliver a high dose of X-ray to tumors, while limiting the dose exposed to the surrounding healthy organs. Inaccurate localization of the prostate could result in wrong dose delivery, and thus incur under-treatment or even serious side-effects (e.g. rectum bleeding). To ensure the high efficacy of treatment, accurate prostate segmentation from CT images is critical. On the other hand, traditionally, the prostate and surrounding organs are often manually segmented by physician(s). This process is time-consuming and also suffers from both intra- and inter-observer variations [2]. Therefore, automatic and accurate prostate segmentation is highly desired in IGRT.

Despite the importance in IGRT, automatic and accurate prostate segmentation from CT images is still a challenging task due to the following three reasons. First, the image contrast between the prostate and surrounding structures is low, as shown in

---

Y. Shao and Y. Gao—Co-first authors.

© Springer International Publishing Switzerland 2014
B. Menze et al. (Eds.): MCV 2014, LNCS 8848, pp. 127–136, 2014.
DOI: 10.1007/978-3-319-13972-2_12

(a)–(c) of Fig. 1. Second, the motion of the prostate is unpredictable for different patients. Third, due to the uncertainty in the existence of bowel gas, the prostate appearance is highly variable, as can be seen by comparing (a) and (c) of Fig. 1.

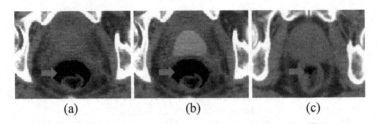

(a)   (b)   (c)

Fig. 1. Typical prostate CT images. The green area in (b) indicates the manual segmentation of prostate by a physician for the same image in (a). Image in (c) shows the prostate image of another patient with less bowel gas than both (a) and (b). Here, the red arrows indicate the bowel gas (Colour figure online).

To address these challenges, many prostate segmentation methods have been proposed for CT images. The methods in [3–5] use patient-specific information to localize the prostate. For these methods, images from the same patient are exploited to facilitate prostate segmentation. Feng et al. [3] leveraged the population and patient-specific image information for deformable segmentation of prostate. Liao et al. [4] collected the previous segmentations of the same patient to update the training images, under a hierarchical sparse label propagation framework, for accurate prostate segmentation. Gao et al. [5] employed the previous prostate segmentations of the same patient as patient-specific atlases to segment the prostate in CT images. Since no previous images from the same patient are available in planning stage, the methods in [3–5] cannot be directly applied to the prostate segmentation in planning CT images. Therefore, it is critical to develop a population-based segmentation method. Costa et al. [6] presented a non-overlapping constraint from nearby bladder on a coupled deformable models for prostate localization. Lu et al. [7] applied information theory to boundary inference process for pelvic organ segmentation. Chen et al. [8] adopted a Bayesian framework with anatomical constraints from surrounding bones to segment the prostate.

Recently, motivated by random forest [9], the regression-based voting strategy achieves promising results in medical image segmentation. For example, Criminisi et al. [10] employed the regression forest to vote the centers of organs' bounding boxes. Lindner et al. [11] adopted the regression forest to predict the optimal positions of global and local models for accurate proximal femur segmentation. These works all train one regression forest for each specific point (e.g. center of the bounding box or point of the deformable model). However, it is difficult to extend this schema to boundary detection, especially in 3D case, since there might be a large number of points on the boundary.

In this paper, we present a new voting strategy to detect the weak boundary for prostate segmentation. Different from the previous methods, our method learns only a single global regression forest to estimate and vote the nearest boundary points for enhancing the entire prostate boundary, then guiding the later deformable segmentation. The advantages of our method include: (1) our method does not require point-to-point correspondences for learning the regression forest, thus avoiding the difficulty in capturing the correspondences of the 3D prostate boundary points from different subjects in the boundary regression; (2) our method does not require the effort to train one regression forest for each boundary point of 3D object, thus avoiding the training of a large number of regression forests.

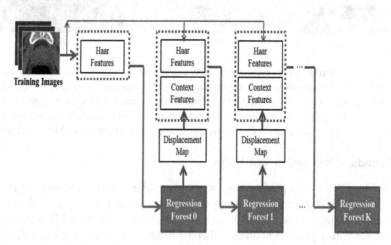

Fig. 2. Training a sequence of regression forests in our proposed method.

2 Method

To accurately segment the prostate from CT images, we first propose a boundary regression method, based on the regression forest, to estimate and vote the nearest prostate boundary points from each image point according to its local image appearance. A boundary voting map is thus obtained to enhance the whole prostate boundary in each CT image (as demonstrated in Fig. 3). Then, to further boost the performance of our boundary regression method, we combine the regression forest with the auto-context model [12] to achieve a more accurate boundary voting map. Specifically, in the training stage (Fig. 2), we train a sequence of regression forests, each of which can estimate a 3D displacement vector from each image point to its nearest prostate boundary, using the local appearance (of this image point). Different from the previous works [10, 11], which often use only the image appearance features, our method further utilizes the context features from the output displacement map of the previous regression forest to train next regression forest. Iteratively, our method improves the estimation of displacement vectors in the whole image, and finally obtains an improved boundary voting map. In the testing stage, given a testing image, the learned regression forests could be sequentially applied to estimate the 3D displacement vector for each point. As more regression forests are applied, the prediction of the 3D displacement vectors in the whole image can be more accurate, and thus can be used in the regression voting strategy to generate a better boundary voting map. Finally, a deformable model, which has been trained in the training stage, can be applied to the obtained boundary voting map for final prostate segmentation.

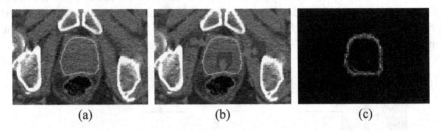

(a)   (b)   (c)

Fig. 3. Demonstration of our boundary regression and voting for prostate. (a) shows the original image and the manual contour (green). (b) demonstrates our boundary regression by local image patches (blue cubes). Red arrows indicate the displacement vectors (regression target) from the centers of local image patches to their corresponding nearest boundary points. (c) shows the boundary voting map of our method using only image appearance features (Colour figure online).

2.1 Boundary Regression and Voting

Motivated by [10], we propose to employ the regression forest for voting the prostate boundary. A regression forest is used to learn a non-linear mapping from the local patch of each image point to its nearest prostate boundary point, obtaining a 3D displacement. Note that, for voting prostate boundary, this 3D displacement is defined as a 3D vector from each image point to its nearest prostate boundary point. Specifically, in the training stage, from each training image, we can first randomly sample a large number of image points $p_i (i = 1, 2 \ldots N)$ around the manually-delineated prostate boundary. Each sampled point p_i is characterized by the extended Haar features f [13], extracted from its $w \times w \times w$ local image patch. Then, the displacement $d_i = (\Delta x_i, \Delta y_i, \Delta z_i)$ between point p_i and its nearest prostate boundary point is considered as the regression target. Based on all pairs of Haar features and displacements, $<f(p_i), d_i>$, from all training images, we can learn a regression forest R_0. For our regression forest, the split node in each decision tree is determined by the best combination of feature and threshold, which can achieve the maximum information gain [10] from splitting. Each leaf node in a decision tree stores the mean displacement of training samples falling into this node. In the testing stage, given a testing image, we use all image points in a region of interest (ROI) for boundary regression and voting. Specifically, for each image point $\widehat{p}$, its extended Haar features $f(\widehat{p})$ can be first extracted using the same way as described in the training stage. Then, the respective displacement $\widehat{d} = R_0(f(\widehat{p}))$ can be predicted by the trained regression forest R_0. Finally, a vote will be accumulated on the position $\widehat{p} + \widehat{d}$ in the boundary voting map. By visiting all possible points in the testing image, we can get a boundary voting map for the prostate, with a typical example shown in Fig. 3.

2.2 Refinement of Boundary Voting Map by the Auto-Context Model

To refine the boundary voting map, we adopt the auto-context model [12] to iteratively train a sequence of regression forests by integrating both image appearance features and the context features extracted from the intermediate displacement map of the previous regression forest. Specifically, we can learn a sequence of regression forests $R_i (i = 0, 1 \ldots K)$ by using the same technique described in Sect. 2.1. The regression forest R_0 (as detailed in Sect. 2.1) is trained by using only the Haar features extracted from the training images, while the latter regression forests $R_i (i = 1, 2 \ldots K)$ are trained by using both the Haar features extracted from the training images and the context features extracted from the respective intermediate displacement maps of the previous regression forest R_{i-1}. The context features used here are again the extended Haar features extracted from the local patch of the intermediate displacement map, instead of the radiation-like features as used in the previous work [12]. This is because the traditional radiation-like auto-context features are the voxel-wise values in the displacement map, which are sensitive to noises in the displacement map. In contrast, the extended Haar features are computed based on local patches, thus more robust to the wrong predictions of displacements produced by the previous regression forest R_{i-1}. Moreover, the extended Haar features provide much richer feature representations than the voxel-wise values for learning the regression forest. Emprically, for the auto-context model, Haar context features achieve faster convergence rate than the traditional radiation-like context features.

Based on the trained regression forests, displacement maps can be sequentially estimated for a testing image. Specifically, the regression forest R_0 is first employed to predict the 3D displacement vectors of the first displacement map, using only the local appearance features from the testing image. Then, by combining the local appearance features (from the testing image) with the context information (from the displacement map of previous regression forest), the latter regression forests $R_i (i = 1, 2 \ldots K)$ could iteratively refine the prediction of the 3D displacement vector for each point in the testing image, and obtain more and more accurate boundary voting maps, as shown in Fig. 4.

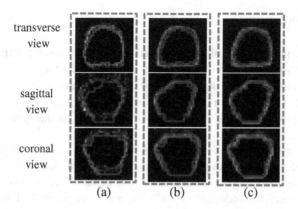

transverse view

sagittal view

coronal view

(a)   (b)   (c)

Fig. 4. Boundary voting maps of a patient generated by the auto-context model at the 1st, 3rd and 5th iterations (a-c), respectively. The green curves indicate the manual segmentations (Colour figure online).

2.3   Deformable Segmentation Based on the Boundary Voting Map

Up to this stage, the boundary voting map for prostate is achieved by the regression-based voting with the auto-context model. Based on the boundary voting map, the prostate can be readily segmented by a deformable model [14]. Specifically, to apply the deformable model, we need to build a shape model, often with thousands of vertices on the surface. To accomplish that, in the training stage, we first use the marching cubes to extract surfaces from all manually-segmented prostates in the training images. Then, a template surface is selected and warped to all other surfaces to establish voxel correspondences [14]. With the established correspondences, each training prostate surface can be affine aligned onto a template surface space. PCA is then used to build a prostate shape subspace by capturing the major shape variations from all aligned training prostate surfaces. In the testing stage, the mean prostate shape is first transformed onto the testing image as the initial shape for the deformable model, by a similarity transform. Here, the similarity transform is evaluated by minimizing the least square distance between six detected landmarks (superior, inferior, left, right, anterior, posterior) and their counterparts on the mean shape. Note that those six landmarks are automatically detected using the landmark detector described in [10], which is learned on six manually-annotated landmarks in all training images. Based on this shape initialization, each vertex in the shape model can be independently deformed on the boundary voting map, along its respective normal direction, to a position with the maximum boundary votes. By adopting the landmark-guided initialization, we can achieve a robust initialization (the DSC between initial shape and the manual segmentation is about 0.78 for our dataset), which largely decreases the chances of falling into bad local minima for deformable model segmentation. In the meanwhile, the deformed shape is also constrained by the learned PCA shape model. By alternating the model deformation and the shape refinement, the shape model can be gradually driven onto the prostate boundary under the guidance of both boundary voting map and the PCA shape subspace.

3   Experiments

To evaluate the performance of our proposed method, we conduct experiments on a prostate dataset with 70 planning CT images from 70 different patients with prostate cancer. Each image has voxel size $0.938 \times 0.938 \times 3.0$ mm^3 which was isotropically resampled to $2.0 \times 2.0 \times 2.0$ mm^3 for the experiment. A clinical expert manually delineated the prostates in all 70 images, which we use as the ground truth in our experiment.

In the experiments, we use four-fold cross-validation to evaluate the performance of our method. The parameters adopted in our method are as follows: the number of trees in each regression forest is set as 10; the maximum depth of each tree is 15; the number of candidate features for node split is 1000; the minimum number of samples in each leaf is 5; the patch size w for extracting Haar features is 30; the number of samples drawn around the prostate boundary in each training image is $N = 10000$; the number of iterations in the auto-context model is 5 (i.e., $K = 4$); the PCA shape subspace captures 98 % shape variation, regarding about 18 eigen-modes; and the number of iterations used for deformable model is 20. The ROI for boundary regression and voting is determined by the tightest bounding box that covers the initial shape of the deformable model.

3.1 Boundary Regression Vs Prostate Classification

Since the image contrast between prostate and the surrounding structures is low, prostate boundary is not clear and even ambiguous in the CT images, which renders difficulty for accurate prostate segmentation. In the literature [5], to address this tough problem, classification-based method has been proposed to distinguish prostate from the background by assigning each image point (voxel) a prostate likelihood value. Specifically, a classifier is trained by using the positive samples from prostate and the negative samples from background. In the testing stage, the learned classifier can be used to voxel-wisely classify the new testing image for producing a classification response map, which is then utilized by the deformable model to finally segment the prostate. To evaluate the effectiveness of our proposed boundary regression method, we conduct a comparative experiment between the prostate classification method and our proposed boundary regression method. Specifically, in the prostate classification method, we use classification forest as the classifier with the same setting (e.g., number of trees, number of features and thresholds, splitting stop criterion) as boundary regression to estimate the posterior probability of each voxel belonging to the prostate. Then, the generated classification response map is used to guide the deformable segmentation by finding the voxel along the normal with the maximum gradient. In contrast, our boundary regression method uses the obtained boundary voting map to guide the deformable segmentation by searching the voxel along the normal with the maximum boundary votes. Note that both methods use the same sampling strategy, features and shape models, as well as the same auto-context model. Table 1 shows the quantitative segmentation results for the two methods, where Dice Similarity Coefficient (DSC) measures the overlap between automated and manual segmentations. ASD denotes Average Surface Distance between automated and manual segmentations.

Table 1. Quantitative comparison between classification and boundary regression.

Method	DSC	ASD
Classification	0.82 ± 0.07	2.47 ± 1.06
Boundary regression	$\mathbf{0.85 \pm 0.06}$	$\mathbf{2.01 \pm 0.81}$

From Table 1, we can see that our boundary regression method allows for better segmentations, in terms of higher DSC and lower ASD, than the prostate classification method. Also, the performance improvement of our method regarding DSC and ASD is statistically significant ($p < 0.05$). This result proves that our proposed method is more effective to produce a guidance map for steering the deformable segmentation.

3.2   Effectiveness of Using the Auto-Context Model

To show the effectiveness of using the auto-context model for iteratively refining the boundary voting map, in Fig. 4, we have shown three prostate boundary voting maps estimated at the 1st, 3rd and 5th iterations with the auto-context model. As we can see, with the increase of iteration, the prostate boundary becomes clearer and closer to the manual ground-truth. For quantitative evaluation on the final segmentation results, we perform deformable segmentation based on each intermediate boundary voting map, which is generated at each iteration in the auto-context model. As shown in Fig. 5, the accuracy of prostate segmentation increases with iterations (the DSC increases and the ASD decreases). This result shows the effectiveness of the auto-context model in both enhancing the boundary voting map and facilitating the final prostate segmentation.

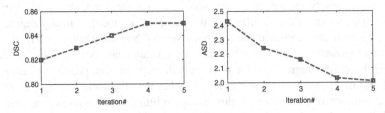

Fig. 5. Iterative improvement of segmentation accuracy with the auto-context model. The left panel shows DSC and the right shows ASD.

3.3   Comparison with Other State-of-the-Art Methods

Due to the unavailability of either source codes or the datasets used by other prostate segmentation methods, it is difficult to directly compare them with the proposed method quantitatively. In order to get a rough understanding of the status in CT prostate segmentation, we list the segmentation accuracies reported by other works in Table 2. To quantitatively evaluate the methods, except the aforementioned DSC and ASD, we also employ other three metrics: sensitivity (SEN), positive predictive value (PPV), and false positive ratio (FPR).

$$\text{SEN} = \frac{TP}{TP + FN} \quad (1) \quad \text{PPV} = \frac{TP}{TP + FP} \quad (2) \quad \text{FPR} = \frac{FP}{TP + FP} \quad (3)$$

where TP is the number of correctly labeled prostate voxels, FP is the number of falsely labeled organ voxels (i.e., labeling background voxels as prostate voxels), and FN is the number of falsely labeled background voxels (i.e., labeling prostate voxels as background voxels).

As can be seen in Table 2, our method achieves competitive segmentation accuracy to the state-of-the-art methods under comparison, although we utilize only one organ (prostate), without incorporating the constraints from the nearby structures as Costa et al. [6] and Chen et al. [8] do.

Table 2. Quantitative comparison between our method and other methods. *NA* indicates that the respective metric is not reported in the publication.

Method	Mean SEN	Median SEN	Mean ASD	Median ASD	Mean PPV	Median FPR
Costa et al. [6]	0.75	*NA*	*NA*	*NA*	0.80	*NA*
Lu et al. [7]	*NA*	*NA*	2.37	2.15	*NA*	*NA*
Chen et al. [8]	*NA*	0.84	*NA*	**1.10**	*NA*	0.13
Our method	**0.84**	**0.87**	**2.01**	1.85	**0.86**	**0.10**

4 Conclusion and Discussion

We have presented a new boundary voting method for CT prostate segmentation. Compared with the previous point regression methods that train one regression forest for each specific point, we learn a single global regression forest for the detection of the entire prostate boundary. To boost the boundary regression performance, we further combine the regression forest with the auto-context model for iteratively refining the boundary voting map of the prostate. Finally, the deformable model is also adopted to segment the prostate under the guidance of both the boundary voting map and the learned prostate shape subspace. Validated on 70 CT images from 70 different patients, our proposed method achieves better segmentation accuracy than the traditional prostate classification method, as well as competitive performance to several state-of-the-art methods under comparison. In this study, due to the relatively stable shapes of the prostates, we use PCA for shape modeling. However, for other organs with complex shape variations (e.g., rectum), a recently proposed shape modeling technique [15, 16], namely sparse shape composition, might be better. This will be our future work.

References

1. A Snapshotof Prostate Cancer. http://www.cancer.gov/researchandfunding/snapshots/pdf/ Prostate-Snapshot.pdf
2. Foskey, M., Davis, B., Goyal, L., Chang, S., Chaney, E., Strehl, N., Tomei, S., Rosenman, J., Joshi, S.: Large deformation three-dimensional image registration in image-guided radiation therapy. Phys. Med. Biol. **50**, 5869 (2005)
3. Feng, Q., Foskey, M., Chen, W., Shen, D.: Segmenting CT prostate images using population and patient-specific statistics for radiotherapy. Med. Phys. **37**, 4121–4132 (2010)
4. Liao, S., Gao, Y., Lian, J., Shen, D.: Sparse patch-based label propagation for accurate prostate localization in CT images. IEEE Trans. Med. Imaging **32**, 419–434 (2013)
5. Gao, Y., Liao, S., Shen, D.: Prostate segmentation by sparse representation based classification. Med. Phys. **39**, 6372–6387 (2012)
6. Costa, M.J., Delingette, H., Novellas, S., Ayache, N.: Automatic segmentation of bladder and prostate using coupled 3D deformable models. In: Ayache, N., Ourselin, S., Maeder, A. (eds.) MICCAI 2007, Part I. LNCS, vol. 4791, pp. 252–260. Springer, Heidelberg (2007)

7. Lu, C., Zheng, Y., Birkbeck, N., Zhang, J., Kohlberger, T., Tietjen, C., Boettger, T., Duncan, J.S., Zhou, S.: Precise segmentation of multiple organs in CT volumes using learning-based approach and information theory. In: Ayache, N., Delingette, H., Golland, P., Mori, K. (eds.) MICCAI 2012, Part II. LNCS, vol. 7511, pp. 462–469. Springer, Heidelberg (2012)

8. Chen, S., Lovelock, D.M., Radke, R.J.: Segmenting the prostate and rectum in CT imagery using anatomical constraints. Med. Image Anal. **15**, 1–11 (2011)

9. Breiman, L.: Random forests. Mach. Learn. **45**, 5–32 (2001)

10. Criminisi, A., Shotton, J., Robertson, D., Konukoglu, E.: Regression Forests for Efficient Anatomy Detection and Localization in CT Studies. In: Menze, B., Langs, G., Tu, Z., Criminisi, A. (eds.) MICCAI 2010. LNCS, vol. 6533, pp. 106–117. Springer, Heidelberg (2011)

11. Lindner, C., Thiagarajah, S., Wilkinson, J.M., Consortium, T., Wallis, G., Cootes, T.: Fully automatic segmentation of the proximal femur using random forest regression voting. IEEE Trans. Med. Imaging **32**, 1462–1472 (2013)

12. Tu, Z., Bai, X.: Auto-context and its application to high-level vision tasks and 3d brain image segmentation. IEEE Trans. Pattern Anal. Mach. Intell. **32**, 1744–1757 (2010)

13. Zhan, Y., Dewan, M., Harder, M., Krishnan, A., Zhou, X.S.: Robust automatic knee mr slice positioning through redundant and hierarchical anatomy detection. IEEE Trans. Med. Imaging **30**, 2087–2100 (2011)

14. Shen, D., Herskovits, E.H., Davatzikos, C.: An adaptive-focus statistical shape model for segmentation and shape modeling of 3-D brain structures. IEEE Trans. Med. Imaging **20**, 257–270 (2001)

15. Zhang, S., Zhan, Y., Dewan, M., Huang, J., Metaxas, D.N., Zhou, X.S.: Towards robust and effective shape modeling: sparse shape composition. Med. Image Anal. **16**, 265–277 (2012)

16. Zhang, S., Zhan, Y., Metaxas, D.N.: Deformable segmentation via sparse representation and dictionary learning. Med. Image Anal. **16**, 1385–1396 (2012)

Precise Lumen Segmentation in Coronary Computed Tomography Angiography

Felix Lugauer[1,2](✉), Yefeng Zheng[3], Joachim Hornegger[1],
and B. Michael Kelm[2]

[1] Pattern Recognition Lab, University of Erlangen-Nuremberg, Erlangen, Germany
felix.lugauer@fau.de
[2] Imaging and Computer Vision, Siemens AG, Corporate Technology,
Erlangen, Germany
[3] Imaging and Computer Vision, Siemens Corporate Research, Princeton, USA

Abstract. Coronary computed tomography angiography (CCTA) allows for non-invasive identification and grading of stenoses by evaluating the degree of narrowing of the blood-filled vessel lumen. Recently, methods have been proposed that simulate coronary blood flow using computational fluid dynamics (CFD) to compute the fractional flow reserve non-invasively. Both grading and CFD rely on a precise segmentation of the vessel lumen from CCTA. We propose a novel, model-guided segmentation approach based on a Markov random field formulation with convex priors which assures the preservation of the tubular structure of the coronary lumen. Allowing for various robust smoothness terms, the approach yields very accurate lumen segmentations even in the presence of calcified and non-calcified plaques. Evaluations on the public Rotterdam segmentation challenge demonstrate the robustness and accuracy of our method: on standardized tests with multi-vendor CCTA from 30 symptomatic patients, we achieve superior accuracies as compared to both state-of-the-art methods and medical experts.

Keywords: CCTA · Lumen segmentation · Markov random field · Tubular surface

1 Introduction

Coronary artery disease (CAD) is a leading cause of death in the western world according to the American Heart Association [2]. CAD is indicated by the build-up of coronary plaque which is accompanied by an inflammatory process in the vessel wall. It may result in a local narrowing of the lumen, known as stenosis, which in turn may cause an ischemic heart failure.

The diagnostic standard in current clinical practice is invasive coronary angiography (ICA) which requires catheterization. Besides the degree of stenosis,

---

Felix Lugauer: The author has been with Siemens Corporate Technology for this work.

B. Menze et al. (Eds.): MCV 2014, LNCS 8848, pp. 137–147, 2014.
DOI: 10.1007/978-3-319-13972-2_13

pressure differences across lesions can be measured under induced hyperemia. Fractional flow reserve (FFR) is computed as the pressure ratio and has been shown to be indicative for ischemia-causing stenoses. However, the procedure is costly and involves considerable risks and inconvenience for the patient.

Alternatively, with coronary computed tomography angiography (CCTA) a volumetric image of the contrasted coronary vessels is acquired which allows for a non-invasive identification and analysis of coronary stenoses. Usually, stenoses with grades (degree of anatomical obstruction) above 50 % are considered hemodynamically relevant. Recently, the non-invasive computation of FFR has been proposed as an alternative to ICA. This is achieved by simulating coronary blood flow using computational fluid dynamics (CFD) based on lumen geometry extracted from CCTA. Latest studies show that CFD provides a better accuracy in identifying ischemia-causing stenoses than the anatomical grade [8]. Both grading and CFD heavily depend on the accuracy of the extracted coronary lumen. As manual segmentation is very time-consuming and prone to high variability among medical experts, automatic and robust methods are desirable.

There exists a substantial body of research on vessel extraction and segmentation algorithms [5]. For brevity, we only mention related methods and approaches that have been applied to coronary artery segmentation using the standardized evaluation framework proposed by Kirişli et al. [4]. Previous approaches tend to focus on healthy vessels and often fail to correctly segment the lumen in diseased vessels, i.e. in the presence of calcified, non-calcified and mixed plaques. This can be partially accounted for by explicitly modeling or suppressing calcified plaque before segmentation [7,9,10]. Many of the proposed approaches also involve post-processing and refinement of the segmentation results for fixing artifacts. Shazad et al. [10], for example, propose a voxel-based graph-cut segmentation followed by a radial resampling and smoothing which patches non-tubular segmentation results (e.g. dissected lumen segmentations) and artifacts due to the voxel-level accuracy. A shape prior as included in the model-based level set approach proposed by Wang et al. [12] helps to avoid leakages and allows for a robust lumen extraction even in low contrast (ambiguous) regions. Similarly, Mohr et al. [9] employ a level-set approach based on results from a tissue classification and calcium segmentation step. Lugauer et al. [7] apply boundary detection and calcium removal within the segmentation approach of Li et al. [6] which strictly enforces topological constraints. However, this closed-set formulation only allows to apply a particular ("ε-insensitive") smoothness prior, which is not well-suited for suppressing the high amount of noise encountered in coronary lumen segmentation. Post-smoothing of the segmentation results is thus suggested in [7].

For an optimal accuracy, all prior information should be considered by the segmentation approach and post-processing should not be required. We propose a method that addresses the above mentioned issues by (1) explicitly accounting for calcified-plaque, (2) enforcing a tubular structure, and (3) providing robust surface regularization suitable for coronary lumen segmentation by adopting a general Markov random field (MRF) [3] formulation to tubular segmentation.

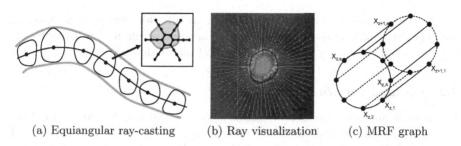

(a) Equiangular ray-casting   (b) Ray visualization   (c) MRF graph

Fig. 1. (a) Radial candidate positions along rays in cross-sectional slices orthogonal to the given centerline. (b) Associated boundary probabilities for rays within a slice. (c) Cylindrical element of a tubular MRF graph where each node represents the selection of a candidate position along a certain ray and edges implement smoothness priors.

2   Method

A set of centerlines (CTLs) approximately describing the curve of the coronary artery tree initializes the proposed surface extraction method. The lumen geometry is modeled on the basis of generalized cylinders with radially varying contours along the given centerline for each vessel segment. A discrete number of radial candidate positions along equiangular rays in orthogonal slices (Fig. 1a) are constructed and represented as random variables of a corresponding MRF graph (Fig. 1c). Using learning-based boundary detectors (Fig. 1b) and robust semi-convex regularization terms, this formulation allows for an optimal surface segmentation within polynomial time using well-known min-cut/max-flow solvers. We first describe the learning-based boundary detection model, followed by details on the MRF-based optimal surface generation.

2.1   Detection Model

The probability of a lumen wall is estimated in every cross-sectional slice for a vessel segment comprising Z slices using a fixed number of A equiangular rays with R equally-spaced (δ_r) radial candidate positions. While fixed terms based on image gradient and structural information could be used [6], we propose a learning-based probabilistic estimate based on steerable features. These are a collection of low-level image features sampled on a ray-oriented pattern [13]. Probabilistic boosting trees [11] are trained on manually segmented lumen contours by bootstrap aggregation and tested at every of the $Z \cdot A \cdot R$ candidate positions to estimate the probability $P_B(z, a, r)$ of lying on the lumen boundary. In order to improve the detection of boundaries from diseased lumen, the same amount of training samples were randomly selected from healthy and diseased (calcified or soft-plaque) lumen tissue. A calcium removal step, as proposed in [7], ensures the exclusion of calcified plaque from the segmented lumen by modifying the boundary probabilities. Essentially, every ray is analyzed for intersections with calcium and, if found, boundary probabilities are exponentially damped at these positions in outbound direction.

Since vessel segments were processed in parallel for performance reasons, enforcing matching contours at vessel furcation points would require a tree topology scheduled processing which has been omitted for simplicity.

2.2   Optimal Surface Generation

Finding the lumen surface is now cast as a combinatorial optimization problem: for every ray an optimal candidate position has to be selected. The trade-off between image-based likelihood (*w.r.t.* the boundary probabilities) and the prior assumption that the true lumen surface is smoothly varying, is best expressed with a first order Markov random field.

MRF Formulation. Let $G = (V, E)$ denote an undirected graph with a set of vertices V and undirected edges $E \subset V \times V$. Each vertex $v \in V$ is associated with a multivariate random variable $X_v = X_{z,a} = r$ where $r \in [1 \ldots R]$ describes its state while a and z denote the angular position and the slice of a certain ray. Edges are constructed according to the generalized cylinder model within and across contour slices as depicted in Fig. 1c. For computational efficiency, we propose to use a first order MRF energy formulation as in Ishikawa [3]

$$E(X) = \sum_{(u,v)\in E} \gamma_{uv} g(X_u - X_v) + \sum_{v \in V} h(v, X_v), \tag{1}$$

where $g(\cdot)$ is a convex function of the label difference of vertex u and v. The first sum represents the smoothness prior, whereas the second sum, the data term, incorporates the observations (*i.e.* the boundary likelihood). The constant edge weight factors γ_{uv} have been used to trade between intra-slice γ_a and inter-slice smoothness γ_z. Energy functions of this form can be minimized exactly within polynomial time by a *min-cut/max-flow* algorithm [3]. As convex priors that penalize label differences $d = X_u - X_v$ across edges, we considered

$$g(d) = \beta |d| \qquad \text{(L1-norm)} \tag{2}$$

$$g(d) = \beta \begin{cases} 0 & |d| \le \alpha \\ (|d| - \alpha) & |d| > \alpha \end{cases} \qquad (\epsilon\text{-insensitive for } \beta \gg 1) \tag{3}$$

$$g(d) = \beta \begin{cases} (d/\alpha)^2 & |d| \le \alpha \\ 2|d/\alpha| - 1 & |d| > \alpha \end{cases} \qquad \text{(Huber)} \tag{4}$$

with threshold and slope parameters α and β (see Fig. 4a). While any kind of convex function could be used, the above three are especially well suited due to their robust nature and computational advantages which will be discussed later.

Flow Graph Construction. As shown in [3], a transformation of the undirected graph G into a directed graph H (flow graph) results in an s-t min-cut problem which can be solved exactly by min-cut/max-flow algorithms. The flow graph $H = (V_H, E_H)$ is derived from G such that for any vertex $v \in V$, $R - 1$ vertices $V_{z,a,r} \in V_H$ are created. Two special vertices s, t mark the source and the sink of the flow graph summing up to $Z \cdot A \cdot (R - 1) + 2$ vertices in total. H consists of directed edges $(u, v) \in E_H$ (from vertex u to v) with positive capacity $c(u, v)$.

The graph is constructed in a way such that every s-t cut in H (a cut separating source and sink) corresponds to a configuration (variable assignment) $X \in \mathcal{X}$ of the MRF and the cost of the cut—sum of all edge capacities $c(u, v)$ in the cut—is the cost of this configuration according to (1). Note that, differing from [3], we omit a layer of superfluous vertices in our description (by merging data- and constraint-edges of the first of R layers which connects the source and $Z \cdot A$ vertices).

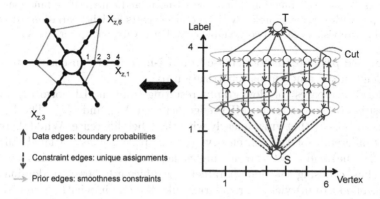

Fig. 2. Exemplary 2D flow graph for a single slice ($a = 6$ rays, $r = 4$ radial candidates) using the L1-norm prior (2). The cut represents an MRF configuration and, thus, uniquely describes a particular contour ($x_{z,1-3} = 2, x_{z,4-5} = 3, x_{z,6} = 4$). By analogy, a cut plane in the 3D flow graph defines a vessel surface geometry.

Potentials of the MRF are incorporated using three types of edges. *Data Edges* implement the observations $h(v, X_v)$ by sink-directed (vertical) edges with capacities equal to the negative log-likelihood of the boundary probabilities, while *Constraint Edges* impose a unique assignment by source-directed edges with infinite capacities. *Prior Edges* incorporate the prior terms $\gamma_{uv} g(X_u - X_v)$ of (1). Their capacities are second-order differences of the convex prior function (2)–(4) and are computed as

$$\text{cap}(d) = \frac{g(d + 1) - 2g(d) + g(d - 1)}{2}, \tag{5}$$

where $d = r_1 - r_2$ is the radial offset between vertices that represent the variables $X_{z,a_1} = r_1$ and $X_{z,a_2} = r_2$, i.e. the edge $(V_{z,a_1,r_1}, V_{z,a_2,r_1})$ in H (see Fig. 2 for an exemplary construction in 2D). Prior edges must be considered in two directions and potentially between all pairs of vertices in two neighboring columns. But since edges with capacity $\text{cap}(d) = 0$ can be omitted, prior terms with linear ranges result in fewer flow graph edges and, ultimately, in a faster min-cut/max-flow computation. The proposed prior functions (2)–(4) exhibit linear ranges (Fig. 4a) of varying extent. That means, the computational complexity of

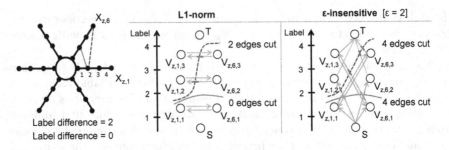

Fig. 3. Prior edges are only added for label differences with non-zero second-order differences of the prior function. Using the L1-norm and ε-insensitive functions yields flow graphs with varying complexity. The resulting costs for label variations (difference of 0 and 2) are visualized by two example cuts. For clarity, only prior edges are drawn.

the proposed priors tends to increase from L1-norm over ε-insensitive to Huber dependent on the function parametrization (α).

Figure 3 compares the flow graphs resulting from the L1-norm (2) and the ε-insensitive (3) priors for an MRF edge between $X_{z,6}$ and $X_{z,1}$. The L1-norm prior induces costs that grow linearly with the label difference. While there is no penalty difference for the ε-insensitive ($\epsilon = 2$) prior between a label difference of $d = 2$ (blue) and $d = 0$ (green), higher label differences would induce higher costs. Thus, choosing the slope parameter β sufficiently large (to dominate any data likelihood term) yields a regularizer like the one implicitly assumed by Li *et al.* [6]. The impact of that choice on the segmentation result is visualized in Fig. 4. While the L1-norm and Huber priors yield smooth, nearly circular contours, applying the ε-insensitive prior results in contours which are highly varying and more susceptible to noise (data-affine).

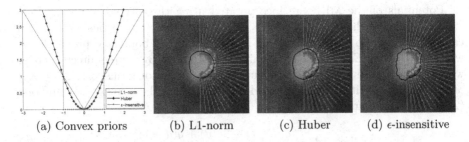

(a) Convex priors   (b) L1-norm   (c) Huber   (d) ε-insensitive

Fig. 4. (a) Different convex penalty functions can trade noise-robust (b) & (c) for data-affine (d) segmentations (right half colored with the boundary likelihood in blue-to-red) (Color figure online).

3   Experimental Results

The segmentation accuracy of the proposed method was tested using the publicly accessible standardized coronary artery evaluation framework which allows

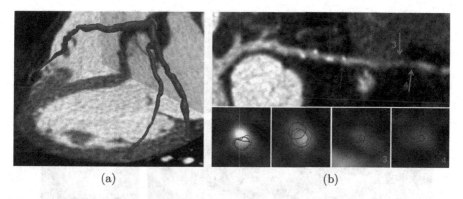

(a)   (b)

Fig. 5. (a) Surface visualization of the segmented left main coronaries with the LCX and LAD branch of the training dataset #10. (b) The upper part of the LAD is affected by mild mixed plaque while the lower end is narrowed by moderate soft-plaque (CPR, top). (b) Cross-sectional views with expert annotations in green, red and yellow along with our segmentation (blue) through mixed (1, 2) and soft plaque (3, 4). The proposed method effectively minimizes the variability within expert annotations (Color figure online).

for the comparison with current segmentation algorithms on 48 multi-protocol/-vendor CTA image volumes [4]. Annotations by three medical experts were provided on the main coronary vessels[1] for the first 18 training datasets which were used for training of the boundary detectors. The hyper-parameters were empirically chosen and in particular the Huber function parameters were a trade-off between graph-cut-induced computation time and accuracy *w.r.t.* an independent set of reference annotations: slice distance 0.3 mm, $A = 64$ rays with $R = 50$ candidates at $\delta_r = 0.1$ mm, Huber prior (4) with $\alpha = \beta = 1$ and $\gamma_a = 0.5$, $\gamma_z = 0.1$. The graph-cut solver was implemented in C++ as described in the original work [1]. We used CTLs obtained from the automatic tracking algorithm described by Zheng *et al.* [14].

Qualitative results are presented for pathological data from the training set in Fig. 5 and from the testing dataset in Fig. 6. Figure 5a shows a surface geometry view of the left coronaries using the proposed segmentation while Fig. 5b shows a curved planar reformation (CPR) of the—by mixed and soft plaque affected—LAD along with cross-sectional views through these lesions. The expert contours which were annotated from the same set of centerlines vary considerably while our contours (blue) rather minimizes the variability towards a consensus segmentation (as all annotations were used for training). In Fig. 6 segmented vessels of two patients with calcified and non-calcified plaques are shown. The lumen is smoothly segmented while calcified plaques are precisely circumscribed.

In Table 1, the maximum/mean surface distance (MAXSD/MSD) and the volumetric overlap (DICE) report the accuracies separately for healthy (H) and

---

[1] Left main (LM), left anterior descending (LAD), right coronary (RCA), left circumflex (LCX) artery.

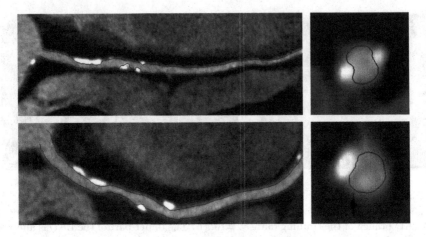

Fig. 6. Segmented lumen of calcified arteries for two patients as obtained by the proposed algorithm visualized from different projections (left: CPR, right: cross-section).

diseased (D) arteries averaged over the 30 testing/18 training datasets (hereafter we refer to testing results). The evaluation framework computes these measurements separately *w.r.t.* annotations of the three medical experts and averages them [4]. The proposed method achieves the best rank[2] compared to all other automatic methods and ranks higher than two of the three medical experts. Among the automatic methods it performs best (results marked bold) on diseased vessel segments for all error measures[3]. Since only the main vessels were compared with the reference, a mismatch between the labels of our applied CTL tracing and the reference causes a large error bias for datasets (20, 28, 30, 31, 32, 41, 47) (can partly be seen in Fig. 7) and deteriorates the MSD and MAXSD error measures in particular for the healthy vessels. Our training results are consistent (only slightly better) with those for testing which indicates that no over-fitting occurred.

While manual segmentation requires substantial expertise and time and is prone to high inter- and intra-user variability, our automatic method yields a robust segmentation in under a minute per patient. The box-and-whiskers plots in Fig. 7 show that our method performs equally well or even better than the best medical expert on most datasets. Apparently, the consensus learned from the annotations of the three experts yields superior performance when compared on the testing data. Our method effectively averages individual annotation biases during training and, thus, avoids the considerable inter-user variability seen in the expert annotations.

---

[2] Rank denotes the performance in comparison to all other participants where a rank of 1.0 means that this method yields the best measures for all subjects and vessels.

[3] Latest results can be found at: http://coronary.bigr.nl/stenoses/results/results.php.

Table 1. Three error measures are reported separately for diseased (D) and healthy (H) vessels (boldface marks best among automatic methods). Rank lists the overall segmentation ranking compared to all participating methods (*w.r.t.* testing results). Measures are averaged over 30 testing (18 training) datasets (listed testing/training).

Method	Rank avg. ⇓	DICE D [%]	DICE H [%]	MSD D [mm]	MSD H [mm]	MAXSD D [mm]	MAXSD H [mm]
Expert3	3.5/4.5	79/76	81/80	.23/.24	.21/.23	3.00/3.07	3.45/3.25
Proposed	3.8/4.0	**76/75**	**75/77**	**.32/.27**	.51/.32	**2.47/1.96**	3.67/2.79
Expert1	4.4/5.4	76/74	77/79	.24/.26	.24/.26	2.87/3.29	3.47/3.61
Lugauer [7]	4.5/5.2	74/72	73/74	.35/.28	.55/.35	2.99/2.02	3.73/2.88
Mohr [9]	4.5/5.6	70/73	73/75	.40/.29	**.39/.45**	2.68/1.87	**2.75/3.73**
Expert2	6.1/7.3	65/66	72/73	.34/.31	.27/.25	2.82/2.70	3.26/3.00
Shahzad [10]	6.4/7.9	65/66	68/70	.39/.37	.41/.32	2.73/2.49	3.20/3.04
Wang [12]	6.9/9.0	69/68	69/72	.45/.43	.55/.56	3.94/4.06	6.48/5.23

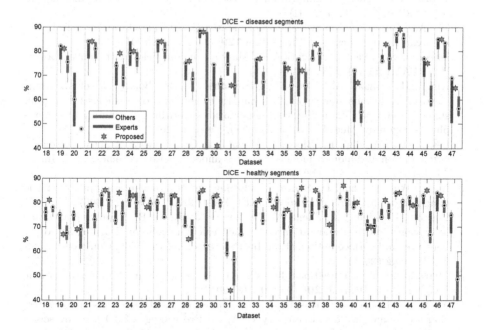

Fig. 7. Inter-user variability boxplots between the three medical experts and the four best-ranking methods (others) in comparison to our results (star) *w.r.t.* DICE measure for each subject of the testing data. Circles indicate medians, the box edges the 25th and 75th percentiles and whiskers extend to outliers. Note, very low and missing results are mostly due to label differences between the reference and the CTL tracking method.

4   Conclusion

A novel method for segmenting the lumen of the coronary arteries in computed tomography angiography has been proposed. While enforcing a tubular structure of the segmentation, the approach allows for a flexible choice of robust smoothness priors. Combined with a learning-based boundary detection, excellent performance is achieved on public challenge data [4]. Our analysis shows that the automatic segmentation results are as accurate as those from medical experts. While the proposed method is evaluated for coronary vessels only, it is readily applicable to other tubular structures. An extension to evolving arbitrary surfaces under local smoothness constraints is easily possible. The precise segmentation of our new approach will improve automatic stenosis detection and enable an improved non-invasive simulation of coronary blood flow, which is left to be evaluated in future work.

References

1. Boykov, Y., Kolmogorov, V.: An experimental comparison of min-cut/max-flow algorithms for energy minimization in vision. IEEE Trans. Pattern Anal. Mach. Intell. **26**(9), 1124–1137 (2004)
2. Go, A., et al.: Heart disease and stroke statistics-2014 update a report from the american heart association. Circulation **129**(3), e28–e292 (2014)
3. Ishikawa, H.: Exact optimization for Markov random fields with convex priors. IEEE PAMI **25**(10), 1333–1336 (2003)
4. Kirişli, H., Schaap, M., Metz, C., Dharampal, A., Meijboom, W., et al.: Standardized evaluation framework for evaluating coronary artery stenosis detection, stenosis quantification and lumen segmentation algorithms in computed tomography angiography. Med. Image Anal. **17**(8), 859–876 (2013)
5. Lesage, D., Angelini, E., Bloch, I., Funka-Lea, G.: A review of 3D vessel lumen segmentation techniques: models, features and extraction schemes. Med. Image Anal. **13**(6), 819–845 (2009)
6. Li, K., Wu, X., Chen, D., Sonka, L.: Optimal surface segmentation in volumetric images-a graph-theoretic approach. IEEE PAMI **28**(1), 119–134 (2006)
7. Lugauer, F., Zhang, J., Zheng, Y., Hornegger, J., Kelm, B.: Improving accuracy in coronary lumen segmentation via explicit calcium exclusion, learning-based ray detection and surface optimization. In: Proceedings of the SPIE Conference Medical Imaging (2014)
8. Meijs, M., et al.: CT fractional flow reserve: the next level in non-invasive cardiac imaging. Neth. Heart J. **20**(10), 410–418 (2012)
9. Mohr, B., Masood, S., Plakas, C.: Accurate lumen segmentation and stenosis detection and quantification in coronary CTA. In: Proceedings of 3D Cardiovascular Imaging: A MICCAI Segmentation Challenge Workshop (2012)
10. Shahzad, R., Kirişli, H., Metz, C., Tang, H., Schaap, M., van Vliet, L., Niessen, W., van Walsum, T.: Automatic segmentation, detection and quantification of coronary artery stenoses on CTA. Int. J. Cardiovasc. Imaging **29**(8), 1847–1859 (2013)
11. Tu, Z.: Probabilistic boosting-tree: learning discriminative models for classification, recognition, and clustering. In: Tenth IEEE International Conference on Computer Vision, ICCV'05, vol. 2, pp. 1589–1596. IEEE (2005)

12. Wang, C., Moreno, R., Smedby, Ö.: Vessel segmentation using implicit model-guided level sets. In: Proceedings of 3D Cardiovascular Imaging: A MICCAI Segmentation Challenge Workshop (2012)
13. Zheng, Y., Barbu, A., Georgescu, B., Scheuering, M., Comaniciu, D.: Four-chamber heart modeling and automatic segmentation for 3-D cardiac CT volumes using marginal space learning and steerable features. IEEE Trans. Med. Imaging **27**(11), 1668–1681 (2008)
14. Zheng, Y., Tek, H., Funka-Lea, G.: Robust and accurate coronary artery centerline extraction in CTA by combining model-driven and data-driven approaches. In: Mori, K., Sakuma, I., Sato, Y., Barillot, C., Navab, N. (eds.) MICCAI 2013, Part III. LNCS, vol. 8151, pp. 74–81. Springer, Heidelberg (2013)

Confidence-Based Training for Clinical Data Uncertainty in Image-Based Prediction of Cardiac Ablation Targets

Rocío Cabrera-Lozoya[1]([✉]), Jan Margeta[1], Loïc Le Folgoc[1], Yuki Komatsu[2], Benjamin Berte[2], Jatin Relan[2], Hubert Cochet[2], Michel Haïssaguerre[2], Pierre Jaïs[2], Nicholas Ayache[1], and Maxime Sermesant[1]

[1] Inria, Asclepios Team, Sophia Antipolis, France
rocio.cabrera_lozoya@inria.fr
[2] Hôpital Cardiologique du Haut-Lévêque, Institut LYRIC, l'Université Victor Segalen Bordeaux II, Bordeaux, France

Abstract. Ventricular radio-frequency ablation (RFA) can have a critical impact on preventing sudden cardiac arrest but is challenging due to a highly complex arrhythmogenic substrate. This work aims to identify local image characteristics capable of predicting the presence of local abnormal ventricular activities (LAVA). This can allow, pre-operatively and non-invasively, to improve and accelerate the procedure. To achieve this, intensity and texture-based local image features are computed and random forests are used for classification. However using machine-learning approaches on such complex multimodal data can prove difficult due to the inherent errors in the training set. In this manuscript we present a detailed analysis of these error sources due in particular to catheter motion and the data fusion process. We derived a principled analysis of confidence impact on classification. Moreover, we demonstrate how formal integration of these uncertainties in the training process improves the algorithm's performance, opening up possibilities for non-invasive image-based prediction of RFA targets.

1 Introduction

Sudden cardiac arrest (SCA) is a leading cause of death in the world, with 350,000 deaths per year in the USA, and similarly in Europe. Its main cause is cardiac arrhythmia with RFA increasingly being used to treat it but with an unsatisfying success rate due to the difficulty to find the ablation targets. There is therefore a need to identify the arrhythmia substrates and the optimal ablation strategy to substantially improve its success rate.

Most arrhythmias occur on structurally diseased hearts with fibrotic scar, where bundles of surviving tissue promote electrical circuit re-entry. These can be identified using electrophysiological (EP) mapping, a lengthy and invasive method that records cardiac electrical signals through intra-cardiac catheters. LAVA, sharp fractionated bipolar potentials occurring during or after the far-field electrogram, indicate surviving fibres within the scar and have been successfully used as targets for RFA [3].

© Springer International Publishing Switzerland 2014
B. Menze et al. (Eds.): MCV 2014, LNCS 8848, pp. 148–159, 2014.
DOI: 10.1007/978-3-319-13972-2_14

Late-enhancement magnetic resonance imaging (LE-MRI) enables a non-invasive 3D assessment of scar topology and heterogeneity with millimetric spatial resolution. It has been hypothesised that areas of intermediate signal intensity in LE-MRI, referred to as the grey zone, are likely to host both scarred and surviving myocardium related to arrhythmia in ischemic populations [3]. However, consistent EP correlations are still missing. The ability to relate imaging features to LAVA might have direct clinical applications to pre-emptively define mapping and ablation targets, to increase the success rate and to decrease the duration of such procedures (currently>6h). In this manuscript, we evaluated the predictive power of locally computed intensity and texture-based MRI features to identify RFA targets. On the methodological side, we used random forests with advanced image features and classifier parameter estimation using nested cross-validation. However, using machine-learning approaches on such complex multimodal data can prove difficult due to the inherent errors in the training set. We present a detailed analysis of these error sources, due in particular to catheter motion and the data fusion process, their formal integration in the training process, which is rarely done in machine learning approaches, and demonstrate an improved algorithm performance.

2   Clinical Data

Three patients referred for cardiac ablation for post-infarction in ventricular tachycardia were included in this study. They underwent cardiac MRI prior to high-density EP contact mapping of the endocardium (Patients 1 and 2) and epicardium (Patient 3).

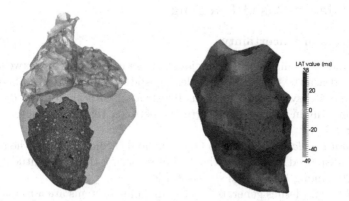

Fig. 1. [left] Anatomical model and EAPs (blue: healthy, red: LAVA) in scar regions (black). [right] CARTO reconstruction of the endocardial cavity, with activation times (Color figure online).

Electrophysiological Data: The CARTO mapping system (Biosense Webster) enables the 3D localization of the catheter tip and provides the distribution of EP signals on cardiac surfaces. Contact mapping was achieved in sinus rhythm on the endocardium (trans-septal approach) and the epicardium (sub-xiphoid approach) with a multi-spline catheter (PentaRay, Biosense Webster). Signals were categorised as normal or LAVA by an experienced electrophysiologist. Table 1 summarizes the characteristics of the electrophysiological datasets for each of the patients in this study.

Table 1. Patient electrophysiological dataset characteristics.

	No. points	Map source	No. healthy	No. lava
Patient 1	91	endocardium	54	37
Patient 2	83	endocardium	50	33
Patient 3	124	epicardium	113	11

Imaging Data: Scar was imaged on a 1.5 T clinical device (Avanto, Siemens Medical Systems) 15 min after the injection of a gadolinium contrast agent. A whole heart image was acquired using an inversion-recovery prepared, ECG-gated, respiratory-navigated, 3D gradient-echo pulse sequence with fat-saturation $(1.25 \times 1.25 \times 2.5\,\mathrm{mm}^3)$. The myocardium was manually segmented on reformatted images of isotropic voxel size $(0.625\,\mathrm{mm}^3)$. Abnormal myocardium (dense scar and grey zone areas) was segmented using adaptive thresholding of the histogram, with a cut-off at 35 % of maximal signal intensity. Segmentations were reviewed by an experienced radiologist, with the option of manual correction.

3   Confidence-Based Learning

3.1   Sources of Uncertainty

We aim to identify differences in regional image characteristics between LAVA inducing and healthy tissue. Nevertheless, despite the integrated catheter localisation in the EP system and previous registration with anatomical data, there remains three main sources of uncertainty between the EP measurements and the imaging data.

Temporal Displacement. Due to breathing and cardiac motions, the recording catheter is displaced throughout the 2.5 s of recording time. Magnitudes varying significantly among EAPs as is shown in Fig. 2.

Data Fusion. Meshes generated by EP mapping systems are a rough approximation of the shape of the ventricular cavity, as seen in Figs. 1 and 2. Therefore, a registration is needed between the EP recording locations and the image segmentation. This is done manually by using landmarks and matching between low voltage areas and scars. Then the EAPs are projected on the image-based mesh by finding the closest cell, and an evaluation of the registration uncertainty is present in the resulting projection distance (PD).

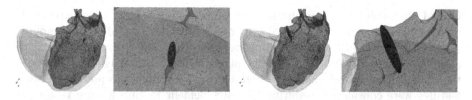

Fig. 2. Location of two EAPs and temporal position variation described by a red ellipsoid (left: low displacement, right: high displacement) (Color figure online).

Sensing Range. The volume of tissue that influences the recording at a particular EAP (catheter's sensing range) is represented by a sphere of 10 mm radius (Fig. 3).

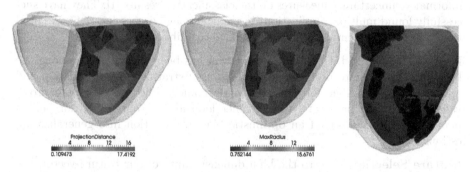

Fig. 3. Posterior endocardial maps for uncertainty attributes [mm] (left: projection distance, centre: major ellipsoid axes). Right: spherical representation of the catheter's hearing range (blue) for a given location. Scar regions are shown in black (Color figure online).

3.2 Image Feature Computation

These properties allow us to define the scale at which the image features will be looked at and how to quantify the errors.

Intensity-based Features: Voxels contained inside the sensing range were used to compute intensity-based features, including minimal, maximal, mean and standard deviation values. Another feature, defined as the standard deviation over the average intensity in the region was included. Myocardium thickness was calculated and the scar transmurality was defined as the extent of scar through the entire myocardium thickness.

Texture-based Features: Grey level co-occurence matrices (GLCM) are matrices of the joint probability of occurrence of a pair of grey values separated by a displacement $d = (dx, dy, dz)$. Haralick features are statistics computed on

GLCM that emphasize specific texture properties and have been extensively used in medical image analysis [7]. In our study, the GLCM were computed around the center of the myocardium were the EAP had been projected using a ROI of window size of $11 \times 11 \times 11$ pixels ($\sim 9.4 \times 9.4 \times 9.4$ mm). Three distances from the central pixel (1, 2 and 4 pixels), 13 directions and 12 Haralick features were considered, resulting in a 468 element texture feature vector per EAP analyzed. Concatenation of the seven intensity and the texture features yielded a final image-based feature vector of 475 dimensions which was used for classification.

3.3   Classification Framework

Random Forests Classifier: Random forests are discriminative classifiers created in an intuitive and easily understandable structure that also provide informative uncertainty measures on the classification results [1]. They have successfully found multiple applications in medical image processing [1,6]. We used the Python implementation from the scikit-learn library [8].

Nested Cross-validation: Cross-validation has been shown to be among the best ways to estimate performance [4]. We used stratified cross-validation and optimized the classifier for precision performance. The use of nested cross-validation, with a parameter-tuning inner loop and an outer loop for performance estimation, avoided an optimistic bias introduction into generalization estimate [9].

Feature Selection: Due to the high dimensionality of our feature vector, the effect of feature space reduction was next assessed. Univariate t-Test statistics were used to assess feature significance [2]. Three reduced datasets were created, including the 50 %, 25 % and the 10 most relevant features (MRF). Additionally, a feature subset was generated containing only the intensity-based features.

Uncertainty Assessment: We derived a principled analysis of confidence impact on classification. Inspired by cost-sensitive learning, we formulate the problem as samples (x, y, c) drawn from a distribution D on a domain $X \times Y \times C$ with X being the input feature space, Y corresponding to the binary output class and C to the confidence associated with each sample. We aim to learn a classifier $h : X \to Y$ which minimizes the new expected classification error:

$$E(x, y, c \sim D)[cI(h(x) \neq y)] \tag{1}$$

Using the Translation Theorem 2.1 in [10] we can compute and draw samples from a distribution D' such that the optimal error rate classifiers for D' are optimal cost minimizers for data drawn from D. We derive how this modifies the training using weights to simulate the expectation of finite data $E(x, y \sim D)[f(x, y)]$ as:

$$E(x, y \sim D)[f(x, y)] = \frac{1}{\sum c} \sum c f(x, y) \tag{2}$$

equivalent to importance sampling for D' using distribution D, so the modified expectation is an unbiased Monte Carlo estimate of the expectation with respect to D' [10]. In random forests, the node split criterion is information gain:

$$IG = H(S) - \sum_{i=1,2} \frac{|S^i|}{|S|} H(S^i) \tag{3}$$

with $|S|$ being the number of samples in a node before split, $|S^i|$ being the number of samples of each children node and $H(S)$ the Shannon entropy:

$$H(S) = - \sum_{c \in C} p(c) log(p(c)) \tag{4}$$

where p(c) is calculated as normalized empirical histogram of labels corresponding to the training points in S, $p(c) = \frac{|S^i|}{|S|}$. Using weighted instances, $p(c)$ is replaced by $p_w(c)$, which has the following formulation:

$$p_w^i(c) = \frac{\sum \text{Weights of samples of class c in node i}}{\sum \text{Weights of samples in node i}} = \frac{\sum_{S_c} W^i}{\sum_S W^i} \tag{5}$$

This yields a sample weighted formulation of the information gain that can be written as:

$$IG = H(W) - \sum_{i=1,2} \frac{\sum_S W^i}{\sum_S W} H(W^i) \tag{6}$$

where W are sample weights at the parent node and W^i are sample weights that have been passed to each child node. $H(W)$ is given by:

$$H(W) = - \sum_{c \in C} p_w(c) log(p_w(c)) \tag{7}$$

To our knowledge, it is the first time such formulation is derived in this context and we believe it strengthens our approach's methodological ground.

We analysed the influence of two factors affecting the certainty in EAPs and imaging data correspondences by weighting our training samples according to the confidence we have on their image features.

Projection Distance. More confidence is assigned to the imaging features computed from EAPs with low PD with respect to those with high values. It is defined as the Euclidean distance between the EAP and the center of the cell in the mesh closest to the given point:

$$PD = \|CellCenter - EAP\| \tag{8}$$

Temporal Displacement. The covariance of the position matrix is obtained and an ellipsoid with radii $2\sqrt{diag(D)}$ is generated, where D is the matrix containing the eigenvalues along the main diagonal. The major ellipsoid radius defines the temporal displacement, as following:

$$TD = max(2\sqrt{diag(D)}) \tag{9}$$

Intuitively, image features from EAPs with smaller major ellipsoid radius are more reliable as they are less affected by movement.

Each EAP is assigned a confidence value by linearly scaling either the PD or the temporal displacement to a weight parameter with range of [0.5, 1] where 0.5 corresponds to the lowest confidence and 1 to the highest. Additionally, a *combined uncertainty* weight is defined as the product of both uncertainty sources. We explore the uncertainty inherently introduced to our dataset due to these factors with three extra experiments by using the previously described sample weighting schemes.

Evaluation Metrics: The results for the classification results will be assessed using precision-recall (PR) and receiver operating characteristic (ROC) curves. A PR curve illustrates the trade-off between the proportion of positively labelled examples that are truly positive (precision) as a function of the proportion of correctly classified positives (recall). A good performance line lies in the upper-right portion of the graph and has a high area under the curve (AUC) value.

A ROC curve depicts relative trade-offs between benefits (true positives) and costs (false positives). Any deviation from the diagonal (representing random guess and with 0.5 AUC) into the plot's upper triangle represents a better performance than chance. Classifiers with higher ROC AUC values are said to have a better average performance.

4   Results and Discussion

The results of classification using the full feature set for each patient are shown in Fig. 4 and their mean AUC values are summarized in Table 2. The AUC PR ranges from 0.75 in Patient 3 to 0.88 in Patient 2. For the AUC ROC metric, values range from 0.80 in Patient 1 to 0.92 in Patient 3. We can therefore argue that an overall good performance was achieved throughout the patients.

By closely looking at the PR curves, we can conclude that the classifier is able to retrieve approximately more than half of the LAVA instances without having a considerable drop in the precision. It is when the totality of the LAVA instances are recovered that precision is compromised. This might correspond to areas in which the LAVA regions are spatially close to healthy ones, therefore finer descriptors of the adjacent areas should be explored. Nonetheless, for our approach some precision can be compromised as the ablation procedure might not be able to distinguish between closely spaced cardiac regions. Plots for Patient 3 show that it presents great variability between folds. Some have perfect scores, probably representing the typical LAVA image signatures, while others perform poorly, possibly due to outlier LAVA present in the testing phase. This can also be due to the patient having an epicardial study compared to the endocardial mapping of Patients 1 and 2.

Results Using Subsets of MRF: The classification results obtained using only 50 %, 25 % and the top 10 MRF in each dataset are summarized in Table 2.

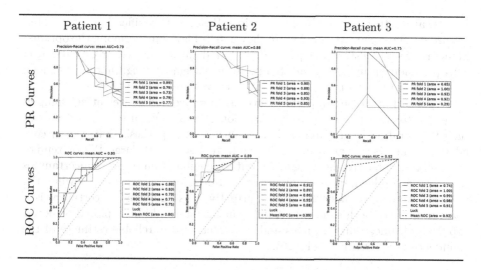

Fig. 4. Precision-recall and ROC curves for patients 1–3 after nested cross-validation with precision optimisation. Line colors represent each fold (curves with AUC = 1 are aligned with axes) and the dotted line represents the average curve for all folds (Color figure online).

Table 2. Area under the curves for Precision-Recall and ROC.

	PR AUC			ROC AUC		
	Patient 1	Patient 2	Patient 3	Patient 1	Patient 2	Patient 3
Full Features	0.79	0.88	0.75	0.80	0.89	0.92
50% MRF	0.72	0.86	0.72	0.76	0.86	0.91
25% MRF	0.73	0.91	0.81	0.73	0.91	0.91
10 MRF	0.69	0.80	0.66	0.73	0.81	0.88
Intensity Features	0.78	0.75	0.31	0.73	0.78	0.63

The purpose of this task was to investigate the redundancy in the feature set. In general, the use of 50 % of MRF resulted only in a small drop in AUC PR and AUC ROC scores, suggesting some feature redundancy. Nonetheless, while Patient 2 and 3 had a slight increase in performance when using its 25 % MRF, all patients suffered a considerable drop in score when using 10 MRF. Due to the characteristics of our current feature selection scheme (univariate filtering method), it failed to assess groups of features that work together to better discriminate between classes.

The results for the assessment of intensity feature importance w.r.t. the full set of features are included in Table 2. Using only intensity features for classification led to a large drop in overall classification performance. This shows that advanced texture patterns are required to describe the complex intertwining of myocardial fibres in scarred and grey zone areas responsible of LAVA generation.

Uncertainty Impact on the Prediction: Results of classification with the full feature set and weighted samples are shown in Table 3. Furthermore, the optional random forests construction parameters found during nested cross validation with precision optimization and temporal displacement weighting are included in Table 4 and the resulting PR and ROC curves are shown in Fig. 6.

A general increase in performance is observed when weighting samples according to their proximity to the location of image feature computation and their temporal position stability. This confirms our hypothesis that a lower confidence should be assigned during training to EAPs with large PD or temporal displacements. Weighting samples with a combination of both uncertainties results in a similar improvement in the classification performance as when the elements were used independently. Currently, this combined uncertainty is a naive product of both elements. A different fusion should be explored to better exploit both uncertainty sources and construct a more reliable estimate of the confidence of a given EAP (Fig. 5).

Table 3. Classification performance scores using sample uncertainty weights.

Confidence-based training						
Area under the curves	Patient 1		Patient 2		Patient 3	
	PR	ROC	PR	ROC	PR	ROC
No confidence weighting	0.79	0.80	0.88	0.89	0.75	0.92
Projection distance weighting	0.85	0.85	0.94	0.94	0.96	0.99
Temporal displacement weighting	0.86	0.87	0.95	0.95	0.95	0.99
Combined uncertainty weighting	0.84	0.87	0.94	0.94	0.94	0.99

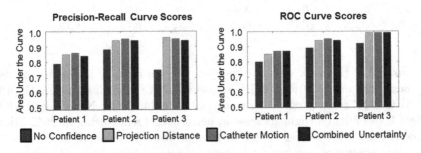

Fig. 5. Bar plots for classification performance scores using sample uncertainty weights

A visual interpretation of the results obtained using temporal displacement weighting and their comparison to ground truth are shown in Fig. 7. The central image is a preliminary output to be used in a clinical environment. The endocardial map shows regions classified as being in risk of presenting LAVA and that should be ablation targets. The rightmost image shows that prediction errors are primarily present in regions with low classification confidence.

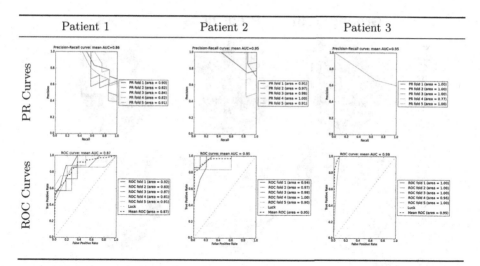

Fig. 6. Precision-recall and ROC curves for patients 1–3 after nested cross-validation with precision optimisation and temporal displacement weighting. Line colors represent each fold (curves with AUC = 1 are aligned with axes) and the dotted line represents the average curve for all folds (Color figure online).

Table 4. Random forests construction parameters when performing nested cross validation with precision optimization and temporal displacement weighting.

Random forest construction parameters					
	PR score	No. trees	No. features	Split criteria	No. inner folds
Patient 1	0.86	25	60	entropy	5
Patient 2	0.95	25	60	entropy	5
Patient 3	0.95	10	20	gini	5

5 Conclusions

We presented the use of intensity and texture-based local imaging features in the vicinity of myocardial scar and grey zones towards the prediction of RFA target localisation. Additionally, we detailed the uncertainty in the data and explored its impact on the classification results. For both PR AUC and ROC AUC, we scored above 0.75 and an extra 0.05 was gained when using uncertainty evaluation to weight the training data. Finally, a preliminary output with visual interpretation and potential use in a clinical environment was presented.

The aim of the current work was to analyse the feasibility of classification using solely image-based features on complex multi-modal data. So far, the choice of features produced encouraging results but a further refinement and exploration of different texture filters is considered for the following stages of the project to better describe the underlying tissue inhomogeneity. In the feature selection

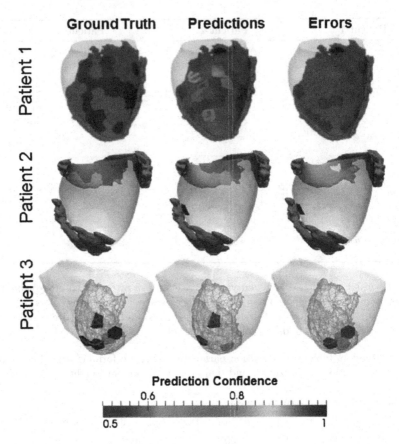

Fig. 7. [left] LAVA regions from ground truth. [center] LAVA regions from predictions. [right] Prediction errors. (Color coding by classification confidence) (Color figure online)

stage, the use of wrapper methods should be explored to evaluate the impact in the classification performance of feature subsets rather than individual features [5]. Future work also includes the improvement of the weighting scheme to better exploit uncertainties on catheter position and motion.

We are aware that an increase in the size of the patient database is required in order to aim for inter-patient analysis, but this work serves as a proof of concept with results good and encouraging enough to warrant further investigation and open up possibilities for non-invasive cardiac arrhythmia ablation planning.

Acknowledgments. Part of this work was funded by the European Research Council through the ERC Advanced Grant MedYMA 2011-291080 (on Biophysical Modeling and Analysis of Dynamic Medical Images).

References

1. Criminisi, A., Shotton, J., Konukoglu, E.: Decision Forests for Classification, Regression, Density Estimation, Manifold Learning and Semi-Supervised Learning, MSR-TR-2011-114 (2011)
2. Guyon, I., Elisseeff, A.: An introduction to variable and feature selection. J. Mach. Learn. Res. **3**, 1157–1182 (2003)
3. Jais, P., Maury, P., Khairy, P., Sacher, F., Nault, I., Komatsu, Y., Hocini, M., Forclaz, A., Jadidi, A.S., Weerasooryia, R., Shah, A., Derval, N., Cochet, H., Knecht, S., Miyazaki, S., Linton, N., Rivard, L., Wright, M., Wilton, S.B., Scherr, D., Pascale, P., Roten, L., Pederson, M., Bordachar, P., Laurent, F., Kim, S.J., Ritter, P., Clementy, J., Haissaguerre, M.: Elimination of local abnormal ventricular activities: a new end point for substrate modification in patients with scar-related ventricular tachycardia. Circulation **125**(18), 2184–2196 (2012)
4. Kohavi, R.: A study of cross-validation and bootstrap for accuracy estimation and model selection. In: Proceedings of the 14th International Joint Conference on Artificial Intelligence (IJCAI), pp. 1137–1143 (1995)
5. Kohavi, R., John, G.: Wrappers for feature subset selection. In: Artificial Intelligence, pp. 273–324 (1997)
6. Lempitsky, V., Verhoek, M., Noble, J.A., Blake, A.: Random forest classification for automatic delineation of myocardium in real-time 3D echocardiography. In: Ayache, N., Delingette, H., Sermesant, M. (eds.) FIMH 2009. LNCS, vol. 5528, pp. 447–456. Springer, Heidelberg (2009)
7. Ludvik, T., Smutek, D., Shimizu, A., Kobatake, H.: 3D extension of haralick texture features for medical image analysis. In: Proceedings of the Fourth IASTED International Conference on Signal Processing, Pattern Recognition, and Applications SPPRA, pp. 350–355 (2007)
8. Pedregosa, F., Varoquaux, G., Gramfort, A., Michel, V., Thirion, B., Grisel, O., Blondel, M., Prettenhofer, P., Weiss, R., Dubourg, V., Vanderplas, J., Passos, A., Cournapeau, D., Brucher, M., Perrot, M., Duchesnay, E.: Scikit-learn: machine learning in Python. J. Mach. Learn. Res. **12**, 2825–2830 (2011)
9. Ruschhaupt, M., Huber, W., Poustka, A., Mansmann, U.: A compendium to ensure computational reproducibility in high-dimensional classification tasks. Stat. Appl. Genet. Mol. Biol. **3**, Article 37 (2004)
10. Zadrozny, B., et al.: Cost-sensitive learning by cost-proportionate example weighting. In: Proceedings of the 3rd IEEE Conference on Data Mining, pp. 435–442 (2003)

VISCERAL Session

Rule-Based Ventral Cavity Multi-organ Automatic Segmentation in CT Scans

Assaf B. Spanier[✉] and Leo Joskowicz

The Rachel and Selim Benin School of Computer Science and Engineering,
The Hebrew University of Jerusalem, Jerusalem, Israel
{assaf.spanier,leo.josko}@mail.huji.ac.il
http://www.cs.huji.ac.il/~caslab/site/

Abstract. We describe a new method for the automatic segmentation of multiple organs of the ventral cavity in CT scans. The method is based on a set of rules that determine the order in which the organs are isolated and segmented. First, the air-containing organs are segmented: the trachea and the lungs. Then, the organs with high blood content: the spleen, the kidneys and the liver, are segmented. Each organ is individually segmented with a generic four-step pipeline procedure. Our method is unique in that it uses the same generic segmentation approach for all organs and in that it relies on the segmentation difficulty of organs to guide the segmentation process. Experimental results on 20 CT scans of the VISCERAL Anatomy2 Challenge training datasets yield an average Dice volume overlap similarity score of 90.95. For the 10 CT scans test datasets, the average Dice scores is 88.5.

1 Introduction

The increasing amount of medical imaging data acquired in clinical practice constitutes a vast database of untapped diagnostically relevant information. To date, only a small fraction of this information is used during clinical routine for research due to the complexity, richness, high dimensionality, and data size [1].

Content-based image retrieval (CBIR) techniques have been proposed to access this information and to identify similar cases to assist radiologists in the clinical decision support process [2]. The segmentation of individual ventral cavity organs in CT scans is expected to improve the diagnostic accuracy and performance of CBIR systems. While the manual delineation of these organs is considered the gold standard, this is a tedious and very time-consuming process which is impractical for all but a few dozen datasets for research. Consequently, a plethora of methods for automatic segmentation of ventral body cavity organs in CT scans have been proposed. Liver segmentation methods are thoroughly summarized and reviewed by Mharib et al. [4]. Lungs segmentation from CT scans has been addressed by Sluimer et al. [5]. Kidney segmentation methods are described in Freiman et al. [6]. While very different from each other, all these methods target a single type of organ and do not use information about other organs' segmentations. Thus, multi-organ segmentation requires a specific

© Springer International Publishing Switzerland 2014
B. Menze et al. (Eds.): MCV 2014, LNCS 8848, pp. 163–170, 2014.
DOI: 10.1007/978-3-319-13972-2_15

method for each organ, which yields variable quality results and quickly becomes unmanageable as the number of organs to be segmented grows. It is thus desirable to develop a single, generic approach that can be customized for each organ and that shares information between organs.

The rule-based approach to medical image segmentation calls for using each organ's anatomical context and prior knowledge about its location and extension for enhancing, improving, and automating the segmentation process. This is a pipeline-oriented approach, the organs of interest are successively extracted from the CT scan. Previous research has focused mainly on liver segmentation [3]. In this paper, we extend and generalize the rule-based approach to the automatic segmentation of multiple ventral cavity organs in CT scans.

2   Method

Our approach extends the rule-based technique by providing a unified, generic four-step method that is customized for each organ and incorporates information about other organs' prior segmentation. In our method, simple and "context-free" organs are segmented first, followed by more complex and context-based identification and delineation.

We describe below the steps of the general framework, followed by the detailed implementation of seven ventral cavity organs: the trachea, the left and right lungs, the left and right kidneys, the spleen, and the liver.

2.1   Generic Organ Segmentation Framework

The segmentation of each organ is performed in four successive steps:

1. ROI Identification - The region of interest (ROI) is extracted and constitutes a coarse initial segmentation. This step is organ dependent, and is based on the location of the organ in the ventral cavity.
2. Thresholding - After ROI identification, we threshold the CT image to fine tune the coarse segmentation of the organ based on its unique gray level characteristics. Naturally, the thresholding value is organ specific.
3. 2D Seed Identification - A representative 2D axial slice of the organ in the CT scan is identified. The segmentation result of step two is confined to this slice then used as a 2D seed for region growing segmentation.
4. Slice Region Growing - The final organ segmentation by 3D region growing starting from the 2D-seed and clustering classification algorithms are used to obtain the final segmentation of the organ.

2.2   Detailed Implementation

We start with a preprocessing step to isolate the patient's body from the background (air and scan gantry) based on location and intensity values. The generic four-step framework is then applied to the ventral body cavity organs in the following order. First, the breathing system organs are segmented: the trachea and the lungs. Next, the organs with high blood content are segmented: the kidneys, the spleen, and the liver. This organ segmentation order prevents ambiguous assignment of the same image region to multiple organs, as previously segmented image regions are excluded from the segmentation process. We describe each step in detail next:

Step 1: ROI Identification. A coarse initial segmentation of the organ is obtained.

Lungs and Trachea: The breathing system organ's ROI relies on the fact that these organs mostly contain air represented by low HU value (bellow $-300HU$). Therefore, the ROI is constitutes of the consecutive axial slices (starting from the top of the scan) which contain gray-levels of $-300HU$ and below. Figure 1a shows a representative example of the breathing system's ROI.

Kidney, liver and spleen: We focus on the axial slices between the widest and narrowest bones skeleton perimeters Fig. 2a. For each slice define first a line that passes through the center of the spinal column at $45°$. Then we define two ROIs as follows: The left kidney and the spleen ROIs are the regions in the left hand side of the line. Figure 2b. The liver and the right Kidney ROIs are the regions in the right hand side of the line. Figure 2c. To eliminate penetration of ROIs to the rib cage region, we exclude the rib cage from the ROIs by simple thresholding with the value of $1000HU$ and above.

Step 2: Thresholding. We threshold the CT image to refine the coarse segmentation obtained by the ROI.

Lungs and Trachea: After the slices that contain the air organs are identified by the ROI, a threshold is applied to include all voxels with values of $-500HU$ and below, then the largest connected component is selected. This results two regions that consist of course segmentation of the lungs and trachea. Figure 1b illustrates this step.

Kidney, Liver and Spleen: First we estimate the ROI of the heart, that is defined by the enclosure region between the two lungs. We then use this ROI's gray level mean, μ_{heart}, and standard deviation, σ_{heart}, to define the threshold for the kidneys, the liver and the spleen. For the kidneys, we threshold the image by including only the voxels in the range $[\mu_{heart}, \mu_{heart} + \sigma_{heart}]$ and for the liver and spleen we include only the voxels in the range $[\mu_{heart} - \sigma_{heart}, \mu_{heart}]$. Figure 2b illustrates a representative example this step.

Step 3: 2D-seed Identification. The 2D-seed for each organ is defined as follow; A 2D axial slice in the CT scan is first selected. Then, the intersection between the result of the previous step is conned and this slice is used as the 2D-seed of the organ. The 2D axial slice selection is organ specific as described below:

Lungs and Trachea: In the coarse segmentation of the lungs and trachea defined in step-2 the axial slice with the narrowest perimeter is selected as the

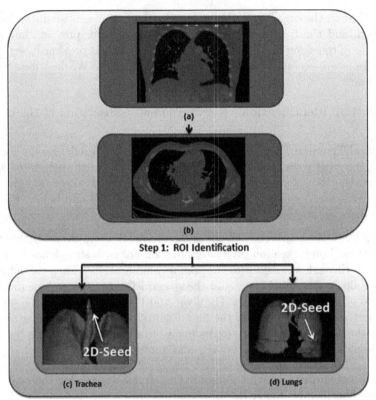

Fig. 1. Illustration of the first three steps for the of the segmentation of air containing organs, Top: A collection of consecutive axial slices that constitute the breathing system ROI in coronal (a) and axial (b) views. Bottom: The result of the thresholding step is shown (red), and the 2D-seed is marked in green for the trachea (c) and lungs (d) (Color figure online).

2D axial slice for the trachea. The axial slice with the widest perimeter is selected as the 2D slice for the lungs. Note that the 2D axial slice of the lungs contains two connected components, for the left and right lungs Fig. 1c–d.

Kidneys: Within the ROI the axial slice with the widest perimeter is selected as the 2D slice for the kidneys.

Liver and Spleen: The first slice above the kidney is selected as the 2D-seed for the liver and spleen.

Figure 2b shows a representative example for the 2D-seed for the kidneys, liver and spleen.

Step 4: Slice Region Growing. For each organ, we perform region growing from the 2D-seed. The seed is extended slice by slice along the axial direction,

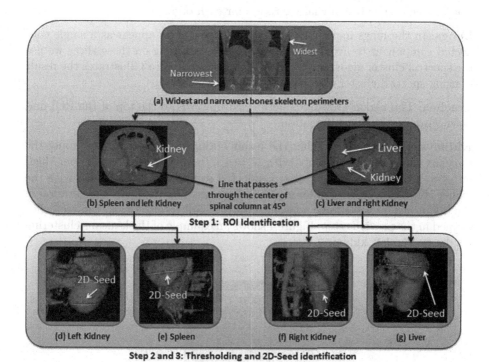

Fig. 2. The first three steps of the blood containing organs segmentation. Top: A collection of consecutive axial slices that constitute the blood containing organs (a). Middle: The ROI is divided by a line that passes through the center of the spinal column at 45°, leading to two ROIs (b–c). Bottom: Applying the thresholding step results with a coarse segmentation for each organ (red), where the 2D-seed for step 3 is marked in green for left kidney (d), spleen (e), right kidney (f) and liver (g) (Color figure online).

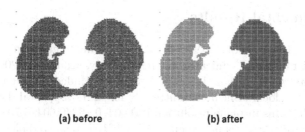

Fig. 3. Results of the spectral cluster algorithm to isolate each lung – in a axial slice view

within the coarse segmentation obtained in step 2 to include the entire organ. The unique segmentation characteristics for each organ are:

Lungs: In the lungs inevitably, some axial slices might appear as a single connected component to avoid this and to isolate each lung on those slices we use the spectral cluster algorithm [7] with two clusters. Figure 3 illustrates the result of using spectral cluster algorithm.

Trachea: The region growing is performed upwards to the top of the ROI and downwards to the first bifurcation.

Kidneys: For each slice within the result obtained after step 2, we apply the k-means clustering algorithm – with K = 3 – to cluster each region (per slice) into two groups. Then, the largest connected component of the group with the higher HU values is selected for each slice, constituting the final segmentation of the organ, where we enforce continuity of the segmentation from the seed slice defined in the previous step. Figure 4 shows an example of the k-means clustering results for the left kidney.

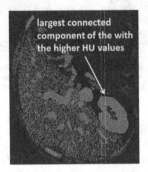

Fig. 4. K-means clustering (axial view) for the left kidney. The yellow group is the one with largest connected component with the higher HU values (Color figure online)

3   Experimental Results

We evaluated our method the VISCERAL Anatomy2 challenge. The training datasets consist of 20 CT clinical scans, respectively, acquired in 2004–08. Datasets of patients younger than 18 years were not included following the recommendation of the local ethical committee (S-465/2012, approval date Feb. 21th 2013). The CT scans in-plane resolution is 0.604–0.793/0.604–0.793 mm; the in-between plane resolution is geq3mm. A VISCERAL team radiologist manually produced ground-truth segmentations for each scan.

Table 1 summarizes the results for the training datasets, left lung, right lung, trachea, spleen, kidneys and the liver. Note that the DICE similarity coefficients

Table 1. Results: Mean Dice similarity coefficient and standard deviation for the training datasets on each organ.

Training dataset	Left lung	Right lung	Trachea	Spleen	Left kidney	Right kidney	Liver
	97.4	97.6	79.5	89.2	92.8	89.2	83.5
Test dataset	Left lung	Right lung	Trachea	Spleen	Left kidney	Right kidney	Liver
	97.0	96.8	85.1	82.2	82.9	87.0	NaN (See Footnote 1)

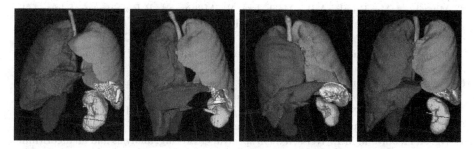

Fig. 5. Multi-organ segmentation results of four representative datasets of the VISCERAL Anatomy2 Challenge.

are high or very high. Figure 5 shows four representative examples of the multi-organ segmentation results.[1]

4   Conclusions

We have developed a generic framework for the segmentation of ventral body cavity organs in CT scans. Our approach consists of a four-step pipeline method that takes into account prior information about the locations of the organs and their appearance in CT scans. We have shown that the method is applicable to a variety of ventral body cavity organs including the trachea, the left and right lungs, the spleen, the left and right kidneys, and the liver. For the segmentation of air containing organs (i.e. lungs and trachea) in CTce we ranked first among other methods that participated in the challenge. Current and future research incorporating other structures and more modalities such as MRI and non-enhanced CT.

---

[1] Test results for Liver segmentations are not available due to an unforeseen technical error.

References

1. Langs, G., Hanbury, A., Menze, B., Müller, H.: VISCERAL: towards large data in medical imaging — challenges and directions. In: Greenspan, H., Müller, H., Syeda-Mahmood, T. (eds.) MCBR-CDS 2012. LNCS, vol. 7723, pp. 92–98. Springer, Heidelberg (2013)
2. Rubin, D.L., Akgül, C.B., Napel, S., Beaulieu, C.F., Greenspan, H., Acar, B.: Content-based image retrieval in radiology: current status and future directions. J. Digit. Imaging **24**(2), 208–222 (2011)
3. Schmidt, G., Athelogou, M., Schoenmeyer, R., Korn, R., Binnig, G.: Cognition network technology for a fully automated 3D segmentation of the liver. In: Proceedings of the MICCAI Workshop on 3D Segmentation in the Clinic: A Grand Challenge, pp. 125–133 (2007)
4. Mharib, A.M., Ramli, A.R., Mashohor, S., Mahmood, R.B.: Survey of liver CT image segmentation methods. Artif. Intell. Rev. **37**(2), 83–95 (2012)
5. Sluimer, I., Schilham, A., Prokop, M., van Ginneken, B.: Computer analysis of computed tomography scans of the lung: a survey. IEEE Trans. Med. Imaging **25**(4), 385–394 (2006)
6. Freiman, M., Kronman, A., Esses, S.J., Joskowicz, L., Sosna, J.: Non-parametric iterative model constraint graph min-cut for automatic kidney segmentation. In: Jiang, T., Navab, N., Pluim, J.P.W., Viergever, M.A. (eds.) MICCAI 2010, Part III. LNCS, vol. 6363, pp. 73–80. Springer, Heidelberg (2010)
7. Ng, A.Y., Jordan, M.I., Weiss, Y.: On spectral clustering: analysis and an algorithm. In: Advances in Neural Information Processing Systems, vol. 2, pp. 849–856 (2002)

Multi-atlas Segmentation and Landmark Localization in Images with Large Field of View

Tobias Gass$^{(\boxtimes)}$, Gabor Szekely, and Orcun Goksel

Computer Vision Lab, ETH Zurich, Zurich, Switzerland
{gasst,szekely,ogoksel}@vision.ee.ethz.ch

Abstract. In this work, we present multi-atlas based techniques for both segmentation and landmark detection in images with large field-of-view (FOV). Such images can provide important insight in the anatomical structure of the human body, but are challenging to deal with since the localization search space for landmarks and organs, in addition to the raw amount of data, is large. In many studies, segmentation and localization techniques are developed specifically for an individual target anatomy or image modality. This can leave a substantial amount of the potential of large FOV images untapped, as the co-localization and shape variability of organs are neglected. We thus focus on modality and anatomy independent techniques to be applied to a wide range of input images. For segmentation, we propagate the multi-organ label maps from several atlases to a target image via a large FOV Markov random field (MRF) based non-rigid registration method. The propagated labels are then fused in the target domain using similarity-weighted majority voting. For landmark localization, we use a consensus based fusion of location estimates from several atlases identified by a template-matching approach. We present our results in the IEEE ISBI 2014 VISCERAL challenge as well as VISCERAL Anatomy1 and Anatomy2 benchmarks.

1 Introduction

Both segmenting images into anatomical regions and detecting anatomical landmarks are key steps in medical image processing. Segmentations are widely used to semantically interpret image data, which can critically support clinical applications such as diagnosis, implant design and radiotherapy planning [1]. Landmarks can provide important cues for correspondence establishment in longitudinal studies, multi-modal fusion and inter-patient knowledge transfer. They are especially useful in cases where dense correspondences can not be guaranteed or are difficult to estimate, which is a common challenge in image registration. Many studies in the literature investigate anatomy and modality specific methods, which allow for task-specific performance evaluation and tuning. However, the ongoing improvement of data acquisition and storage facilities leads to an increased availability of high-quality images covering a large field of view (FOV), with full-body scans being the limit case. Such images allow for studying anatomy at a large scale, with the potential of discovering and exploiting

© Springer International Publishing Switzerland 2014
B. Menze et al. (Eds.): MCV 2014, LNCS 8848, pp. 171–180, 2014.
DOI: 10.1007/978-3-319-13972-2_16

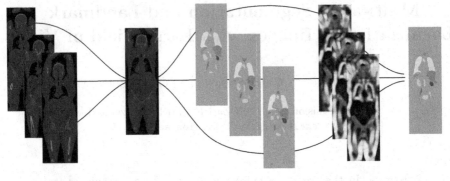

(a) Non-rigid registration of atlas images to target   (b) Deforming atlas segmentations   (c) Fusing segmentations with LNCC-based weights

Fig. 1. Multi-atlas segmentation pipeline. Whole-body registrations are computed for separately for each atlas-target image pair. In the employed LNCC-weighted majority voting segmentation fusion, all anatomical labels compete with each other.

inter-organ relationships. This has been facilitated by the public availability of such data in the VISCERAL (Visual Concept Extraction Challenge in Radiology) project[1]. In order to best utilize such data in a wide range of applications, our work focuses on generic segmentation and landmark detection methods that are independent of the image modality and do not require much effort for customization. The presented methods are applied on the landmark localization and organ segmentation challenges organized by the VISCERAL consortium. Extending our previous article presented at the ISBI VISCERAL workshop [2], we present results from both the IEEE ISBI challenge, as well as the VISCERAL Anatomy1 and Anatomy2 benchmarks in this paper.

2   Multi-atlas Segmentation

We use a multi-atlas segmentation method to segment all structures in a target image simultaneously. This was shown to achieve reliable and accurate segmentations in the literature [3]. Each atlas is registered individually to a target image, where we utilize our own implementation of the MRF-based non-rigid registration algorithm presented in [4]. The ground-truth annotations from each atlas are then propagated to the target coordinate frame using the registrations from the previous step. We then fuse the propagated multi-organ labels from several atlases based on similarity weighted max-voting using local normalized cross-correlation (LNCC) [5]. The pipeline is illustrated in Fig. 1.

---

[1] http://www.visceral.eu.

2.1   Atlas-Based Registration via MRF

The registration of an atlas A_n to an image X can be written as the minimization of a registration energy $E(T, X, A_n)$ with respect to the displacement vector field T. An efficient method for solving such energy minimization problems are Markov Random Fields (MRFs), which do not rely on the gradient of the criterion and are therefore less prone to poor local optima, for example due to poor initialization. MRFs are defined as discrete optimization problem on graphs, with unary potentials (ψ) assigned to graph nodes and pair-wise (Ψ) potentials assigned to edges as follows: In order to use MRFs for solving the minimization problem, this energy is decomposed into unary and pairwise potentials over discrete labels as follows:

$$E(T, X, A_n) = \sum_{p \in \Omega} \left(\psi_p(l_p) + \sum_{q \in \mathcal{N}(p)} \lambda \Psi_{pq}(l_p, l_q) \right), \tag{1}$$

where Ω is the discretized image space. The continuous displacement space is sampled discretely, so that each registration label l in the set of all registration labels L_R maps to a unique displacement vector d. The unary potentials measure the fit between the deformed atlas image and the target image at a location p. The pairwise potentials, weighted by λ, correspond to prior assumptions over the displacement field, which is often required to be smooth. In MRFs, this can be implemented by penalizing the displacements of nodes in the neighborhood $\mathcal{N}$ based on the squared Euclidean distance between their displacements.

Solving (1) on the pixel level is prohibited by computational demands since the graph size and the label space become too large. To overcome this, an efficient method was proposed in [4] that seeks the displacements d of control points in an iterative, multi-resolution cubic B-spline framework. We use our implementation of this method with four levels of detail, where the coarsest grid resolution has three nodes along the shortest edge of an input image and a spacing as isotropic as possible given that a control-point is required on each corner of the image. The images are downsampled by a factor of 2^3, and both image and control grid resolutions are doubled in each following level of the resolution hierarchy. At each level of detail, we sample four displacements in each of the six cardinal direction, yielding 25 displacement samples in total. Within each direction, samples are equidistant, with the largest displacement set to 0.4 times the control grid spacing. This was shown to guarantee diffeomorphic deformations [6]. For each level of detail, we re-run the MRF registration four times, with the displacements being re-scaled by the golden ratio 0.618, and composing the result onto the previous deformation. This guarantees that the result is still diffeomorphic and sub-pixel accuracy can be achieved. The normalized cross-correlation (NCC) of patches centered around each control point is used as unary potential. The discrete energy minimization of each instance is computed using tree-reweighted message passing (TRW-S) [7], which allows for minimizing arbitrary (non-submodular) potential functions.

2.2   Label Fusion

Deforming the atlas segmentation S_{A_n} with the final MRF-optimized registration $\hat{T}_n$ results in a segmentation candidate of the target image X:

$$S_{X,n} = S_{A_n}(\hat{T}_n). \tag{2}$$

Due to the locally optimal registration, poor initialization or gross differences between atlas and target can lead to unsatisfactory segmentation results from a single candidate. In machine learning, it is a well-known fact that a combination of multiple weak information sources can yield very good results. In medical image segmentation, this has led to the successful application of multi-atlas segmentation [3].

We compute N segmentation candidates $S_{X,n}$ of a target image X from N atlases via (2). Such segmentations can then be fused using majority voting (MV), where the most frequently assigned anatomical label out of the set $L_S = \{1, \ldots, N_S\}$ is assigned to each location p: To account for the difference in registration quality, we additionally weigh each segmentation candidate by the local post-registration similarity. This assumes that segmentations are locally more reliable when the atlas fit is good. The resulting weighted majority vote (wMV) can then be formalized as follows:

$$S_X^{\text{wMV}}(p) = \arg\max_{l_S \in L_S} \sum_n w_n(p)\, \delta\big(l_S, S_{X,n}(p)\big). \tag{3}$$

We use local normalized cross correlation (LNCC, [5]) between image X and deformed atlas $A_n(T_n)$ to obtain the weights w. The advantages of LNCC are its smoothness and fast computation time due to convolution with Gaussian kernels:

$$\text{LNCC}(X,Y,p) = \frac{\langle X,Y \rangle(p)}{\sigma_X(p)\,\sigma_Y(p)} \qquad \langle X,Y \rangle(p) = \overline{X \cdot Y}(p) - \overline{X}(p) \cdot \overline{Y}(p)$$

$$\overline{X} = \mathcal{G}_{\sigma_G} * X \qquad \sigma_X^2(p) = \overline{X^2}(p) - \overline{X}^2(p), \tag{4}$$

where $*$ is the convolution operator and $\mathcal{G}_{\sigma_G}$ is a Gaussian kernel with standard deviation σ_G. From the LNCC metric, we compute the normalized weights: $w_n(p) = \left(\frac{1 - \text{LNCC}_\sigma\big(X, A_n(T_n), p\big)}{2} \right)^\gamma$, where γ is used to scale the similarity such that contributions from individual segmentations are well spread [8].

3   Landmark Detection

We use a template based approach for anatomical landmark detection. Similarly to our segmentation method, we fuse multiple location estimates obtained from several atlases based on their consensus. Formally, we want to localize the unknown voxel coordinates p^ℓ of landmark ℓ in the target image X. For each atlas A_n, we first perform a template matching procedure to generate location estimates, followed by the location fusion.

Table 1. Specifics of template and search ROI, where $|\cdot|$ represents image dimensions (per axis).

ROI box (cropped image)	Centered at	Targeted half-width (d_{HW})	Max size ($n_{\max}$)
Template image A_n^ℓ	$p_{A_n}^\ell$	20 mm	41^3 voxels
Search region X^ℓ	$p_{A_n}^\ell \cdot \frac{|X|}{|A_n|}$	–	241^3 voxels

3.1 Template Matching

We use a box-shaped image region A_n^ℓ in the current atlas as template and similarly define a box-shaped search region X^ℓ in the target image. Both such regions are chosen targeting a physically isotropic region of interest (ROI) in the corresponding images, while limiting the maximum number of voxels in the ROI to ensure efficient computation.

The template half-width was empirically set to 20 mm via cross-validation in multiple modalities using different template sizes (e.g., 10, 20, 30, ...). Further specifics of the ROI selection are given in Table 1. We center the search region around the normalized voxel coordinates of the landmark from the atlas, which can be used as a gross estimate of the landmark location using the fact that both the atlas and the target have similar fields of view (i.e. both abdomen, thorax, or whole body). Note that our large search region covers most or all of the image in many modalities (e.g. in MRce) or at least a quadrant thereof (e.g. in CT), such that the searched landmark can be guaranteed to exist therein.

The atlas template is then compared to each template location i in the target image. Two independent similarity metrics, *sum of squared differences* (SSD) and *normalized cross-correlation* (NCC) are efficiently computed using convolution. Both values are then normalized linearly to $[0,1]$ such that they are both 1 at the best match location. A combined similarity metric $\mathrm{SSD}^a \cdot \mathrm{COR}^b$ is then computed, where the parameters $a = 2$ and $b = 3$ were determined empirically via cross-validation with several powers. The maximum of this combined metric then indicates the best matching location estimate p_n^ℓ for landmark ℓ with respect to atlas A_n.

3.2 Candidate Location Fusion

The *median* operator was empirically determined to be the best method for fusing location estimates. We performed cross-validation trials with different statistical fusion techniques such as the mean and weighted average of location estimates. Accordingly, each axis coordinate of the target landmark location is found as the median value of those axes from atlas estimates. The entire process is summarized in the following:

- Repeat for each atlas A_n:
    - → Crop landmark template A_n^ℓ centered at given landmark location $p_{A_n}^\ell$ in atlas image A_n

Table 2. Segmentation overlap (Dice) results of the presented method in the VIS-CERAL Anatomy1, ISBI challenges and Visceral Anatomy2 challenge.

Modality	Anatomy1				ISBI challenge				Anatomy2			
	Ctce	MR	CT	MRce	Ctce	MR	CT	MRce	Ctce	MR	CT	MRce
Kidney (L)	0.903	0.73	0.81	0.78	0.89	0.55	0.76	0.89	0.91	0.71	0.78	0.85
Kidney (R)	0.88	0.73	0.75	0.79	0.83	0.59	0.68	0.73	0.91	0.71	0.75	0.88
Spleen	0.80	0.67	0.69	0.69	0.80	0.65	0.68	0.79	0.78	0.62	0.67	0.66
Liver	0.90	0.82	0.83	0.85	0.88	0.82	0.80	0.86	0.91	0.74	0.83	0.84
Lung (L)	0.96	0.53	0.95	0.65	0.96	0.49	0.96		0.96	0.52	0.95	
Lung (R)	0.97	0.90	0.96	0.66	0.97	0.91	0.97		0.97	0.81	0.96	
Urinary bladder	0.68	0.66	0.64	0.28	0.66	0.58	0.64	0.33	0.68	0.65	0.66	0.20
Lumbar Vert. 1	0.60	0.40	0.35	0.06	0.55	0.62	0.33	0.08	0.62	0.33	0.41	0.08
Thyroid	0.25	0.37	0.47		0.32	0.49	0.44		0.19	0.32	0.45	
Pancreas	0.47		0.44	0.36	0.44		0.47	0.36	0.46	0.20	0.42	0.37
Psoas major (L)	0.81	0.80	0.77	0.64	0.80	0.77	0.77	0.65	0.82	0.73	0.78	0.64
Psoas major (R)			0.79				0.78				0.75	
Gallblader	0.33	0.02	0.10	0.04	0.21	0.04	0.08	0.00	0.38	0.00	0.19	0.04
Sternum	0.60	0.36	0.65		0.61	0.36	0.63		0.64	0.00	0.63	
Aorta	0.79	0.74	0.72	0.62	0.79	0.78	0.72		0.78	0.69	0.74	0.53
Trachea	0.85	0.74	0.82		0.84	0.75	0.84		0.85	0.73	0.84	
Adren. gland (L)	0.20	0.11	0.17	0.00	0.10	0.14	0.28		0.25	0.00	0.07	0.02
Adren. gland (R)	0.16	0.22	0.14	0.11	0.02	0.27	0.13		0.18	0.01	0.18	0.02

→ Crop a large search region X^ℓ centered around a grossly approximated location in X

→ Compute $\mathrm{SSD}\big(A_n^\ell, X^\ell\big)$ and $\mathrm{COR}\big(A_n^\ell, X^\ell\big)$

→ $p_n^\ell = \arg\max_i \big(\, \mathrm{SSD}[i]^2 \cdot \mathrm{COR}[i]^3 \,\big)$

• $p^\ell = \mathrm{median}\,\big\{ p_n^\ell \mid \forall_n \big\}$

4   Results and Discussion

Our methods have been evaluated in the VISCERAL challenge and benchmarks, the setup of which are explained in [9]. Throughout the results, the following abbreviations are used for the image modalities: whole-body CT images (CT), thorax+abdomen contrast-agent CT images (CTce), abdominal T1-weighted contrast-agent MR images (MRce), and whole-body T1-weighted MR images (MR).

Each individual image modality was treated separately from the others, e.g. only CT atlas images were used for the segmentation of a CT target image. We used the training images from Anatomy1 benchmark as atlases, i.e. depending on the modality of the test image, six atlases for CTce and seven for CT, MR, MRce. Furthermore, the segmentation and landmark detection challenges were solved separately as detailed above.

Segmentation Task: We combined all organ segmentations for each atlas into a single multi-label segmentation image, which was then deformed using the atlas-to-target registration $\hat{T}$ described in Sect. 2.1. In Table 2, Dice overlap metric

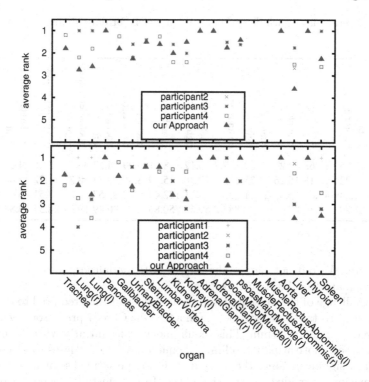

Fig. 2. Average segmentation rank (by Dice coefficient) for each participant and organ for the CT (top) and CTce (bottom) modalities in the ISBI segmentation challenge. An average rank of 1 indicates a method that yields the best Dice metric for all input images.

results regarding our segmentation approach reported by VISCERAL for the test images can be seen for the VISCERAL Anatomy1 and Anatomy2 benchmark and the ISBI challenge. It is notable that the multi-atlas fusion has significantly lower segmentation accuracy for organs which have low volume, e.g. urinary and gall bladders, and the adrenal glands. One possible explanation is that such small structures are difficult to register using full-body images. Due to such misalignments, overlap between multiple deformed atlas segmentations for such label can be small, resulting in the weighted majority voting not selecting that label.

In order to compare our technique to other participants' in the ISBI challenge, we computed an average rank per organ per participant. For each given test image, we assigned a rank to each method, i.e. $\{1, 2, ..., P\}$ where P is the number of participants submitted a (non-blank) result for that test image. In Fig. 2 the average of such ranks for all given test images is seen per anatomy. Our submission was *the only entrant that aimed to segment all images in all modalities* and it achieved competitive results for many organs as seen in the

Table 3. Average landmark detection errors in voxels for our submission to the ISBI challenge.

Modality	aorta bifurcation	aortic arch	clavicle left	clavicle right	crista iliaca left	crista iliaca right	symphysis	trachea bifurcation	trochanter major left	trochanter major right	trochanter minor left	trochanter minor right	Average
CT	19.05	17.68	9.27	5.69	7.7	6.12	8.01	3.99	34.37	36.18	5.16	4.06	13.11
CTce	36.22	16.18	16.26	32.35	13.93	10.38	15.59	3.35	37.84	38.31	11.22	12.64	20.36
MR	252.49	43.67	13.05	23.31	23.29	19.21	122.45	61.2	29.57	44.4	18.51	62.4	59.46
MRce	61.28				88.92	57.65	50.86		30.49	59.81	28.54	34.84	51.55

given figure. We did not plot ranks for the MR modalities, since we were the only participant to submit such results.

One challenge of the presented approach is the run-time required to compute multiple atlas-to-target registrations. On a 2.8 Ghz Core i7 processor, each registration requires about 40 min. This requirement scales linearly with the number of used atlases, motivating us to limit the number of used atlases to seven. This is especially significant since the computations are performed sequentially on the virtual machine provided for the challenges. In circumstances where a parallel processing is available and increased segmentation accuracy can be traded off with increased run-time, more atlases can potentially be used. One advantage, however, of the described method is that it requires a single registration per atlas to identify *all labels* in the target image. This means the complexity does not scale with the number of anatomical labels, which can be of importance for densely segmented volumes.

Landmark Detection Task: In the Anatomy1 and ISBI challenges organized by the VISCERAL project, our landmark localization achieved in whole-body CT images an impressive 11 and 13 voxel average error, respectively in these challenges. This is comparable to the best result out of multiple submissions of a competing participant in the Anatomy1 challenge, who also achieved a 11 voxel average error, albeit omitting the difficult clavicle landmark. For the ISBI challenge, mean landmark localization error is presented in Table 3. We also report the landmark localization error in the recent VISCERAL Anatomy2 benchmark in Table 4, where we achieved similar results on a much larger number of landmarks. In both Anatomy1 and ISBI challenges, our submission was the only one to tackle the challenging task of landmark detection in MR and MRce images. Even though the mean error of our method is much higher on the MR data in comparison to CT and CTce, it should be noted that the minimum errors for multiple landmarks on the trachea and trochanter are between 3 and

Table 4. Median landmark localization errors in voxels for our submission to the VISCERAL Anatomy2 benchmark.

CT				MRT				MRT1cefs	
aorta_bifurcation	23.78	sternoclavicular_left	7.58	aorta_bifurcation	76.93	sternoclavicular_left	112.31	aorta_bifurcation	47.00
aortic_arch	12.71	sternoclavicular_right	5.83	aortic_arch	24.31	sternoclavicular_right	117.47	aorticvalve	192.35
aorticvalve	49.28	symphysis	9.52	aorticvalve	179.87	symphysis	207.98	crista_iliaca_left	46.86
bronchus_left	4.16	Th1	14.16	bronchus_left	67.33	Th1	205.24	crista_iliaca_right	21.70
bronchus_right	10.90	Th2	22.85	bronchus_right	53.07	Th2	23.91	ischiadicum_left	40.77
C2	22.10	Th3	8.89	C2	13.32	Th3	16.08	ischiadicum_right	54.87
C3	13.58	Th4	12.07	C3	18.52	Th4	25.53	L1	51.45
C4	17.44	Th5	17.36	C4	330.30	Th5	58.56	L2	28.20
C5	9.05	Th6	20.29	C5	15.34	Th6	79.27	L3	57.96
C6	6.89	Th7	32.19	C6	67.19	Th7	167.28	L4	54.49
C7	9.20	Th8	46.45	C7	338.38	Th8	230.31	L5	54.88
clavicle_left	5.26	Th9	51.43	clavicle_left	7.75	Th9	72.48	renalpelvis_left	73.60
clavicle_right	4.01	Th10	75.04	clavicle_right	12.25	Th10	161.37	renalpelvis_right	44.67
coronaria	17.26	Th11	32.11	coronaria		Th11	98.67	symphysis	37.04
crista_iliaca_left	7.75	Th12	35.52	crista_iliaca_left	30.89	Th12	34.33	Th6	178.79
crista_iliaca_right	10.38	trachea_bifurcation	3.92	crista_iliaca_right	18.52	trachea_bifurcation	5.95	Th7	156.32
eye_left	91.77	trochanter_major_left	5.36	eye_left	279.49	trochanter_major_left	26.14	Th8	177.44
eye_right	97.99	trochanter_major_right	4.30	eye_right	282.47	trochanter_major_right	26.59	Th9	166.52
ischiadicum_left	8.45	trochanter_minor_left	8.50	ischiadicum_left	25.26	trochanter_minor_left	33.13	Th10	86.72
ischiadicum_right	10.64	trochanter_minor_right	6.46	ischiadicum_right	34.31	trochanter_minor_right	129.02	Th11	63.23
L1	35.92	tuberculum_left	9.61	L1	32.16	tuberculum_left	12.81	Th12	60.85
L2	3.92	tuberculum_right	11.54	L2	23.59	tuberculum_right	11.13	trochanter_major_left	111.00
L3	33.52	vci_bifurcation	13.62	L3	32.65	vci_bifurcation	96.72	trochanter_major_right	46.61
L4	25.39	ventricle_left	7.39	L4	67.32	ventricle_left	24.52	trochanter_minor_left	71.01
L5	20.55	ventricle_right	7.10	L5	5.44	ventricle_right	40.73	trochanter_minor_right	16.28
renalpelvis_left	47.69	xyphoideus	24.41	renalpelvis_left	10.11	xyphoideus	228.08	vci_bifurcation	71.63
renalpelvis_right	100.68			renalpelvis_right	37.61			xyphoideus	214.49

(Color scale legend: 0, 20, 40, 60, 80, 100, 120, 140, 160, 180, 200, 220, 240, 260, 280, 300)

13 voxels, according to VISCERAL challenge results. More detailed results can be found on the VISCERAL page[2].

5   Conclusions

In this paper, our submissions for the VISCERAL Anatomy1, Anatomy2 and ISBI challenges were described. We employed two generic methods for both segmentation and landmark localization that utilize the information contained in multiple atlases. The large FOV of the images provides both challenges and benefits: Computational aspects have to be considered when dealing with the substantial amount of data and the large search space. Meanwhile, the co-localization of organs can be an important cue for successful processing of such data.

Acknowledgements. The research leading to these results has received funding from the European Union Seventh Framework Programme (FP7/2007–2013) under grant agreement n° 318068. This work has also received funding from the Swiss National Center of Competence in Research on Computer Aided and Image Guided Medical Interventions (NCCR Co-Me) supported by the Swiss National Science Foundation.

References

1. Pekar, V., McNutt, T.R., Kaus, M.R.: Automated model-based organ delineation for radiotherapy planning in prostatic region. Int. J. Radiat. Oncol. Biol. Phys. **60**(3), 973–980 (2004)

---

[2] http://www.visceral.eu.

2. Goksel, O., Gass, T., Szekely, G.: Segmentation and landmark localization based on multiple atlases. In: Goksel, O. (ed.) Proceedings of the VISCERAL Challenge at ISBI. CEUR Workshop Proceedings, Beijing, China, pp. 37–43, May 2014
3. Heckemann, R.A., Hajnal, J.V., Aljabar, P., Rueckert, D., Hammers, A.: Automatic anatomical brain MRI segmentation combining label propagation and decision fusion. NeuroImage **33**(1), 115–126 (2006)
4. Glocker, B., Komodakis, N., Tziritas, G., Navab, N., Paragios, N.: Dense image registration through MRFs and efficient linear programming. Med. Image Anal. **12**(6), 731–741 (2008)
5. Cachier, P., Bardinet, E., Dormont, D., Pennec, X., Ayache, N.: Iconic feature based nonrigid registration: the PASHA algorithm. Comput. Vis. Image Underst. **89**(2–3), 272–298 (2003)
6. Rueckert, D., Aljabar, P., Heckemann, R.a., Hajnal, J.V., Hammers, A.: Diffeomorphic registration using B-splines. In: Proceedings of the Medical Image Computing and Computer-Assisted Intervention, pp. 702–709, January 2006
7. Kolmogorov, V.: Convergent tree-reweighted message passing for energy minimization. IEEE Trans. Pattern Anal. Mach. Intell. **28**, 1568–1583 (2006)
8. Iglesias, J.E., Karssemeijer, N.: Robust initial detection of landmarks in film-screen mammograms using multiple FFDM atlases. IEEE Trans. Med. Imaging **28**(11), 1815–1824 (2009)
9. Jimenez del Toro, O.A., Goksel, O., Menze, B., Müller, H., Langs, G., Weber, M.A., Eggel, I., Gruenberg, K., Holzer, M., Jakab, A., Kotsios-Kontokotsios, G., Krenn, M., Fernandez, T.S., Schaer, R., Taha, A.A., Winterstein, M., Hanbury, A.: VISCERAL - VISual Concept Extraction challenge in RAdioLogy: ISBI 2014 Challenge Organization. In: VISCERAL Challenge at ISBI, vol. 1194, pp. 6–15 (2014)

Automatic Liver Segmentation
Using Statistical Prior Models
and Free-form Deformation

Xuhui Li[1,2], Cheng Huang[1], Fucang Jia[1(✉)], Zongmin Li[2],
Chihua Fang[3], and Yingfang Fan[3]

[1] Laboratory for Medical Imaging and Digital Surgery,
Shenzhen Institutes of Advanced Technology,
Chinese Academy of Sciences, Shenzhen 518055, China
fc.jia@siat.ac.cn
[2] College of Computer and Communication Engineering,
China University of Petroleum, Qingdao 266580, China
[3] Department of Hepatobiliary Surgery, Zhujiang Hospital,
Southern Medical University, Guangzhou 510282, China

Abstract. In this paper, an automatic and robust coarse-to-fine liver image segmentation method is proposed. Multiple prior knowledge models are built to implement liver localization and segmentation: voxel-based AdaBoost classifier is trained to localize liver position robustly, shape and appearance models are constructed to fit liver these models to original CT volume. Free-form deformation is incorporated to improve the models' ability of refining liver boundary. The method was submitted to VISCERAL big data challenge, and had been tested on IBSI 2014 challenge datasets and the result demonstrates that the proposed method is accurate and efficient.

Keywords: Liver segmentation · Prior model · Model reconstruction · Model localization · Free-form deformation

1 Introduction

In computer-aided diagnosis and treatment, liver segmentation from CT images is indispensable for volume measurement, resection planning and postoperative effect evaluation etc. The main challenges in automatic segmentation are in that similar intensity values with surrounding issues, large shape variability and pathology.

One advantage of shape models for liver segmentation is their ability to keep regular shape where image information is ambiguous. The shape model may be a single deformable template [1] or Statistical shape model (SSM) [2].

SSM has become a major trend because of its generalization to other new shapes. In MICCAI 2007 liver segmentation competition, SSMs-based method makes a comparable result with some semi-automatic methods (http://www.sliver07.org). However, one drawback is that the segmentation performance of statistical models method becomes inaccurate as shape variability is not covered in the training datasets.

© Springer International Publishing Switzerland 2014
B. Menze et al. (Eds.): MCV 2014, LNCS 8848, pp. 181–188, 2014.
DOI: 10.1007/978-3-319-13972-2_17

In order to overcome this problem, subsequent to SSM fitting, we adopt a free-form deformation to conquer optimal boundary.

In this study, integration of discriminative and generative models in a hybrid scheme was presented to assist liver localization and segmentation: machine learning based voxel classier, active shape model (ASM) [3] including statistical shape model (SSM) prior and local appearance model. Finally, the final fitted model was free-form deformed to true liver boundary under appearance model guidance. The coarse-to-fine liver image segmentation framework including liver localization, model reconstruction, model fitting and free-form deformation is illustrated in Fig. 1.

The VISCERAL project (http://www.visceral.eu) organizers organized a benchmark on organ segmentation and landmark detection. We participated in the challenge and got intermediate evaluation result at 2014 IEEE International Symposium on Biomedical Imaging (ISBI). Experiment results are presented in Sect. 4.

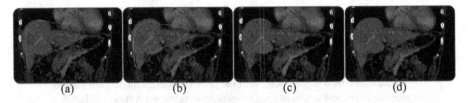

(a)   (b)   (c)   (d)

Fig. 1. The four steps of liver segmentation framework: (a) liver model localization; (b) registration with liver distance map; (c) models fitting; (d) free-form deformation.

2   Construction of Prior Models

The liver segmentation works under the guidance of statistical shape and appearance prior models. However, the pose of original images, including the spatial position and rotation angle, vary with each individual. Pose training method described in [4] was utilized to resample all the images using rigid transform and provide the initial alignment for liver pose.

The SSM was constructed from a set of converted simplex meshes after the binary manual segmentations were converted to triangular meshes. However, correct correspondence establishment between all triangular meshes is the most challenging part of model construction, influencing model quality such as generalization ability, specificity, and segmentation robustness. Traditional point matching algorithm like iterative closest point (ICP) applies to affine transformation, which cannot fully describe liver shape variability. Here, a deformable mesh alignment method was applied, starting from a multi-resolution B-spline deformable registration between a liver atlas and original CT volume of patients with Mattes mutual information metric [5]. A homeomorphic topology between the input meshes was guaranteed since they are generated from identical landmarks placed on the reference atlas.

However, the mesh after B-spline transformation is often unable to extend to the exact boundary, a modified deformable model scheme, additional to a threshold force based on binary manual segmentation, was proposed. We deform the simplex mesh according to forces computed from every vertex P_i. In our case, the total force applied on P_i was expressed as follows

$$f(P_i) = \alpha f_{int}(P_i) + \beta f_{ext}(P_i) + \kappa f_{threshold}(P_i) \qquad (1)$$

Where f_{int} is the internal force ensuring smoothness of the mesh, and the f_{ext} derived from image gradient aims at recovering correct boundary. The threshold force is defined as

$$f_{threshold}(P_i) = \begin{cases} f_{normal}(P_i), & 0.01 \leq I(P_i) \leq 1 \\ -f_{normal}(P_i), & others \end{cases} \qquad (2)$$

Where the f_{normal} is the normal vector of vertex P_i, and vertices would be shifted along the normal direction according to their intensity values $I(P_i)$. The mesh alignment results are good enough for constructing multiple prior knowledge models.

When shape correspondence completed, Statismo toolkit [6] was used to reconstruct the SSM in which principal component analysis (PCA) was used to generate a compact model of the shape variability. The SSM was used to constrain the model fitting during segmentation.

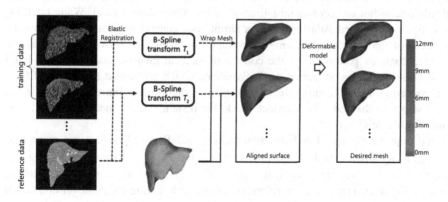

Fig. 2. Flowchart of correspondence establishment between surfaces. The final results demonstrate deformable model is fitted well for detail optimization.

A model of the appearance of liver boundary tissue is essential for shape model to be fitted to new data. Conventional statistical appearance models were to sample profiles perpendicular to the surface in all training images and process these profiles in a PCA fashion. However, the profiles do not ideally obey to Gaussian distribution due to the presence of pathologies or neighborhood organ similarity in appearances, and shape is not necessarily correlated with appearance. As an alternative, we employ a K Nearest Neighbor (KNN)-classifier to model intensity or gradient profiles into three classes as follows: for each landmark, the profiles are sampled equidistantly over a length of 16.5 mm and stored as the boundary model. To shift the profiles towards the inside and outside of the liver yield internal and external samples respectively.

3   Method

3.1   Localization of Liver Model

In order to locate the liver model in the whole body or abdominal CT images, a multi-resolution registration approach starting with an abdominal volume atlas image $I_{reference}$ in contrast enhanced CT modality was used. The target volume I_{target} is the CT volume in either non-contrast or contrast enhanced CT volume, then the spatial relative location between the target and atlas images is estimated.

$$\mu^* = \arg\max_\mu \mathbb{C}\left(T_\mu; I_{reference}, I_{target}\right) \tag{3}$$

Where $\mathbb{C}$ is a similarity measure of the parameterized coordinate transformation T_μ. The correlation coefficient histogram metric returned the cost with optimal position in parameter space which is generated by the one plus one evolutionary. The goal of the registration is to find a translation parameter vector μ^* so that the atlas image could match the abdominal region of CT volume. Then the abdominal interest of region (ROI) $I_{abdomen}$ is obtained according to the atlas image.

Most researches emphasized on the final liver segmentation accuracy instead of organ position recognition [7]. In practice, the shape-based method often failed completely due to not so accurate initialization of the mean shape model. Wang et al. [8] recently demonstrated AdaBoost was a simple but general approach to improve the accuracy of automatic image segmentation algorithm which has shown excellent ability to learn complex patterns from the context of medical images. AdaBoost is to build strong classifiers from sufficient weak classifiers, which are trained from a set of local and contextual image features such as the neighborhood mean intensity, the variance, the distance to the abdominal surface mask, the distance of the mean intensity to the one of other neighbors etc.

To improve the speed and the robustness of AdaBoost algorithm, we preprocess $I_{abdomen}$ using down sampling and median filter, and $I'_{abdomen}$ as shown in Fig. 2a was got by matching the intensity with the atlas image using the histogram matching method [9], such that pixels representing the same homologous point on abdominal image have the similar intensity on both the training and target volume. Finally, $I'_{abdomen}$ was processed by AdaBoost method to generate a liver probability map. The binary mask can be obtained at threshold 0.3, the liver region was obtained by largest connected region labeling to exclude other tissues or organs. The liver centroid was computed as follows.

$$z_{index} = \arg\max_{z_{index}} \iiint_\Omega p(I)dv, subject to \tag{4}$$

$$\Omega = \left\{(x, y, z) | 0 \leq x \leq 0.6x_{size}, 0 \leq y \leq y_{size}, z_{index} \leq z \leq z_{index} + 80/z_{spacing}\right\}$$

where $p(I)$ is the largest probability map, Then a liver narrow band (as shown in Fig. 2b) with $80/z_{spacing}$ height is detected by counting maximum liver pixels. This approach provides robust initialization for the mean liver shape of SSM (Fig. 3).

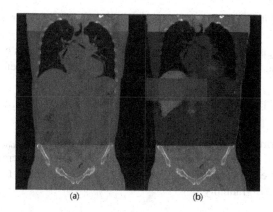

(a)   (b)

Fig. 3. Coronal views of position recognition, (a) shows purple upper part derived from volume CT by atlas image registration. (b) A red narrow band with 25 pixels size in the Z-axis direction was colored, and the largest connect region of liver probability map was labeled with green (Color figure online).

3.2 Model Fitting

In order to propagate the segmentation of the mean liver shape segmentation to a new image $I'_{abdomen}$, A coarse-to-fine strategy is employed in the framework. The SSM registration is used to extract the liver contours first. This section consists of two stages: distance map model fitting and appearance model fitting.

In the first step, a global transformation $T_{distance}$ is obtained by the reference mesh to the distance map image registration and $T_{distance}$ is decomposed as $T_{distance} = T_{SSM} \circ T_{rigid}$ where T_{SSM} is a statistical shape model transformation and T_{rigid} is a rigid transformation. The transformation parameters are optimized by minimizing the following energy function:

$$E(T_{distance}) = \alpha \log \text{Err}(T_{SSM}) + \int_v D(T_{translation})dv + \beta\, R(T_{rotation}) \quad (5)$$

Where the $\text{Err}(T_{SSM})$ is the error function of SSM parameters. α is the weight of the shape term which measure the importance of T_{SSM}. $D(T_{translation})$ is the value of the vertex sets in the distance map image. $R(T_{rotation})$ is a regularization term, which prevents the liver shape from excessive rotation to leak to heart region. Therefore, the distance map image was registered to the point sets of the mean liver shape model, and the mesh vertices of deformed mean shape were fitted to liver boundary location with major shape variation constraints. Here, we only used 95 % components for the shape model to avoid over fitting.

In the following, the appearance model was used to drive the model moving toward the precise liver boundary. The displacement vector field ΔV is computed on the basis of previous trained kNN-classifier. The category and probability of current vertex can be estimated by 10 nearby profiles in the classifier. As a result, the landmarks were shifted inside or outside based on the class label until reaching to the maximum boundary probability. After completing the deformation of liver shape based on appearance model, a model fitting $T_{appearance}$ is obtained by the reference mesh to deformed mesh registration method and nearest neighbor points was established by kD tree algorithm. The metric for SSM fitting registration can be written as follows:

$$E(T_{appearance}) = \alpha \log \text{Err}(T_{SSM}) + \int_v Kd(T_{translation})dv \qquad (6)$$

where the first term is same as the that of $E(T_{distance})$. $Kd(T_{translation})$ represents the Euclidean distance of the nearest neighbor points. In order to increase the generalization of SSM, in each iteration, the number of freedom degrees of the transformation model was increased gradually.

3.3   Free-Form Deformation

The PCA approach of constructing SSMs seeks for only those modes of variation that are shown in the training sets [10]. The final step, called free-form deformation, aimed at updating the position for each landmark up to confidence threshold. The deformation process was achieved by double constraint forces, shape and appearance constraints, to capture the optimal liver delineation. The internal force strived to keep the deformable mesh close to regularity of liver shape. Previous kNN-classifier was integrated as external force to conquer local specific variation of liver boundary. Free-form deformation was based on deformable simplex mesh segmentation [11]. The external force is defined as:

$$F_{ext} = \begin{cases} \beta \langle \vec{\nabla} G, \vec{n} \rangle \vec{n} + \kappa \vec{n} &, \quad vertex \in inside \\ \beta \langle \vec{\nabla} G, \vec{n} \rangle \vec{n} &, \quad vertex \in boundary \\ -\kappa \vec{n} &, \quad vertex \in outside \end{cases} \qquad (7)$$

where $\vec{\nabla} G$ is the image gradient and $\vec{n}$ is the normal vector of current vector. The class of the vertex is determined by the KNN-classifier. Therefore, the external force of inside vertex is the combination of image gradient and appearance model constraint. Instead, the outside vertex was only up to the appearance model in case of the effect of non-liver region gradient.

4   Experiment and Result

In this section, the experiments on the VISCERAL Anatomy benchmark were presented, which provided a benchmark to compare the performance of algorithms for automated multiple organ segmentation. Currently, the segmentation framework only tested on liver in CT and CTce modalities. Seven CT and seven CTce datasets were employed to train AdaBoost classifier. Fifteen whole body common CT and 15 abdomen contrast enhanced CT from the VISCERAL benchmark and additional manually segmented 50 contrast enhanced clinical datasets were used to train the shape and appearance prior models. There were 1252 landmarks in the liver shape model, each profile was sampled with 11 points along the landmark normal direction in the appearance model.

Table 1. kNN-classifier accurancy of the intensity and gradient profiles.

	Intensity	Gradient
Inside	0.88	0.79
Outside	0.83	0.87
Boundary	0.81	0.82
Mean	0.84	0.83

We compared the performance of kNN-classifiers on intensity and gradient profiles. For the parameters setting of kNN, the maximum neighbor k is 5, the number of test ratio is 10 %. The accuracy in discriminating three kinds (inside, boundary, outside) of samples are presented in in Table 1. The results show that the kNN-classifiers with the intensity feature are better than with the gradient feature, can distinguish liver boundary from non-boundary landmark well.

Table 2. Liver segmentation evaluation result in CT and CTce image modality.

Modality	DICE	MSD	ICC	ARI
CT	0.911 ± 0.010	0.313 ± 0.047	0.911 ± 0.010	0.909 ± 0.010
CTce	0.922 ± 0.011	0.290 ± 0.123	0.922 ± 0.011	0.918 ± 0.012

We participated in the ISBI 2014 challenge. During the challenge, a testing set of volumes, including 5 whole body CT and 5 abdominal CTce volumes, needed to be segmented automatically. Table 2 reported the quantitative results (DICE: DICE coefficient, MSD: Mean Surface distance, ICC: Interclass Correlation, ARI: Adjusted Rand Index) of our segmentation in the challenge. Total segmentation results have been published online (http://www.visceral.eu/assets/assets/VISCERAL-at-ISBI-segmentation-results.pdf).

5   Discussion and Conclusions

We proposed a robust and automatic liver segmentation method integrating of multiple prior information models. In training stage, the pose of all training datasets were corrected and resampled with the reference image. And the mesh generated from manual segmentation is aligned by deformable mesh alignment. The method exploits AdaBoost classifiers to represent contextual clues in liver model localization. Two main priors, profile appearance and shape variation of liver model, were used. The segmentation is based on different registration for model fitting and deformation.

Moreover, the proposed method has some room for improvement. The kNN classification result demonstrated the accuracy of appearance model is not enough. Profile samples were just classified into three categories without considering the local region priors. Therefore, an advanced clustering method, such as Expectation Maximization (EM), could improve the robustness. Future more, our SSMs method can be applied to other organ segmentation not needing many parameters adjustment.

In summary, the method has been validated on ISBI 2014 VISCERAL challenge and the executable have been submitted to the Azure cloud computing sever for unseen large data testing. The ISBI 2014 benchmark demonstrates that the method has comparable performance with the other state-of-the-art methods.

Acknowledgments. The work was supported by the 12th Five-Year National High-tech R&D Program of China (863 Program) (No.2012AA022305) and Guangdong Provincial Scientific & Technology Project (No.2012A080203013 and No.2012A030400013).

References

1. Gauriau, R., Cuingnet, R., Prevost, R., Mory, B., Ardon, R., Lesage, D., Bloch, I.: A generic, robust and fully-automatic workflow for 3D CT liver segmentation. In: Yoshida, H., Warfield, S., Vannier, M.W. (eds.) Abdominal Imaging 2013. LNCS, vol. 8198, pp. 241–250. Springer, Heidelberg (2013)
2. Kainmüller, D., Lange, T., Lamecker, H.: Shape constrained automatic segmentation of the liver based on a heuristic intensity model. In: Hiemann, T., Styner, M., van Ginneken, B. (eds.) 3D Segmentation in the Clinic: A Grand Challenge, pp. 109–116 (2007)
3. Cootes, T.F., Taylor, C.J., Cooper, D.H., Graham, J.: Active shape models-their training and application. Comput. Vis. Image Understand. **61**(1), 38–59 (1995)
4. Huang, C., Jia, F., Fang, C., Fan, Y., Hu, Q.: Automatic liver detection and segmentation from 3D CT images: a hybrid method using statistical pose model and probabilistic atlas. Int. J. Comput. Assist. Radiol. Surg. **8**(S1), 237–238 (2013)
5. Thevenaz, P., Unser, M.: Optimization of mutual information for multiresolution image registration. IEEE Trans. Image Process. **9**(12), 2083–2099 (2000)
6. Luthi, M., Blanc, R., Albrecht, T., Gass, T., Goksel, O., Buchler, P., Kistler, M., Bouslei-man, H., Reyes, M., Cattin, P., Vetter, T.: Statismo - A framework for PCA based statistical models. Insight J. **1**, 1–18 (2012)
7. Ben Younes, L., Nakajima, Y., Saito, T.: Fully automatic segmentation of the Femur from 3D-CT images using primitive shape recognition and statistical shape models. Int. J. Comput. Assist. Radiol. Surg. **9**(2), 189–196 (2014)
8. Wang, H., Das, S.R., Suh, J.W., Altinay, M., Pluta, J., Craige, C., Avants, B., Yushkevich, P.A.: A learning-based wrapper method to correct systematic errors in automatic image segmentation: Consistently improved performance in hippocampus, cortex and brain segmentation. Neuroimage **55**(3), 968–985 (2011)
9. Nyúl, L.G., Udupa, J.K., Zhang, X.: New variants of a method of MRI scale standardization. IEEE Trans. Med. Imag. **19**(2), 143–150 (2000)
10. Berendsen, F.F., van der Heide, U.A., Langerak, T.R., Kotte, A.N.T.J., Pluim, J.P.W.: Free-form image registration regularized by a statistical shape model: application to organ segmentation in cervical MR. Comput. Vis. Image Understand. **117**(9), 1119–1127 (2013)
11. Montagnat, J., Delingette, H.: Volumetric medical images segmentation using shape constrained deformable models. In: Troccaz, J., Mösges, R., Grimson, W.L. (eds.) CVRMed-MRCAS 1997. LNCS, vol. 1205. Springer, Heidelberg (1997)

Hierarchic Multi–atlas Based Segmentation for Anatomical Structures: Evaluation in the VISCERAL Anatomy Benchmarks

Oscar Alfonso Jiménez del Toro[1,2]([✉]) and Henning Müller[1,2]

[1] University of Applied Sciences Western Switzerland (HES–SO), Sierre, Switzerland
[2] University and University Hospitals of Geneva, Geneva, Switzerland
{oscar.jimenez,henning.mueller}@hevs.ch

Abstract. Computer–based medical image analysis is often initialized with the localization of anatomical structures in clinical scans. Many methods have been proposed for segmenting single and multiple anatomical structures. However, it is uncommon to compare different approaches with the same test set, namely a publicly available one. The comparison of these methods objectively defines the advantages and limitations for each method. A hierarchic multi–atlas based segmentation approach was proposed for the segmentation of multiple anatomical structures in computed tomography scans. The method relies on an anatomical hierarchy that exploits the inherent spatial and anatomical variability of medical images using image registration techniques. It was submitted and tested in the VISCERAL project Anatomy benchmarks. In this paper, the results are analyzed and compared to the results of the other segmentation methods submitted in the benchmark. Various anatomical structures in both un–enhanced and contrast–enhanced CT scans resulted in the highest overlap with the proposed method compared to the other evaluated approaches. Although the method was trained with a small training set it generated accurate output segmentations for liver, lungs and other anatomical structures.

Keywords: Multi–atlas based segmentation · Image registration · VIS-CERAL

1 Introduction

As part of their daily clinical workload, health providers visually inspect medical images to support a diagnostic hypothesis. This task has time limitations and it can not be scaled for big data repositories [2]. Without an objective interpretation of these medical images, more advanced research is limited to a small subset of patient cases. It is then fundamental to have a first automatic interpretation and selection of the images before performing a more in–depth image analysis [7]. Many computer–aided diagnosis techniques thus initially require the identification and segmentation of anatomical structures.

B. Menze et al. (Eds.): MCV 2014, LNCS 8848, pp. 189–200, 2014.
DOI: 10.1007/978-3-319-13972-2_18

There are already various methods that have been proposed for segmenting anatomical structures. Some approaches are based on shape modeling or random decision forests, while others combine intensity feature selection with dynamic programming [1,6,8]. Even though some of the available approaches have obtained high segmentation overlap, the results are frequently obtained in private data sets. Many of these methods are also targeted towards the segmentation of a single anatomical structure. Extending their implementation for other organs is not straightforward and might require extensive re–training of the algorithm.

The Visual Concept Extraction Challenge in Radiology(VISCERAL[1]) benchmarks aim at evaluating the available state–of–the–art segmentation methods on a large public data set [5]. The VISCERAL data set includes multiple anatomical structures manually annotated by expert radiologists. These annotations were considered the 'gold truth' against which the output segmentations from the submitted methods are compared. The manual annotations include multiple organs (e.g. lungs, kidney, liver...) and relevant anatomical structures (e.g. some muscles and bones) in different imaging modalities such as computed tomography (CT) and magnetic resonance (MR).

A fully automatic segmentation approach for multiple anatomical structures is presented in this paper. It is implemented using multi–atlas registration in a hierarchic pipeline that includes *a priori* anatomical localization knowledge. It maximizes the information contained in each patient scan, exploiting the inherent anatomical variability and spatial distribution of the structures. The results from the method are presented and compared to those of the other segmentation methods submitted in the VISCERAL Anatomy Benchmarks.

2   Materials and Methods

The proposed method is divided into three steps: 1. Pre–processing, 2. Hierarchic anatomical registration and 3. Label fusion. Each step is detailed in the following paragraphs. The algorithm has already been described in [12].

2.1   Preprocessing

The test or target volumes were resampled to obtain isometric voxels in all dimensions. The volumes were then downscaled half their size to improve the algorithm speed and reduce the search area for the image registrations. The volumes were upscaled to their original size for the final label fusion step of the method.

2.2   Hierarchic Anatomical Registration

Multi–atlas Based Registration. Multi–atlas based segmentation is an approach that estimates the unknown location of a structure in a target image

---

[1] http://www.visceral.eu/, as of 5 October 2014.

using multiple reference atlases. Each atlas includes a patient volume and a label volume, created by manual annotation. The label volume had annotated the location of one or more structures in the patient volume. Parameterized image registration based on a cost function was used to increase the spatial relationship between the target and atlas volume. The cost function was optimized in each step using the adaptive stochastic gradient descent optimizer proposed in [3] with a multi–resolution approach. Normalized cross–correlation was used as a similarity metric for the cost function in CT scans. The label volumes were then transformed taking the coordinate transformation obtained from the registration. The image registration was performed using the implementation and method of Elastix software[2] [4].

Both affine and non–rigid registrations were carried out for the final label estimation. Affine registration allowed scaling, rotation and translation. It was used as an initial alignment for both the global and local transformations. The non–rigid B–spline registrations defined the final output label and were used only in the local anatomical regions–of–interest (ROI) created for each structure. This registration pipeline generates a robust initial estimation for each anatomical structure with multiple and faster to compute rigid registrations. Global and local rigid registrations improve the starting point for the computationally more expensive non–rigid registrations. However, the final non–rigid registrations are only performed locally increasing the overall speed of the algorithm.

Anatomical Hierarchy. In [11] it was shown how some structures influence the distribution of the multiple organs in the thorax and abdomen. This anatomical property was exploited to create a hierarchic segmentation pipeline. The advantage of such a hierarchy is that the smaller and harder to segment structures can benefit from a previous initialization made with a bigger surrounding anatomical structure. It also maximizes the information contained in the training set, since each structure is registered within their own anatomical ROI (see Fig. 1). Therefore, the registrations are less affected by global inconsistencies between the atlases and target volumes.

A global affine registration is followed by individual affine registrations using local binary masks to enforce the spatial correlation of each anatomical structure separately. These masks are obtained from the morphological dilation of the intersection in the output labels from the different atlases registered with rigid registrations. After each anatomical structure has its own independent ROI mask, the volumes are registered again but using a non–rigid B–spline transformation model. The new transformed label volumes for each structure constitute the individual votes that will be used for the label fusion step. The information regarding the hierarchic anatomical pipeline was initially described in [12]. A graphical representation of this hierarchy is presented in Figure(see Fig. 2). It shows the anatomical hierarchy and the type of registrations used in the algorithm for all the 20 available anatomical structures in the VISCERAL Anatomy benchmarks. It includes thoracic, abdominal and pelvic organs such as liver,

---

[2] Elastix:http://elastix.isi.uu.nl, 2014. [Online; accessed 5–October–2014].

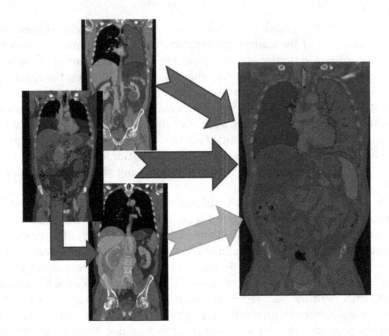

Fig. 1. Hierarchic anatomical registrations. The registrations of the bigger structures are used as a initialization for the smaller structures, which are harder to segment. Smaller anatomical structures show a higher anatomical variability and lower contrast, the latter is particularly evident in un–enhanced medical scans. In the proposed method, most of the registrations of structures like liver, lungs and urinary bladder will be reused, which makes it faster and more robust for the segmentation of structures like kidneys and gallbladder

lungs and the urinary bladder; bone structures like the sternum and first lumbar vertebra and abdominal muscles like the rectus abdominis and psoas major.

2.3 Label Fusion

After the multi–atlas registration there is a label estimation for each of the atlases in the training set. It has been shown that fusing the multiple estimation labels generates a more accurate segmentation when compared to the best result obtained from a single estimation label. Although there are many label fusion methods available, setting a majority voting threshold has proven to be an effective straightforward solution [9]. The thresholds are implemented on a per–voxel basis and were optimized in the training set. In this approach we selected five different thresholds, one for each of the allowed configurations in the VISCERAL Anatomy[1] and Anatomy[2] benchmarks.

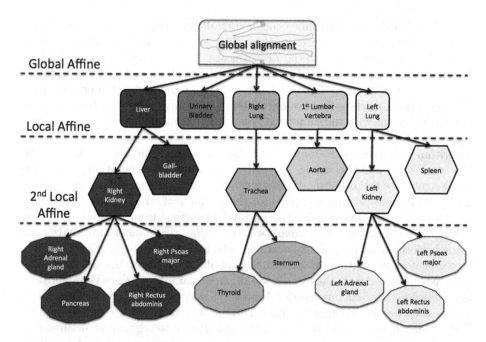

Fig. 2. Hierarchic anatomical correlations included in the algorithm for the Anatomy[2] benchmark. The hierarchy is designated in accordance to a medical expert according to the anatomical locations and shape features of the different structures in the VIS-CERAL data set. For example, after an initial global alignment between the atlas and the target image, the ROI for one of the bigger structures like the liver is created with the intersection of the morphologically dilated liver labels after the correspondent coordinate transformation in the atlas. Then, the images will be rigidly registered again using the liver ROI as a mask for both images. The process is repeated afterwards for the right kidney using the liver coordinate transformation as a starting point. The kidney rigidly registered images will then be the initialization for the pancreas, adrenal glands, right psoas major and rectus abdominis muscles

3 Experimental Setup

3.1 Data Set

Seven volumes were provided for both un–enhanced and contrast–enhanced computed tomography (ceCT) in the initial VISCERAL Anatomy[1] benchmark. For each scan there were originally up to 15 anatomical structures in each 3D volume manually annotated by expert radiologists. The number of volumes was increased to 20 volumes per modality for the Anatomy[2] benchmark with up to 20 annotated structures per volume. These structures include organs like liver, lungs and kidneys, and bones or muscles like the first lumbar vertebra and the abdominal muscles. The complete data set structure list and detailed description of the medical images is described in [10].

Both VISCERAL Anatomy benchmarks allowed participants to select the tasks and anatomical structures in which they wish to participate. The proposed method was trained only with the 7 ceCT scans of the trunk released for the first benchmark. Ten structures fully included in the field–of–view of these volumes were selected. The liver, right and left kidneys, right and left lungs, urinary bladder, spleen, trachea, first lumbar vertebra and gallbladder were segmented in trunk ceCT scans with the submitted approach in Anatomy[1] benchmark. For the Anatomy[2] benchmark the number of training volumes was maintained but the algorithm was updated to segment all the annotated structures from ceCT of the trunk scans and also whole-body CT scans. This implementation process for more structures and other modalities was added in the algorithm using the same methodology and principles applied for the anatomical structures of Anatomy[1].

The main modifications in the original algorithm from Anatomy[1] to the algorithm for Anatomy[2] benchmark were regarding the number of optimization steps performed during the registrations. The increased amount of time needed to segment all 20 anatomical structures from all the CT scans un–enhanced and contrast–enhanced from the test set was of particular interest since the algorithm is intended for big data repositories. However, less optimization can have an effect in the accuracy of the registrations in the search to speed up the algorithm. This trade–off was chosen because of the importance to segment structures like the adrenal glands, the thyroid and abdominal aorta in the clinical practice. The method is now generalized to all CT volumes and the overall execution time of the full method was maintained from the first benchmark with double the amount of possible output segmentations.

3.2   Evaluation

The participants received a virtual cloud–computing 8–core CPU instance with 16 GB RAM. Both the executable and required libraries were installed by the participants in the provided virtual machines (VM). The organizers took over the VMs and ran the executables for all the target volumes in the test set for a pre–defined time period. Once the evaluation phase had finished, the results were published in the VISCERAL project website (Anatomy[1] Results[3]) and (Anatomy[2] Results[4]). The goal of this framework is to generate an objective and un–biased evaluation of the different algorithms with the same test set and computing capabilities for all the participants.

The test set from the Anatomy[1] benchmark included 12 ceCT volumes of the trunk. The results from the proposed method are presented and compared to those of other organ segmentation approaches submitted in the benchmark. For the Anatomy[1] benchmark, five other methods were submitted that segmented anatomical structures in ceCT scans. The methods proposed by Gass et al.(GG),

---

[3] http://www.visceral.eu/closed-benchmarks/benchmark-1/benchmark-1-results/, as of 5 October 2014.

[4] http://www.visceral.eu/closed-benchmarks/anatomy2/anatomy2-results/, as of 5 October 2014.

Table 1. DICE coefficient average results in trunk ceCT test set of the VISCERAL Anatomy[1] benchmark. The proposed hierarchic multi–atlas based method (JM Jimenez del Toro et al. in grey) submitted output segmentations for ten anatomical structures. Highlighted in white are the best overlap obtained for 4 structures: right and left kidney, liver, gallbladder. The left lung and right lungs obtained also high overlap among the submitted methods. SJ Spanier et al., HJ Huang et al., W Wang et al., Kechichian et al. and GG Gass et al. (Benchmark Anatomy1 Results, http://www.visceral.eu/closed-benchmarks/benchmark-1/benchmark-1-results/, as of 5 October 2014).

Participant	Modality	Region	left kidney	right kidney	spleen	liver	left lung	right lung	urinary bladder	muscle body of left rectus abdominis	muscle body of right rectus abdominis	lumbar Vertebra 1	thyroid	pancreas	left psoas major muscle	right psoas major muscle	gallbladder	sternum	aorta	trachea	left adrenal gland	right adrenal gland
			29663	29662	86	58	1326	1302	237	40358	40357	29193	7578	170	32249	32248	187	2473	480	1247	30325	30324
Measure	DICE coefficient																					
SJ	Ctce	ThAb	0.631	0.663	0.690	0.747	0.848	0.975											0.785			
HJ	Ctce	ThAb					0.891															
W	Ctce	ThAb	0.804	0.872	0.873	0.898	0.965	0.969	0.805						0.792	0.811		0.713				
JM	Ctce	ThAb	0.921	0.913	0.852	0.918	0.955	0.965	0.700			0.522					0.566			0.836		
K	Ctce	ThAb	0.747	0.632	0.768	0.806	0.856	0.892	0.718	0.130	0.171	0.447	0.004	0.155	0.706	0.633	0.281	0.454	0.505	0.696	0.000	0.007
GG	Ctce	ThAb	0.903	0.877	0.802	0.899	0.961	0.968	0.676			0.604	0.252	0.465	0.811		0.334	0.595	0.785	0.847	0.204	0.164

Huang et al.(HJ), Kechichian et al.(K), Spanier et al.(SJ) and Wang et al.(W) segmented at least one anatomical structure in ceCT. Most of these participant methods have different implementations and use alternative techniques than those presented in this paper. However the methods proposed by Gass et al. and Kechichian et al. also use atlas–based segmentation approaches. Some of the other techniques used for organ segmentation include level set and shape priors (Wang et al.), rule–based segmentation (Spanier et al.) and prior knowledge models (Huang et al.). More information regarding each of the submitted methods is available in the VISCERAL Anatomy benchmarks results webpage mentioned earlier.

For the Anatomy[2] benchmark the testset included 10 ceCT volumes of the trunk and 10 whole–body un–enhanced CT scans (wbCT). Six other methods were submitted that segmented at least one anatomical structure in ceCT scans. The method proposed by Haworth et al.(H) was added to the previous methods submitted for the Anatomy[1] benchmark (SJ, LHJ formerly HJ, WS formerly W, KDV formerly K and GGS formerly GG). Four of these methods (LHJ, WS, H and GGS) segmented at least one anatomical structure in both contrast–enhanced and un–enhanced CT scans.

The DICE coefficient, adjusted rand index, interclass correlation and average distance error were computed and published for each anatomical structure contained in the test set.

Table 2. Minimum average distance error in trunk ceCT test set of VISCERAL Anatomy[1] benchmark. Highlighted in white are the lowest averaged distance errors obtained with the proposed algorithm (JM Jimenez del Toro et al. in grey). Six of the ten submitted structures (right and left kidney, liver, left lung, gallbladder and trachea) got the lowest distance error with a very low error also for right lung. SJ Spanier et al., HJ Huang et al., W Wang et al., Kechichian et al. and GG Gass et al. (Benchmark Anatomy1 Results, http://www.visceral.eu/closed-benchmarks/benchmark-1/benchmark-1-results/, as of 5 October 2014)

Participant	Modality	Region	left kidney	right kidney	spleen	liver	left lung	right lung	urinary bladder	muscle body of left rectus abdominis	muscle body of right rectus abdominis	lumbar Vertebra 1	thyroid	pancreas	left psoas major muscle	right psoas major muscle	gallbladder	sternum	aorta	trachea	left adrenal gland	right adrenal gland
			29663	29662	86	58	1326	1302	237	40358	40357	29193	7578	170	32249	32248	187	2473	480	1247	30325	30324
Measure			Average distance error																			
SJ	Ctce	ThAb	12.98	11.53	17.13	4.39	11.72	0.05												2.60		
HJ	Ctce	ThAb					0.74															
W	Ctce	ThAb	1.61	0.65	0.51	0.42	0.16	0.08	0.85													
JM	Ctce	ThAb	0.15	0.24	0.66	0.30	0.09	0.06	1.61			5.36					2.36			0.30		
K	Ctce	ThAb	2.82	6.13	1.95	1.96	1.18	0.96	1.74	17.77	16.10	5.50	19.69	24.19	2.51	4.38	9.49	6.63	5.88	2.34	28.97	8.45
GG	Ctce	ThAb	0.28	0.75	1.12	0.58	0.22	0.43	1.65				2.47	5.74	4.64	0.67	8.36	1.40	0.92	0.57	5.52	6.08

4 Results

4.1 Anatomy[1] Results

The results for the 10 anatomical structures had a total average DICE coefficient of 0.815 in ceCT. The DICE coefficients and average distance error tables for the ceCT test set are shown in Tables 1 and 2 respectively. The ranking of the different methods participating in each of anatomical structure are presented in Table 3. The hierarchic multi–atlas based segmentation approach obtained the best overlap in four clinically important anatomical structures: liver, right and left kidneys and gallbladder. Almost all the other segmented structures were in the top–three ranking among the submitted methods. The method also computed the smallest total average distance error with 1.11 average for the 10 structures. Seven of the submitted structures were in top position for this evaluation metric in VISCERAL Anatomy[1].

4.2 Anatomy[2] Results

The results for all the possible anatomical structures had a total average DICE coefficient of 0.67 in ceCT and 0.68 in wbCT. The DICE coefficients results for both modalities are shown in Tables 4 and 5 respectively. The proposed method obtained the best overlap in six anatomical structures in ceCT: thyroid, trachea, left and right adrenal glands and left and right rectus abdominis muscles. Eleven structures in wbCT had the best overlap with the hierarchic anatomical registration method in the Anatomy[2] benchmark: both lungs, lumbar vertebra 1,

Table 3. Segmentation ranking in ceCT test set of VISCERAL Benchmark 1 Anatomy. According to the DICE overlap this is the ranking for the ten submitted structures. The other methods that had output segmentations for these structures are mentioned in the far–left tab: SJ Spanier et al., HJ Huang et al., W Wang et al., Kechichian et al. and GG Gass et al. (Benchmark Anatomy1 Results, http://www.visceral.eu/ closed-benchmarks/benchmark-1/benchmark-1-results/, as of 5 October 2014)

Anatomical structure	Rank Anatomy 1	Other participating methods
left kidney	*1st*	SJ, W, K, GG
right kidney	*1st*	SJ, W, K, GG
liver	*1st*	SJ,HJ, W, K, GG
gallbladder	*1st*	K, GG
trachea	2nd	SJ, K, GG
spleen	2nd	SJ, W, K, GG
1st lumbar vertebra	2nd	K, GG
left lung	3rd	SJ, W, K, GG
urinary bladder	3rd	W, K, GG
right lung	4th	SJ, W, K, GG

thyroid, gallbladder, sternum, aorta, trachea, left and right adrenal glands and left and right rectus abdominis muscles. The hierarchic anatomical registration method was the only method in the Anatomy[2] benchmark that obtained an score for all the possible anatomical structures in the benchmark in both wbCT and ceCT.

5 Discussion and Conclusions

The main contributions of this hierarchic anatomical segmentation approach are:

- A robust automatic segmentation approach for multiple anatomical structures. The method was benchmarked against different segmentation approaches for single or multiple anatomical structures. It obtained the best overlap and smallest average distance error for most of the structures it segmented in the publicly available VISCERAL Anatomy[1] test set for ceCT scans. It was also produced the best overlap for various kind of organs like the lungs and thyroid, bone structures like the sternum and first lumbar vertebra and the abdominal muscles included in the data set in wbCT.
- A hierarchy for anatomical structure segmentation was defined based on the organ size and tissue contrast. This hierarchy can be extended for more anatomical structures and implemented also with other medical imaging modalities such as MR. The competitive results of the method particularly

Table 4. DICE coefficient average results in trunk ceCT test set of the VISCERAL Anatomy[2] benchmark. The proposed method (JM in grey) obtained the highest overlap for 6 of the 20 anatomical structures (results in white). Particularly for small anatomical structures like the adrenal glands and thyroid it produces better estimation than the other participant methods. The hirarchic method was the only one producing an score for all the structures in the data set. This characteristic of the implementation highlights the method's flexibility to be adapted for any kind of anatomical structure (Anatomy2 Results, http://www.visceral.eu/closed-benchmarks/anatomy2/anatomy2-results, as of 5 October 2014).

Participant	Modality	Region	left kidney	right kidney	spleen	liver	left lung	right lung	urinary bladder	muscle body of left rectus abdominis	muscle body of right rectus abdominis	lumbar Vertebra 1	thyroid	pancreas	left psoas major muscle	right psoas major muscle	gallbladder	sternum	aorta	trachea	left adrenal gland	right adrenal gland
			29663	29662	86	58	1326	1302	237	40358	40357	29193	7578	170	32249	32248	187	2473	480	1247	30325	30324
Measure			DICE coefficient																			
SJ	CTce	ThAb	0.829	0.870	0.822		0.970	0.968												0.851		
LHJ	CTce	ThAb			0.937																	
WS	CTce	ThAb	0.930	0.923	0.874	0.930	0.967	0.966	0.870						0.820	0.845			0.773			
H	CTce	ThAb	0.912	0.885		0.912	0.956	0.964							0.808	0.806			0.760			
JM	CTce	ThAb	0.910	0.884	0.730	0.887	0.959	0.963	0.679	0.474	0.453	0.523	0.549	0.423	0.794	0.799	0.276	0.721	0.762	0.855	0.331	0.342
KDV	CTce	ThAb	0.856	0.805	0.839	0.933	0.957	0.953	0.774	0.134	0.257	0.486	0.039	0.544	0.792	0.711	0.143	0.634	0.578	0.624	0.000	0.000
GGS	CTce	ThAb	0.913	0.914	0.781	0.908	0.961	0.965	0.683			0.624	0.184	0.460	0.813		0.381	0.635	0.785	0.847	0.250	0.213

for the smaller structures in the dataset supports the notion that a better initialization leads to more accurate segmentations in these harder to segment structures.
- An efficient exploitation of a small training set based on the inherent anatomical variability of anatomical structures was achieved. This allows enough flexibility to be quickly adapted for new images coming from scanners with different parameter tuning. Also more anatomical structures can be added like it was shown in the implementation with added number of segmented structures from Anatomy[1] to the Anatomy[2] benchmark.

Although the overlap coefficient are consistent for most of the evaluated structures, the smaller and harder to segment structure estimations(e.g. gallbladder, adrenal glands) still need to be improved to be used in a real clinical scenario. It is apparent the reduction of optimization steps used in the Anatomy[1] benchmark compared to the Anatomy[2] results lead to a decrease in the accuracy of the bigger structures like liver. An optimal trade-off between the methods accuracy and the segmentation speed needs to be better defined for future implementations. The method's speed and accuracy can also be improved with a more computationally efficient method for the mathematical morphology and more advanced label fusion techniques.

For future work the method will optimized for a faster implementation and more consistent segmentation results for the initial segmentations of anatomical structures like the liver and spleen. An evaluation of the method for the other modalities (MR and contrast–enhanced MR) is also foreseen with a much bigger test set.

Table 5. DICE coefficient average results in whole–body CT test set of the VISCERAL Anatomy[2] benchmark. The proposed hierarchic anatomical registration method (JM in grey) submitted output segmentations for all the available anatomical structures. Highlighted in white are the best overlap in the benchmark obtained for 11 structures (results in white). The method is particularly robust when compared to other algorithms that segment multiple structures. It generates the best estimations for both large organs like the lungs and small structures like the adrenal glands (Anatomy2 Results, http://www.visceral.eu/closed-benchmarks/anatomy2/anatomy2-results, as of 5 October 2014).

Participant	Modality	Region	left kidney	right kidney	spleen	liver	left lung	right lung	urinary bladder	muscle body of left rectus abdominis	muscle body of right rectus abdominis	lumbar Vertebra 1	thyroid	pancreas	left psoas major muscle	right psoas major muscle	gallbladder	sternum	aorta	trachea	left adrenal gland	right adrenal gland
			29663	29662	86	58	1326	1302	237	40358	40357	29193	7578	170	32249	32248	187	2473	480	1247	30325	30324
Measure		DICE coefficient																				
LHJ	CT	wb				0.831																
WS	CT	wb	0.873	0.904	0.914	0.934	0.960	0.962	0.713						0.833	0.828		0.660				
H	CT	wb	0.906	0.838		0.907	0.959	0.960							0.808	0.786				0.769		
JM	CT	wb	0.784	0.790	0.703	0.866	0.972	0.975	0.698	0.551	0.519	0.718	0.549	0.408	0.806	0.787	0.276	0.761	0.753	0.920	0.373	0.355
GGS	CT	wb	0.778	0.748	0.671	0.831	0.952	0.960	0.666			0.412	0.450	0.415	0.777	0.747	0.191	0.633	0.741	0.840	0.067	0.186

Acknowledgments. The research leading to these results has received funding from the European Union Seventh Framework Programme (FP7/2007–2014) under grant agreement n° 318068 VISCERAL.

References

1. Criminisi, A., Robertson, D., Konukoglu, E., Shotton, J., Pathak, S., White, S., Siddiqui, K.: Regression forests for efficient anatomy detection and localization in computed tomography scans. Med. Image Anal. **17**(8), 1293–1303 (2013)
2. Haux, R.: Hospital information systems—past, present, future. Int. J. Med. Informatics **75**, 268–281 (2005)
3. Klein, S., Pluim, J.P., Staring, M., Viergever, M.A.: Adaptive stochastic gradient descent optimisation for image registration. Int. J. Comput. Vision **81**(3), 227–239 (2009)
4. Klein, S., Staring, M., Murphy, K., Viergever, M.A., Pluim, J.P.: Elastix: a toolbox for intensity-based medical image registration. IEEE Trans. Med. imaging **29**(1), 196–205 (2010)
5. Langs, G., Müller, H., Menze, B.H., Hanbury, A.: Visceral: Towards large data in medical imaging–challenges and directions. Lect. Notes Comput. Sci. **7723**, 92–98 (2013)
6. Linguraru, M.G., Sandberg, J.K., Li, Z., Shah, F., Summers, R.M.: Automated segmentation and quantification of liver and spleen from CT images using normalized probabilistic atlases and enhancement estimation. Med. Phys. **37**(2), 771–783 (2010)
7. Müller, H., Hanbury, A., Shorbaji, N.A.: Methods special topic section, introduction to medical information retrieval. Methods Inf. Med. **51**(6), 516–518 (2012)
8. Oda, M., Nakaoka, T., Kitasaka, T., Furukawa, K., Misawa, K., Fujiwara, M., Mori, K.: Organ segmentation from 3D abdominal CT images based on atlas selection and graph cut. In: Yoshida, H., Sakas, G., Linguraru, M.G. (eds.) Abdominal Imaging. LNCS, vol. 7029, pp. 181–188. Springer, Heidelberg (2012)

9. Rohlfing, T., Brandt, R., Menzel, R., Maurer Jr., C.R.: Evaluation of atlas selection strategies for atlas-based image segmentation with application to confocal microscopy images of bee brains. Neuroimage **23**(8), 983–994 (2004)
10. Jiménez del Toro, O.A., Goksel, O., Menze, B., Müller, H., Langs, G., Weber, M.A., Eggel, I., Gruenberg, K., Holzer, M., Kotsios-Kontokotsios, G., Krenn, M., Schaer, R., Taha, A.A., Winterstein, M., Hanbury, A.: VISCERA—VISual Concept Extraction challenge in RAdioLogy: ISBI 2014 challenge organization. In: Goksel, O. (ed.) Proceedings of the VISCERAL Challenge at ISBI, vol. 1194, pp. 6–15. CEUR Workshop Proceedings, Beijing, China (2014)
11. Jiménez del Toro, O.A., Müller, H.: Multi-structure atlas-based segmentation using anatomical regions of interest. In: Menze, B., Langs, G., Montillo, A., Kelm, M., Müller, H., Tu, Z. (eds.) MCV 2013. LNCS, vol. 8331, pp. 217–221. Springer, Heidelberg (2014)
12. Jiménez del Toro, O.A., Müller, H.: Hierarchical multi-structure segmentation guided by anatomical correlations. In: Goksel, O. (ed.) Proceedings of the VISCERAL Challenge at ISBI, pp. 32–36. CEUR Workshop Proceedings, Beijing, China (2014)

Automatic 3D Multiorgan Segmentation via Clustering and Graph Cut Using Spatial Relations and Hierarchically-Registered Atlases

Razmig Kéchichian[1]([✉]), Sébastien Valette[2], Michaël Sdika[2], and Michel Desvignes[1]

[1] Gipsa-lab: CNRS UMR 5216, Université de Grenoble, Saint-Martin-d'Héres, France
`razmig.kechichian@gipsa-lab.grenoble-inp.fr`
[2] Creatis: CNRS UMR 5220, Inserm U1044, Université de Lyon, Villeurbanne, France

Abstract. We propose a generic method for automatic multiple-organ segmentation based on a multilabel Graph Cut optimization approach which uses location likelihood of organs and prior information of spatial relationships between them. The latter is derived from shortest-path constraints defined on the adjacency graph of structures and the former is defined by probabilistic atlases learned from a training dataset. Organ atlases are mapped to the image by a fast (2+1)D hierarchical registration method based on SURF keypoints. Registered atlases are furthermore used to derive organ intensity likelihoods. Prior and likelihood models are then introduced in a joint centroidal Voronoi image clustering and Graph Cut multiobject segmentation framework. Qualitative and quantitative evaluation has been performed on contrast-enhanced CT images from the Visceral Benchmark dataset.

1 Introduction and Related Work

Clinical practice today, especially whole-body CT and MRI scanning, often generates large numbers of high-resolution images, which makes tasks of efficient data access, transfer, analysis and visualization challenging, especially in distributed computing environments which have seen growing use of handheld terminals for interactive data access and visualization of anatomy. Therefore, there is great interest for efficient and robust medical image segmentation algorithms for the purposes of creating patient-specific anatomical models, clinical applications, medical research and education, and visualization of full-body anatomy [2].

Traditionally single-object or pathology oriented, recent image processing methods [7,9–11,14,16,17] have made the analysis and segmentation of multiple anatomical structures increasingly possible. However, CT and MR images have intrinsic characteristics that render its automatic segmentation challenging. They are commonly degraded by various noise sources and artifacts due to limited acquisition time and resolution, and patient motion which all reduce the

© Springer International Publishing Switzerland 2014
B. Menze et al. (Eds.): MCV 2014, LNCS 8848, pp. 201–209, 2014.
DOI: 10.1007/978-3-319-13972-2_19

prominence of intensity edges in images. Regardless of the imaging modality and related artifacts, many anatomically and functionally distinct structures, especially those corresponding to soft tissues, have similar intensity levels in images and, furthermore, blend into surrounding tissues which have intensities close to their own. It is impossible to identify and segment such structures automatically on the basis of intensity information only. Hence, most advanced segmentation methods exploit some form of prior information on structure location [14,18] or interrelations [7,10,16,17] to achieve greater robustness and precision.

Graph Cut methods, which have been widely applied to single-object segmentation problems [3], rely on a maximum-flow binary optimization scheme of a discrete cost function on the image graph. For a particular class of cost functions which frequently arises in segmentation applications [12], these methods produce provably-good approximate solutions in multiobject [4] and global optima in single-object segmentation. In addition, simultaneous multiobject segmentation approaches are superior to their sequential counterparts in that they raise questions neither on the best segmentation sequence to follow nor on how to avoid the propagation of errors on individual segmentations [7].

We propose a generic method for automatic multiple-organ segmentation based on multilabel Graph Cut optimization which uses location and intensity likelihoods of organs and prior information of their spatial configuration. The spatial prior is derived from shortest-path pairwise constraints defined on the adjacency graph of structures [10], and the organ location likelihood is defined by probabilistic atlases learned from the Visceral Benchmark training dataset [8]. We register organ atlases to the image prior to segmentation using a fast $(2+1)$D registration method based on SURF keypoints [1]. Registered atlases are also used to derive organ intensity likelihoods. Prior and likelihood models are then introduced in a joint centroidal Voronoi image clustering and Graph Cut multi-object segmentation framework. We present the results of qualitative and quantitative evaluation of our method on contrast-enhanced CT images from the Visceral Benchmark dataset.

2   Methods

2.1   SURF Keypoint-Based Image Registration

We first outline our fast $(2+1)$D rigid registration method, which is based on keypoints detection. Features are extracted in 2D volume slices. This has the advantage of being fast and easily parallelizable. Another advantage is that medical data is usually stored in a Picture Archiving and Communication System (PACS) as volume slices instead of full volumes. Our method easily fits into such medical environments. Note that while feature extraction is done in 2D images, registration is still performed in 3D, hence the $(2+1)$D notation.

We currently use the SURF image descriptor [1], but our approach is generic and would work with others. To reduce computation time, we first downsample the input volume to a user-specified dimension. As a rule of thumb, we isotropically resample each volume so that its second longest dimension is equal to the desired resolution R. For example, when $R = 80$, the POPI CT volume [19] of dimensions $482 \times 360 \times 141$ and spacing $0.97\,\text{mm} \times 0.97\,\text{mm} \times 2\,\text{mm}$ is resampled to a $107 \times 80 \times 64$ volume with an isotropic spacing of $4.39\,\text{mm}$.

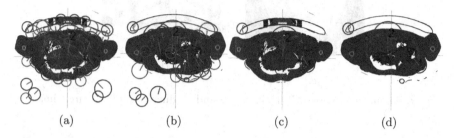

(a)   (b)   (c)   (d)

Fig. 1. Matching two slices of POPI (a) and P1 (b) volumes. (a) and (b) show all features found in both slices (a feature is represented by a circle and its orientation by its radius). (c) and (d) show the three matching features between the two slices.

Next, we extract 2D SURF features from each slice. As these operations are completely independent, this step is carried out in a parallel manner. Figure 1 shows feature extraction on POPI and P1 CT images [15]. The number of extracted features is 1154 and 1079, respectively. Figures 1c and d show the three matching couples found in both images. Once 2D matches are found, we are able to perform volume registration. For robustness purposes, we use a simple scale + translation transformation model:

$$\begin{bmatrix} x' \\ y' \\ z' \end{bmatrix} = s \begin{bmatrix} x \\ y \\ z \end{bmatrix} + \begin{bmatrix} t_x \\ t_y \\ t_z \end{bmatrix} . \tag{1}$$

We estimate the 4 parameters s, t_x, t_y and t_z in similar spirit to the RANSAC method [6], which is an iterative parametric model estimation method known to be very efficient in the presence of outliers. One RANSAC iteration usually consists in randomly picking a small number of samples to estimate the model parameters, and then counting the number of data samples consistent with the model, rejecting outliers. After performing all iterations, the model providing the highest number of consistent data samples is kept as the solution.

2.2   Organ Atlas Construction

Using 20 contrast-enhanced CT images and ground-truth annotations thereof from the Visceral Benchmark dataset [8], we construct a probabilistic atlas for each of the following 20 structures: thyroid; trachea; sternum; liver; spleen; pancreas; gallbladder; first lumbar vertebra; aorta; urinary bladder; right and left lungs, kidneys, adrenal glands, psoas major and rectus abdominis muscle bodies. In addition, we create atlases for three additional image and body regions: background (BKG), thorax and abdomen (THAB) and a body envelope (ENV) from

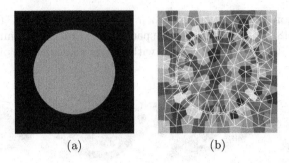

(a)   (b)

Fig. 2. An image-adaptive CVT clustering and its dual graph for a circle image.

annotations generated automatically as follows. BKG is created by thresholding the CT image followed by morphological processing in order to isolate the body region. THAB is created as the dilated union of the aforementioned 20 structures and their bounding 3D ellipse, from which the structures are subtracted after dilation. Finally, ENV is defined as the image minus BKG and THAB. Note that ENV is a crude body envelope that comprises skin, fat, muscle and bone structures. Refer to Fig. 4c for an illustration.

To create atlases, we use a representative image from the dataset as a reference and register remaining images to it via the method described in Sect. 2.1. We register each structure separately in a bounding cube of a given margin in the intensity image, defined according to the corresponding annotation image, and apply the obtained transform subsequently to the annotation image. We accumulate annotations thus registered in a 3D histogram of reference image dimensions which is normalized to produce the corresponding probability map.

2.3   Image Clustering

The full-resolution voxel representation is often redundant because objects usually comprise many similar pixels that could be grouped. Therefore, we simplify the image prior to segmentation by an image-adaptive centroidal Voronoi tessellation (CVT) which strikes a good balance between cluster compactness and object boundary adherence, and helps to place subsequent segmentation boundaries precisely. We have shown that the clustering step improves the overall runtime and memory footprint of the segmentation process up to an order of magnitude without compromising the quality of the result [10].

Let us define a grayscale image as a set of voxels $\mathcal{I} = \{v \mid v = (x, y, z)\}$ and associate to each voxel $v \in \mathcal{I}$ a gray-level I_v from some range $I \subset \mathbb{R}$. Given a grayscale image $\mathcal{I}$ and n sites $c_i \in \mathcal{I}$, a CVT partitions $\mathcal{I}$ into n disjoint clusters C_i associated with each centroid c_i and minimizes the following energy:

$$F(v; c_i) = \sum_{i=1}^{n} \left(\sum_{v \in C_i} \rho(v) \left(\|v - c_i\|^2 + \alpha \|I_v - I_i\|^2 \right) \right) . \tag{2}$$

In (2), $\rho(v)$ is a density function defined according to the intensity-gradient magnitude at voxel v, $\rho(v) = |\nabla I_v|$, α is a positive scalar and I_i is the gray-level of the cluster C_i defined as the mean intensity of its voxels. Refer to Fig. 2 for an illustration in 2D. To minimize (2), we apply a variant of the clustering algorithm in [5] which approximates a CVT in a computationally-efficient manner, involving only local queries on voxels located on boundaries of pairs of clusters.

For referral in later sections, we shall define the graph of a CVT, illustrated in Fig. 2b. Denote the surface of a cluster C_i by ∂C_i. Given a CVT clustering $\mathcal{C}$, let the set $\mathcal{S}$ index its clusters, and let $\mathcal{G} = \langle \mathcal{S}, \mathcal{E} \rangle$ be an undirected graph on cluster centroids where pairs of clusters having nonzero-area common surface define the set of edges $\mathcal{E} = \{\{i, j\} \mid i, j \in \mathcal{S}, |\partial C_i \cap \partial C_j| \neq 0\}$. Consequently, the neighborhood of a node $i \in \mathcal{S}$ is defined as $\mathcal{N}_i = \{j \mid j \in \mathcal{S}, \exists \{i, j\} \in \mathcal{E}\}$.

2.4 Multi-Organ Image Segmentation

We formulate image segmentation as a labeling problem, defined as the assignment of a label from a set of 23 labels L representing the structures to be segmented to each of the variables in a set of n variables, indexed by $\mathcal{S}$, corresponding to the clusters of a CVT-clustered image. Assume that each variable $i \in \mathcal{S}$ is associated with the corresponding node in the graph $\mathcal{G}$ of the CVT defined in Sect. 2.3. An assignment of labels to all variables is called a configuration, and is denoted by $\ell \in \mathcal{L}$. An assignment of a label to a single variable is denoted by ℓ_i. We cast the labeling problem in a maximum a posteriori estimation framework and solve it by minimizing the following energy function of label configurations via the Expansion Moves multilabel Graph Cut algorithm [4]:

$$E(\ell) = t_1 \sum_{i \in \mathcal{S}} D_i(\ell_i) + t_2 \sum_{i \in \mathcal{S}} P_i(\ell_i) + \frac{1}{2} \sum_{i \in \mathcal{S}} \sum_{j \in \mathcal{N}_i} V_{i,j}(\ell_i, \ell_j) . \qquad (3)$$

In (3), t_1 and t_2 are temperature hyperparameters, $\mathcal{N}_i$ is the neighborhood of the variable $i \in \mathcal{S}$. The first and second sums in (3) correspond respectively to organ intensity and location (atlas) likelihood energies, and the third is the energy of a prior distribution of label configurations expressed as a Markov random field w.r.t. the graph $\mathcal{G}$. We shall define these terms in detail.

Spatial Configuration Prior. Pairwise terms of (3) encode prior information on interactions between labels assigned to pairs of neighboring variables encouraging the spatial consistency of labeling with respect to a reference model. We define these terms according to our piecewise-constant vicinity prior model proposed in [10], which, unlike the standard Potts model, incurs multiple levels of penalization capturing the spatial configuration of structures in multiobject segmentation. It is defined as follows. Let $\mathcal{R}$ be the set of symmetric adjacency relations on pairs of distinct labels, $\mathcal{R} = \{r \mid a\,r\,b,\ a, b \in L, a \neq b\}$. $\mathcal{R}$ can be represented by a weighted undirected graph on L, $\mathcal{A} = \langle L, W \rangle$, with the set of edges $W = \{\{a, b\} \mid \exists r \in \mathcal{R}, a\,r\,b, a \neq b\}$ where edge weights are defined by $w(\{a, b\}) = 1$, such that $w(\{a, b\}) = \infty$ if $\nexists r \in \mathcal{R}, a\,r\,b$.

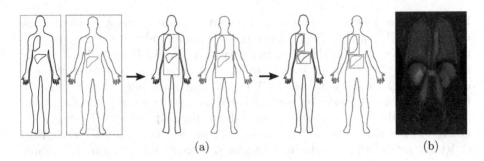

(a)   (b)

Fig. 3. (a) An illustration of our hierarchical registration procedure, and (b) an example of registered organ atlases overlaid on the image.

Given the graph $\mathcal{A}$, we define the pairwise term in (3) as:

$$V_{i,j}(\ell_i, \ell_j) = |\partial C_i \cap \partial C_j| \, \varpi(a, b), \quad \ell_i = a, \, \ell_j = b \ . \tag{4}$$

where $\varpi(a, b)$ is the shortest-path weight from a to b in $\mathcal{A}$. The area of the common surface of adjacent clusters $|\partial C_i \cap \partial C_j|$ is introduced so that the sum of pairwise energies in (3) $\forall a, b \in L$ is equal to the area of the common surface between the corresponding pair of objects multiplied by the shortest-path weight.

Intensity and Location Likelihoods. Unary terms of (3) measure the cost of assigning labels to variables. They are defined as negative log-likelihood functions derived from organ observed intensity and location probabilities:

$$D_i(\ell_i) = -\ln \prod_{v \in C_i} \Pr(I_v \mid \ell_i) \ , \tag{5a}$$

$$P_i(\ell_i) = -\ln \prod_{v \in C_i} \Pr(X_v \mid \ell_i) \ . \tag{5b}$$

In (5b), X_v denotes the object-space coordinates of the voxel v. Conditional probabilities in (5a) and (5b) correspond respectively to those of voxel intensity and location given the structure ℓ_i. To estimate the conditional probability distribution $\Pr(I \mid l)$ for a given label $l \in L$, we first register the corresponding organ atlas to the image, then estimate the conditional probability as a Gauss-smoothed and normalized intensity histogram derived from voxels in high-probability regions of the registered atlas. Conditional probability distributions $\Pr(X \mid L)$ are defined directly from registered atlases. The next section details our hierarchical registration approach which maps organ atlases to the image.

Hierarchical Registration of Organ Atlases. We register probabilistic organ atlases, constructed as described in Sect. 2.2, to the image in a 3-step hierarchical fashion starting at the full image, then on an intermediate level

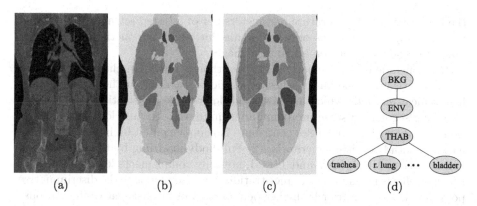

    (a)   (b)   (c)   (d)

Fig. 4. A segmentation of 12 structures from the Visceral Benchmark dataset image 10000109_1_CTce_ThAb. The coronal sections correspond to (a) the image, (b) its segmentation and (c) the associated ground-truth with additional labels for BKG, ENV and THAB. (d) illustrates the adjacency graph used to define the spatial prior model.

Table 1. Mean Dice figures for select organs calculated on 10 segmentations per organ.

Structures	Dice	Structures	Dice	Structures	Dice
Lung (R)	0.95	Kidney (R)	0.81	Urinary bladder	0.77
Lung (L)	0.96	Kidney (L)	0.86	Trachea	0.62
Liver	0.93	Psoas major (R)	0.71	Sternum	0.63
Spleen	0.84	Psoas major (L)	0.79	Aorta	0.57

corresponding to the THAB region, and finally on individual organs. After performing registration on each level, we apply the obtained transform to the corresponding atlas as well as to those of organs contained in the registered region. As in Sect. 2.2, we register each structure separately in a bounding cube of a given margin in the intensity image, defined according to the corresponding atlas. Figure 3 illustrates the hierarchical registration procedure and gives an example of registered organ atlases overlaid on the image to which they have been registered.

3   Results and Conclusions

We have carried out qualitative evaluation on several contrast-enhanced CT images from the Visceral Benchmark training dataset [8]. An example is given in Fig. 4. The number of CVT clusters is equal to 3 % of image voxel count. Temperature parameters t_1 and t_2 are set such that intensity and location likelihood-based unary terms contribute equally to (3). The spatial prior is defined according to the adjacency graph given in Fig. 4d. Table 1 presents the results of quantitative evaluation of our method on contrast-enhanced CT images during the Visceral Anatomy 2 Benchmark. We report results corresponding to the best setting of temperature parameters out of 5 tested settings. In addition, we give mean Dice figures only for organs for which our method successfully produced segmentations on all 10 test images.

We conclude on two remarks. (1) Even though our hierarchical approach to mapping atlases to the image relies on a rigid registration method, unlike many hierarchical methods which use non-rigid deformable registration [13], it helps localizing segmented structure boundaries quite well, because location information roughly registered atlases contribute is complemented by intensity similarity and spatial consistency criteria. (2) Full-body modeling by the introduction of annotations BKG, ENV and THAB, not only complements location information and allows for hierarchical registration, but also increases the discriminative power of the spatial prior by higher penalization of inconsistent configurations.

References

1. Bay, H., Tuytelaars, T., Van Gool, L.: SURF: speeded up robust features. In: Leonardis, A., Bischof, H., Pinz, A. (eds.) ECCV 2006, Part I. LNCS, vol. 3951, pp. 404–417. Springer, Heidelberg (2006)
2. Blume, A., Chun, W., Kogan, D., Kokkevis, V., Weber, N., Petterson, R.W., Zeiger, R.: Google body: 3D human anatomy in the browser. In: ACM SIGGRAPH 2011 Talks, pp. 19:1–19:1 (2011)
3. Boykov, Y., Funka-Lea, G.: Graph cuts and efficient N-D image segmentation. Int. J. Comput. Vis. **70**(2), 109–131 (2006)
4. Boykov, Y., Veksler, O., Zabih, R.: Fast approximate energy minimization via graph cuts. IEEE Trans. Pattern Anal. Mach. Intell. **23**(11), 1222–1239 (2001)
5. Dardenne, J., Valette, S., Siauve, N., Burais, N., Prost, R.: Variational tetraedral mesh generation from discrete volume data. Vis. Comput. **25**(5), 401–410 (2009)
6. Fischler, M.A., Bolles, R.C.: Random sample consensus: a paradigm for model fitting with applications to image analysis and automated cartography. Commun. ACM **24**(6), 381–395 (1981)
7. Fouquier, G., Atif, J., Bloch, I.: Sequential model-based segmentation and recognition of image structures driven by visual features and spatial relations. Comput. Vis. Image Underst. **116**(1), 146–165 (2012)
8. Hanbury, A., Müller, H., Langs, G., Weber, M.A., Menze, B.H., Fernandez, T.S.: Bringing the algorithms to the data: cloud–based benchmarking for medical image analysis. In: Catarci, T., Forner, P., Hiemstra, D., Peñas, A., Santucci, G. (eds.) CLEF 2012. LNCS, vol. 7488, pp. 24–29. Springer, Heidelberg (2012)
9. Iglesias, J.E., Konukoglu, E., Montillo, A., Tu, Z., Criminisi, A.: Combining generative and discriminative models for semantic segmentation of CT scans via active learning. In: Székely, G., Hahn, H.K. (eds.) IPMI 2011. LNCS, vol. 6801, pp. 25–36. Springer, Heidelberg (2011)
10. Kéchichian, R., Valette, S., Desvignes, M., Prost, R.: Shortest-path constraints for 3d multi-object semi-automatic segmentation via clustering and graph cut. IEEE Trans. Image Process. **22**(11), 4224–4236 (2013)
11. Kohlberger, T., Sofka, M., Zhang, J., Birkbeck, N., Wetzl, J., Kaftan, J., Declerck, J., Zhou, S.K.: Automatic multi-organ segmentation using learning-based segmentation and level set optimization. In: Fichtinger, G., Martel, A., Peters, T. (eds.) MICCAI 2011, Part III. LNCS, vol. 6893, pp. 338–345. Springer, Heidelberg (2011)

12. Kolmogorov, V., Zabih, R.: What energy functions can be minimized via graph cuts? IEEE Trans. Pattern Anal. Mach. Intell. **26**(2), 147–159 (2004)
13. Lester, H., Arridge, S.R.: A survey of hierarchical non-linear medical image registration. Pattern Recogn. **32**(1), 129–149 (1999)
14. Linguraru, M.G., Pura, J.A., Pamulapati, V., Summers, R.M.: Statistical 4D graphs for multi-organ abdominal segmentation from multiphase CT. Med. Image Anal. **16**(4), 904–914 (2012)
15. Lynch, R., Pitson, G., Ball, D., Claude, L., Sarrut, D.: Computed tomographic atlas for the new international lymph node map for lung cancer: a radiation oncologist perspective. Pract. Radiat. Oncol. **3**(1), 54–66 (2013)
16. Okada, T., Yoshida, Y., Hori, M., Summers, R.M., Chen, Y.W., Tomiyama, N., Sato, Y.: Abdominal multi-organ segmentation of CT images based on hierarchical spatial modeling of organ interrelations. In: Proceedings of the 3rd International Conference on Abdominal Imaging: Computational and Clinical Applications, pp. 173–180 (2012)
17. Seifert, S., Barbu, A., Zhou, S.K., Liu, D., Feulner, J., Huber, M., Suehling, M., Cavallaro, A., Comaniciu, D.: Hierarchical parsing and semantic navigation of full body CT data. In: SPIE Medical Imaging, Lake Buena Vista, FL, USA, Feb 2009
18. Song, Z., Tustison, N., Avants, B., Gee, J.: Adaptive graph cuts with tissue priors for brain MRI segmentation. In: IEEE ISBI, pp. 762–765, Apr 2006
19. Vandemeulebroucke, J., Sarrut, D., Clarysse, P.: Point-validated pixel-based breathing thorax model. In: International Conference on the Use of Computers in Radiation Therapy (ICCR), pp. 195–199. Toronto, Canada, Jun 2007

Author Index

Ayache, Nicholas 148

Berte, Benjamin 148
Berthold, Michael R. 59

Cabrera-Lozoya, Rocío 148
Cai, Weidong 3
Cochet, Hubert 148
Criminisi, Antonio 116

de Bruijne, Marleen 47
Desvignes, Michel 201
Dowling, Jason A. 105

Fan, Yingfang 181
Fang, Chihua 181
Fripp, Jurgen 105

Gao, Yaozong 22, 97, 127
Gass, Tobias 171
Ghose, Soumya 105
Gilmore, John 13
Gilmore, John H. 22
Glocker, Ben 116
Goksel, Orcun 171
Greer, Peter B. 105

Haïssaguerre, Michel 148
Harmouche, Rola 34
Hornegger, Joachim 137
Huang, Cheng 181

Jaïs, Pierre 148
Jia, Fucang 181
Jiménez del Toro, Oscar Alfonso 189
Joskowicz, Leo 163

Kéchichian, Razmig 201
Kelm, B. Michael 137
Kelm, Michael 3
Komatsu, Yuki 148

Langs, Georg 3, 82
Le Folgoc, Loïc 148
Li, Gang 22
Li, Xuhui 181
Li, Zongmin 181

Lin, Weili 13, 22
Lugauer, Felix 137

Ma, Guangkai 97
Maraci, Mohammad Ali 71
Margeta, Jan 148
Menze, Bjoern 3
Metaxas, Dimitris 3
Montillo, Albert 3
Müller, Henning 3, 189

Napolitano, Raffaele 71
Noble, J. Allison 71

Ofner, Joachim 82

Papageorghiou, Aris 71
Pluim, Josien P.W. 105

Relan, Jatin 148
Rivest-Hénault, David 105
Ross, James C. 34

San José Estépar, Raúl 34
Schlegl, Thomas 82
Sdika, Michaël 201
Sermesant, Maxime 148
Shao, Yeqin 127
Shen, Dinggang 13, 22, 97, 127
Shi, Feng 22
Spanier, Assaf B. 163
Stühler, Elisabeth 59
Szekely, Gabor 171

Valette, Sébastien 201
van Tulder, Gijs 47

Wang, Li 13, 22
Washko, George R. 34
Wu, Guorong 13, 97
Wu, Ligang 97

Yang, Xin 127

Zhang, Shaoting 3
Zheng, Yefeng 137
Zikic, Darko 116

Printed in the United States
By Bookmasters